INSECTS OF THE WORLD

INSECTS OF THE WORLD

THEIR STRUCTURE HABITS AND TRANSFORMATIONS

REV. J.G. WOOD

VOL. II

ATLANTIC PUBLISHERS & DISTRIBUTORS

Published by
ATLANTIC PUBLISHERS AND DISTRIBUTORS
B-2, Vishal Enclave, New Delhi-27
Phone 5413460

Sales Office
4346/4C, Ansari Road, Darya Ganj,
New Delhi-110 002
Phone 3273880, 3285873
Fax 91-11-3285873

ISBN 81-7156-465-8 (Vol. II)
ISBN 81-7156-466-6 (Set)

Typeset at
APD Computer Graphics
B-2, Vishal Enclave, New Delhi-110 027
Printed in India at
Mehra Offset Press
New Delhi

CONTENTS.

PAGE

COLEOPTERA, OR BEETLES—

CH. I.—INTRODUCTION 1
II.—TIGER BEETLES, OR CICINDELIDÆ 6
III.—GROUND BEETLES, OR CARABIDÆ 28
IV.—GROUND BEETLES, OR CARABIDÆ—*continued* 46
V.—HYDRADEPHAGA, OR PREDACIOUS WATER BEETLES . . 65
VI.—PAUSSIDÆ AND BRACHELYTRA, OR ROVE BEETLES . . . 72
VII.—NECROPHAGA, OR CARRION-EATERS 81
VIII.—PECTINICORNES, OR COMB-HORNED BEETLES 91
IX.—LAMELLICORN, OR LEAF-HORNED BEETLES, SOMETIMES CALLED PETALOCERA 109
X.—LAMELLICORNS—*continued* 129
XI.—STERNOXI, OR SKIPJACK BEETLES 146
XII.—MALACODERMI, OR SOFT-SKINNED BEETLES 166
XIII.—HETEROMERA, OR PARTY-LEGGED BEETLES 173
XIV.—RHYNCHOPHORA, OR WEEVILS 193
XV.—WEEVILS—*continued*. 215
XVI.—LONGICORNES, OR LONG-HORNED BEETLES 229
XVII.—PHYTOPHAGA, OR PLANT-EATERS 253
XVIII.—PSEUDOTRIMERA 267

EARWIGS—

CH. I.—DERMAPTERA, OR EUPLEXOPTERA 277

ORTHOPTERA—

CH. I.—BLATTIDÆ, OR COCKROACHES 285
II.—MANTIDÆ, OR LEAF INSECTS 290
III.—AMBULATORIA, OR WALKING-STICK INSECTS 300
IV.—SALTATORIA, OR CRICKETS, GRASSHOPPERS, AND LOCUSTS . 317

THYSANOPTERA—

CH. I.—THRIPIDÆ 347

CONTENTS.

PAGE

NEUROPTERA—

CH. I.—LIBELLULIDÆ 353

II.—MYRMELEONIDÆ, SIALIDÆ, MANTISPIDÆ, AND TERMITIDÆ . 365

HYMENOPTERA—

CH. I.—SAW FLIES 385

II.—ENTOMOPHAGA, OR ICHNEUMONS AND GALL FLIES . . . 393

III.—ACULEATA.—MUTILLAS AND SCOLIAS 417

IV.—FORMICIDÆ, OR ANTS 427

V.—POMPILIDÆ, SPHEGIDÆ, AND BEMBECIDÆ 451

VI.—SOLITARY AND SOCIAL BEES 506

LEPIDOPTERA; OR, BUTTERFLIES AND MOTHS—

CH. I.—PAPILIONIDÆ 535

II.—BUTTERFLIES—*concluded* 598

III.—MOTHS 632

HEMIPTERA; OR, HETEROPTERA 709

HOMOPTERA 733

DIPTERA 749

DESCRIPTION OF PLATES.

PLATE I.

To face p. 11

1. Tetracha punctata.
2. Tetracha punctata, larva.
3. Calochroa princeps.
4. Mormolyce phyllodes.
5. Anthia sex-guttata.
6. Mouhotia glorissa.

PLATE II.

To face p. 125

1. Eucheirus Macleayi.
2. Dynastes Hercules.
3. Golofa hastatus.

PLATE III.

Front.

1. Goliathus Druryii.
2. Dicranocephalus Bowringii.
3. Rhamphorhina Petersiana.
4. Entimus splendidus.
5. Cyphus Linnæi.

PLATE IV.

To face p. 243

1. Acrocinus longimanus.
2. Batocera Celebiana.

PLATE V.

To face p. 290

1. Mantis tinctipennis.
2. Mantis tinctipennis.
3. Dereplatys desiccata.

PLATE VI.

To face p. 325

1. Sanaa imperialis.
2. Acridoxena Hawaiiana.

PLATE VII.

To face p. 356

1. Palpopleura marginata.
2. Palpares Caffer.
3. Ascalaphus Kolyranensis.
4. Ascalaphus Kolyranensis, larva.

PLATE VIII.

To face p. 476

1. Trypoxylon rejector.
2. Parapison rufipes.
3. Eumenes esuriens.
4. Rhynchium nitidulum.

PLATE IX.

To face p. 458

1. Pepsis heros.
2. Pelopæus lætus.
3. Vespa mandarinia (female).

PLATE X.

To face p. 518

1. Chrysantheda frontalis.
2. Xylocopa morio.
3. Centris denudans.
4. Euglossa romandi.

PLATE XI.

To face p. 543

1. Papilio Brookeanus.
2. Papilio Panthous.

PLATE XII.

To face p. 557

1. Papilio Joësa.
2. Papilio Euchenor.

PLATE XIII.

To face p. 585

1. Hestia Idea.
2. Charaxes Eudamippus.

PLATE XIV.

To face p. 595

1. Caligo Eurilochus (upper side).
2. Caligo Eurilochus (under side).

PLATE XV.

To face p. 644

1. Cæquosa Australasiæ.
2. Cyclosia sanguifera.

PLATE XVI.

To face p. 663

1. Attacus Jorulla.
2. Phyllodes consobrina.

PLATE XVII.

To face p. 676

1. Tropæa Leto.
2. Ginanisa Isis.

PLATE XVIII.

To face p. 732

1. Cicada adusta.
2. Hotinus maculatus.
3. Pœciloptera circulata.

PLATE XIX.

To face p. 716

1. Diactor bilineatus.
2. Dalader acuticosta.
3. Pygoplatys lancifer.
4. Oncomeris flavicornis.

PLATE XX.

To face p. 752

1. Pangonia longirostris.
2. Acanthomera magnifica.
3. Mydas giganteus.
4. Phellus glaucus.

HYMENOPTERA.

HYMENOPTERA.

CHAPTER I.

SAW FLIES.

THIS order of insects is easily known by the structure of the wings. These organs are four in number, membranous, and without either scales or hairs. The second pair are always smaller than the first, and have not nearly so many veins. During flight these two pairs of wings are connected together by a series of little hooks, so that they practically form one single pair. The mouth is furnished with horny jaws, and the females possess an ovipositor, which either takes the form of a saw-like instrument, as in the Saw Flies, or a sting, as in the bees, wasps, and ichneumon flies. In some cases, as in the ants, the wings are not present in all the individuals, and the reader will remember that the same is the case with the Termites, which have just been described.

Their number is absolutely enormous, and even in our own country from three to four thousand species of Hymenoptera are known. In this land they do not attain any great size, our largest Hymenopterous insect being the well-known Humble Bee, but in various parts of the world some species grow to a considerable size, as we shall presently see.

We begin our account of the Hymenoptera with the Saw Flies, so called from the curious structure of the ovipositor. This organ is intended for the deposition of eggs in slits which are cut in the bark or the leaf-stems of various trees and plants, and is made in a very beautiful manner. There are scarcely any two genera of Saw Flies in which the ovipositor is made in exactly the same manner, so we must content ourselves with a general description.

At the end of the abdomen, and on the under side, is a pair of horny plates, each edged with teeth like those of a saw. The plates curve slightly upwards, and each slides backwards and forwards in a groove sunk in another horny plate, which thus serves both as a support and a guide. As the saw has to be employed in cutting green wood, it cannot be made simply by a flat plate edged with teeth, like the saws with which dry timber is cut. Each saw is rather thick, and the teeth are arranged very much like those on the back of a sapper's sword. On a closer examination with the microscope the teeth are seen to be further elaborated, each separate tooth being a conical cutting instrument with some eight or ten sharp edges. And in order to secure a wide groove, or "kerf" as carpenters call it, the edges of the saws are furnished with a sharp zigzag projection, something resembling a knife-blade that has been folded in this form, /\/\/\/\/\/, and fixed with its back against the side of the saw.

When used the saws are worked alternately, so that a wide groove is cut in a very short time. Having thus performed the office of the saw, they then assume that of the ovipositor, the blades diverging so as to permit the passage of an egg, which is then placed in the groove. A small drop of some irritant fluid follows the egg, and causes the edges of the groove to swell, and so enclose the egg firmly between them. Here it is kept until the time for hatching, when the young grub crawls out, and betakes itself to the leaves for its subsistence. In our own country these insects are often very injurious, the worst of them all being the dreaded Turnip Fly (*Athalia centifoliæ*), whose grey-black grubs are so well known under the name of Niggers.

We will take a few specimens of these curious insects, and mention a few of their peculiarities as we proceed. The species which is shown on the next page is found in the neighbourhood of Hudson's Bay, and derives its specific name from the shape of the clypeus, which is triangular in the male sex. The head is black and shining, and the thorax and base of the abdomen are also black, but covered with short grey hairs. The rest of the abdomen is dark chestnut with a yellowish tinge. The thighs are black, and the rest of the legs yellow, and the wings are all yellow and glossy.

This is a very large genus, and in the British Museum are a

vast number of species, one of the most remarkable of which is *Cimbex variabilis*, also found near Hudson's Bay. This insect is so exceedingly variable that its definition as a species must have been most difficult. Some specimens are black, with the abdomen white, except a black stripe along the centre. Others are coloured after the same fashion, excepting that mahogany brown takes the place of the black. Others are almost wholly white, while some are black, with white or yellow stripes along the sides.

The larvæ belonging to this genus have twenty-two feet; namely, six on the thorax, fourteen on the abdomen, and two on the last segment. When touched they have the power of

FIG. 186.—Cimbex triangulum.
(Black, last portion of the abdomen chestnut.)

spurting from little holes along their sides a greenish fluid, probably acting as a defence against enemies. Some allied species have this secretion so abundant and so viscid that it perpetually exudes, and when the creature is at rest makes it look just like a lump of slime.

These larvæ are found on the upper surface of the leaves. When they have finished feeding, they spin an oval cocoon of very tough and parchment-like material, in which they pass through the pupal stage. This stage is a very brief one, but that of the larva is very long, the creature retaining its larval form for a considerable period after it has completed the cocoon.

As is the case with many insects, there is a considerable distinction in the antennæ of the two sexes in the genus of which an example is given on the next page. It is a native of

Australia, and is a very beautiful insect. The head, thorax, and upper part of the abdomen are shining blue, like the surface of a watch-spring; and the middle of the body, the scutellum, and a small patch on either side in front of the wings, are bright, shining yellow. In the male insect the antennæ take the beautiful form which is here shown. There are about twenty joints, and each joint is furnished with an appendage, longest in the middle of the antennæ, and shortening gradually towards the tip. As the light shifts about, the shadows play backwards and forwards along the antennæ in a very beautiful manner. A very similar structure of the antennæ is seen in the Rhipidocera, which has been described on page 168. This beautiful structure exists only in the male, the antennæ of the female being quite simple and thread-like.

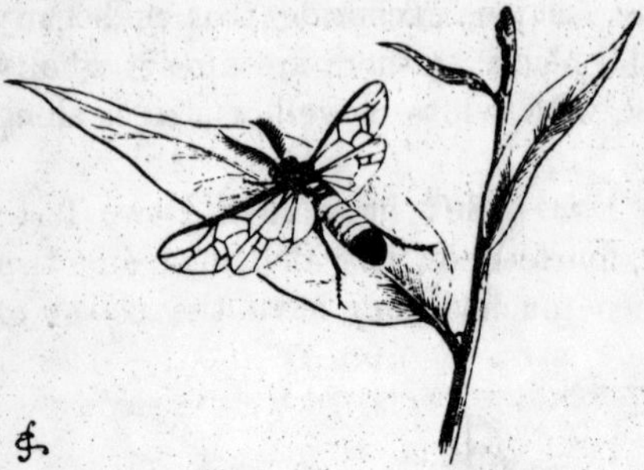

Fig. 187.—Pterygophorus interruptus.
(Shining blue and yellow.)

One species, *Pterygophorus cyaneus*, is all blue, just like a blue-bottle fly.

THE insect which is here drawn is new to science, and is one of a great number of unnamed species of Tenthredo now in the British Museum. It is a native of Darjeeling, in India.

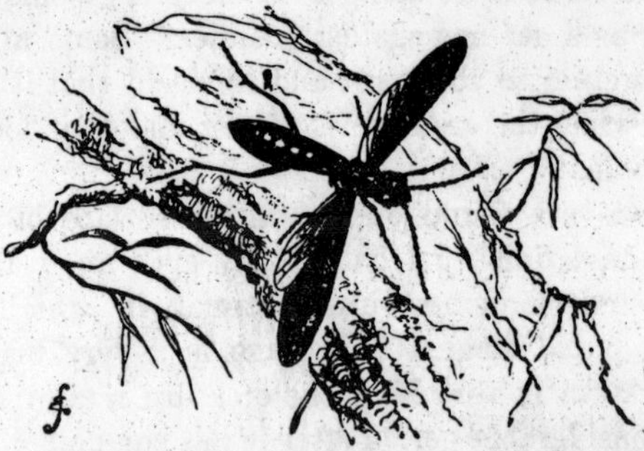

Fig. 188.—Tenthredo coccinocerus. (New species.)
(Green and blue.)

This is a really splendid insect. The head and thorax are metallic green, just like green foil, and the abdomen is burnished blue, glossed with green. The legs are of the same colour as the abdomen, and the antennæ are purple, for which reason I have given it the specific name of *coccinocerus*, or "purple-horn." The wings are brownish, but glossed with green.

OUR last example of the Saw Flies is the *Derecyrta pictipennis*. The example which is here drawn is in the British Museum, and was brought from Ega, in the Amazons, by Mr. Bates.

It is a pretty though not a splendid insect, and derives its beauty quite as much from the wings as from the body. The head is shining and black, looking very much like a little black

FIG. 189.—Derecyrta pictipennis.
(Yellow and brown.)

glass bead. The thorax is yellow, and so is the abdomen, with the exception of a black tip. The wings are mostly brown, but there is a broad yellow patch across the centre, and another, of a similar colour, near the base. The lower wings are coloured in a very similar manner, except that they are more translucent than the upper pair.

ANOTHER group now comes before us, namely, the Uroceridæ. This word literally signifies "horn-tailed," and is given to the insects because the ovipositor projects from the end of the abdomen like a short stout horn. At first sight no organs appear to be more unlike each other than the ovipositor of the Uroceridæ and that of the Saw Flies. A careful examination, however, shows that not only are they identical in their parts, though the structure of those parts is modified, but that the double saw of the Saw Flies, the horn-like projection of the Uroceridæ, the long hair-like ovipositor of the ichneumon flies, and the envenomed sting of the bees and wasps, are but slightly modified variations of the same organ.

It is impossible to give a full description of so complex and beautifully-made a structure as the ovipositor of the Hymenoptera without the aid of many illustrations, and I must therefore only mention the salient points.

As the insects are not required to cut notches into soft wood, as is the case with the Saw Flies, the powerful saws are not needed, and are modified into two small spiculæ, in which the notches or teeth are still preserved, though they are too small for actual use. The two horny plates which strengthen the saws are soldered together, so as to support the central boring instrument. This is a really wonderful piece of mechanism, and I may as well here repeat the description given in my "Insects at Home," and taken from the ovipositor of our fine English species, *Urocerus* (or *Sirex*) *gigas*. It is scarcely needful to observe that this organ is only possessed by the female insect.

"I very strongly recommend any of my readers who may obtain a female insect to disengage the actual borer from its two-bladed sheath, and examine it with the aid of a microscope. A half-inch object-glass will give quite sufficient power. It is straight and stiff, but elastic, as if made of steel, and, if bent, will spring back to its proper form with the elasticity of a Toledo rapier. In form it somewhat resembles the instrument known technically as a 'rymer,' except that the edges are rounded, and not square. But the borer possesses an auxiliary cutting apparatus which places it far above the rymer in point of efficacy.

"Even with an ordinary magnifying lens, it is easy to see that the end of the borer is developed into a sharp head very much resembling that of a boarding-pike, and that the outline of the shaft is broken into a series of notches. The half-inch glass, however, discloses a marvellous example of mechanical excellence. The head of the borer is then seen to be armed with long sharp teeth, slightly curved inwards, and acting just as does the carpenter's ordinary centre-bit.

"So much for the head of the borer: we will now turn to the shaft. It appears that in order to make a clean-cut hole for the reception of the egg, the shaft of the borer has to finish the task which the head begins. Accordingly, it is armed on each of its sides with a series of hard sharp-edged ridges, running diagonally across it, and acting exactly as do the sharp ridges of a coffee-mill. A more effective implement could not have been invented, and the various boring instruments of modern days, however novel they may appear to be, are in reality formed on exactly the same principle as the borer of the Sirex, though perhaps they may not carry out their object with such perfection."

The Uroceridæ all deposit their eggs in trees, the ovipositor first boring a tolerably deep hole, and then placing an egg at its further extremity. As soon as the egg is hatched, the young larva makes its way into the trunk of the tree, where it resides for a considerable time, and causes much damage to the timber by its perforations. Even in this country, where the Uroceridæ are comparatively scarce, whole plantations of fir-trees have been very seriously injured, and in some cases the timber was so filled with perforations that it was useless except for firewood.

There is much doubt among entomologists whether any of the Uroceridæ are genuine inhabitants of this country. A vast amount of fir timber is annually imported, and in that timber great numbers of the larvæ have been known to exist. Consequently, when they emerge in the perfect state and fly into the open air, they instinctively search for growing fir-trees, and proceed to deposit their eggs upon them. Another doubt exists, or rather has existed, respecting these insects, some entomologists thinking that the larvæ do not feed upon the wood, but upon the larvæ of wood-eating beetles that had taken possession of the tree. This conjecture is now considered to be groundless, and it is certain that the structure of the head and jaws is exactly such as would be required by a wood-boring insect. Indeed, the larva of this insect looks almost exactly like that of a wood-eating beetle.

There is a curious point in the structure of the larval jaws. Both are strong, horny, rather square in form, and armed with several teeth and a large horny lobe. But one is compressed and the other depressed, *i.e.* one is flattened as if pinched sideways, and the other as if pressed downwards, so that their mode of action must be very remarkable.

The fine insect which is given as an example of this group of Hymenoptera is a native of North America. It is not only conspicuous on account of its size, but for the beauty of its colouring. The wings are brown glossed with blue, and the abdomen is bright golden yellow, over which are drawn five bands of purple, so deep that it looks black unless a strong light is brought to bear upon it. The head and thorax are yellowish brown, very much granulated, the colour being darker in the middle of the thorax than on the sides. The under surface is black, and the legs are yellow.

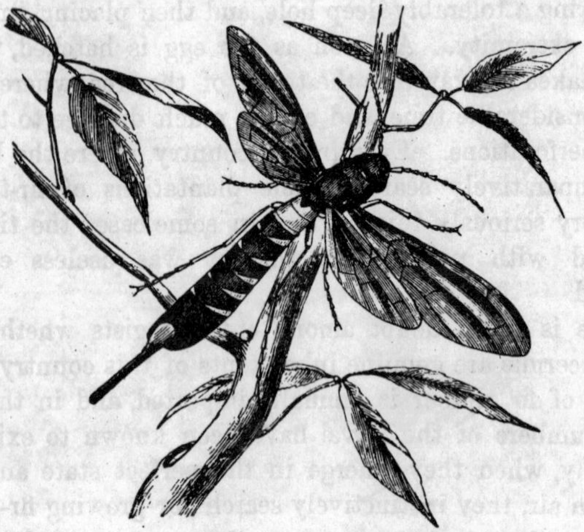

FIG. 190.—Tremex Colomba.
(Purple and yellow.)

As is the case with the British species, this is a most variable insect in point of size, some specimens being not much more than half the length of the others, the difference in size being exactly that of a stout man of six feet high and a weazened dwarf of three feet. In the collection of the British Museum are great numbers of allied species, not differing materially from those of our own country.

CHAPTER II.

ENTOMOPHAGA, OR ICHNEUMONS AND GALL FLIES.

THE large group of Hymenoptera which comes next in order is almost wholly parasitic in its character—most of the species feeding, while in the larval state, on the bodies of other insects. There are, however, many which obtain their subsistence from plants, which are wounded by the mother insect and are developed into the curious growths which are popularly called galls. The arrangement of these insects is singularly intricate, and in many points still affords objects of controversy to systematic entomologists. We will therefore content ourselves with a general rather than a detailed view of those remarkable insects, and place them under the comprehensive name of Ichneumonidæ.

Many of these insects deposit their eggs within the bodies of larvæ that are buried either in wood or in the earth. Anyone would think that the grub of a wood-boring beetle, or the caterpillar of a wood-boring moth, would be quite safe from any external enemies, so long as it remained concealed within the timber. The Ichneumon Flies, however, are able, by some mysterious instinct, not only to discover the exact locality of the hidden larva, but in spite of all obstacles to deposit their eggs within it. Slight and delicate as is the ovipositor in many species, the actual borer being scarcely thicker than a hair, it can make its way even through thick wood, and thus act as a channel through which the egg is conveyed to its destination. The movement by which this operation is conducted is exactly that which is employed by a carpenter when using a brad-awl.

Without going further into details, we will proceed to the examination of the insects which have been selected as typical examples of this vast group.

AUSTRALIA possesses many remarkable species of Ichneumon Flies, one of which is the *Megalyra Shuckardi*, which is here shown of the natural size.

The general colour of this insect is black. The head and thorax are deeply pitted or granulated, very much like the end of a lady's thimble, and are variegated here and there by little patches of short white hairs, the most conspicuous of which are on the two lower angles of the thorax. The abdomen is smooth, shining black, with the exception of the tufts of white hairs which project from beneath the segments on each side, and are

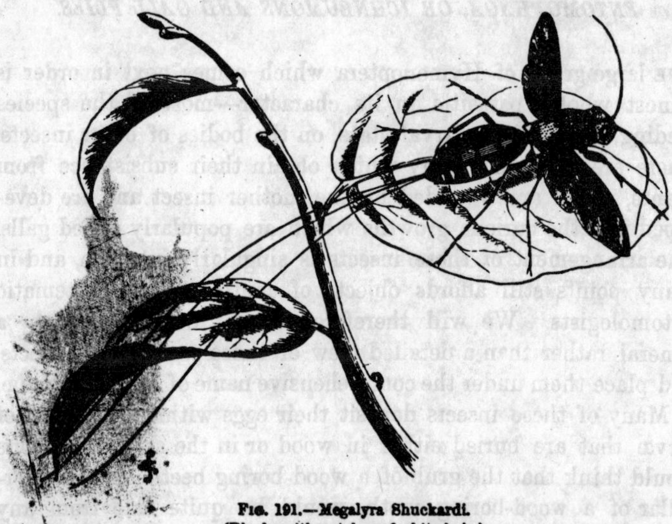

FIG. 191.—Megalyra Shuckardi.
(Black, with patches of white hair.)

exceedingly conspicuous. The wings are dark brown in the middle, and become rather paler towards the edges.

The ovipositor of the female insect is exceedingly long, and is composed of three distinct parts; namely, the actual borer, which occupies the centre, and a pair of sheaths which serve to protect it when not in use. The colour of the borer is pale brown, and that of the sheaths nearly black. Long as they are, they are so slender that the three together are scarcely so thick as a single horsehair. When the insect has been dead for some little time, the parts of the ovipositor are apt to separate and to fall into a lyre-like form; and it is in consequence of this propensity that Mr. Westwood gave to the genus the name of *Megalyra*, or "large lyre."

Formidable as this instrument looks, it is really quite harmless, and, though it can pierce through living timber, cannot produce any injurious effect upon the human skin. Unlike the sting of the bee or wasp, it is not connected with any reservoir of poison, its only use being to introduce the egg into the body of the hidden larva. Many of these insects will, when seized, bend the abdomen and bring the end of the ovipositor against the hand. The movement is, however, nothing more than a menace, and the worst that the insect can do is that a slight prick may be felt. Acting on a similar principle, our common ringed snake will strike at an assailant as fiercely as if it were armed with venomous fangs, and wear so threatening an aspect that even those who know its harmless character cannot avoid a momentary shock.

The male of this species is a very curious creature. Of course he does not possess the ovipositor, but the strangest thing is that he hardly possesses any wings. This is quite a reversal of the usual system. All who have even a slight acquaintance with entomology are aware that in many insects the male possesses wings while the female is wingless.

The reason for this variation of structure is clearly shown by Mr. Westwood :—"An exceedingly interesting species has been communicated to me by M. Audouin, which he discovered to be parasitic in the provisioned nests of Odynerus, Anthophora, and Osmia. The male has most singular antennæ, and minute rudiments of wings; so that it does not quit the cell; but the female is enabled, by means of her full-sized wings, to seek other cells for her progeny. Mr. F. Smith pointed out to me that the nervures of the wings are arranged somewhat differently in the two sexes, the rudimental wings of the male possessing a petiolated cell which does not exist in the fully developed wing of the female."

Another species, *Megalyra fascipennis*, also an Australian insect, is much of the same size and colour, except that there are no patches of white hairs, and that the wings are pale, with a broad dark bar across the middle.

In the insects belonging to the genus Pelecinus, a very singular structure will be observed. Instead of having a short abdomen and a long ovipositor, the abdomen is exceedingly long, and the ovipositor short. The abdomen, indeed, is lengthened so greatly, that at a hasty glance the insect looks exactly like a Dragon Fly. In this respect it bears a singular contrast to the Evanias, which seem to be all thorax and hind-legs, the abdomen being a mere insignificant little appendage to the large thorax. The insects inhabit North America, and in some districts are exceedingly common. The specimen which is here figured was brought from Trenter Falls, New York, by Mr. Doubleday.

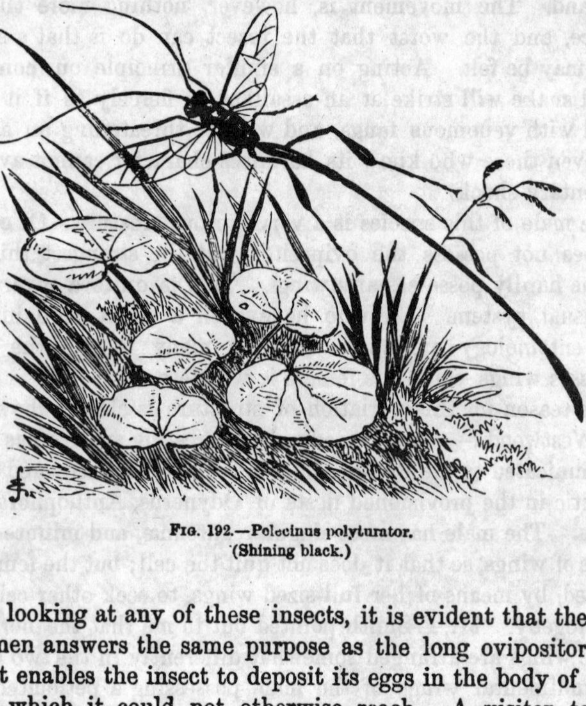

FIG. 192.—Pelecinus polyturator.
(Shining black.)

On looking at any of these insects, it is evident that the long abdomen answers the same purpose as the long ovipositor, and that it enables the insect to deposit its eggs in the body of some larva which it could not otherwise reach. A visitor to the British Museum lately said that in the pine forests of Canada the Pelecini absolutely swarmed, and that hundreds of them might be found on the trunks of the trees dead and stiff, with their abdomen thrust deeply into the burrow made by some wood-boring insect. In some places they were so numerous that a dozen or so could be swept off by a single stroke of the hand down the tree-trunk. This characteristic anecdote at once establishes the exceeding value of the Pelecini in saving the pine forests from insect destroyers, and shows how wonderfully the balance of Nature is preserved as long as man does not interfere.

The colour of the insect is shining black, and the wings are generally translucent, though in some specimens a few dark blotches are seen, varying exceedingly in depth of colour, size, and position. The very remarkable hind-legs must not pass unnoticed, the tibia swelling into a pear-like form, and the whole limb being exceedingly long if contrasted with the head and thorax, though short when compared with the abdomen. The name *Pelecinus* literally means "a pelican," and why it should be applied to the insect is more than I can understand.

One more point must be mentioned. Everything in Nature has its uses. The female Megalyra has a long ovipositor because she is needed to lay eggs in deeply hidden larvæ. The male performs no such task, and consequently has no ovipositor. In the present instance, the greatly elongated abdomen only belongs to the female, that of the male being short and club-shaped.

FIG. 193.—Ichneumon arrogator. (Black and yellow.)

As to the typical genus Ichneumon, it is so vast, and contains such multitudes of species, that the mere sight of the creatures is enough to make anyone recoil in despair from them. Take, for example, the collection at the British Museum. A positive army of Ichneumons is already arranged, while there are multitudes awaiting their turn for being named and classified. None are large, while some are exceedingly minute—being so small that they are fixed on cardboard, the finest pin being too coarse for their tiny bodies.

The species selected for illustration is on account of its being one of the largest of the group, and so gives a good idea of the general form and structure of these insects. Its colour is almost entirely black, but the basal part of the abdomen is yellow, this colour extending to some two-thirds of its length. The wings are dark brown and rather shining. It is remarkable that, although this genus is so enormous, there is scarcely any range of colour, the hues being nothing but black, grey, and yellow; and even the last mentioned hue being of a dull nature.

The present species is a native of Albania.

THE fine insect from which the accompanying illustration was drawn is in the British Museum, and, as far as is known, is an unique specimen. It was brought from Natal.

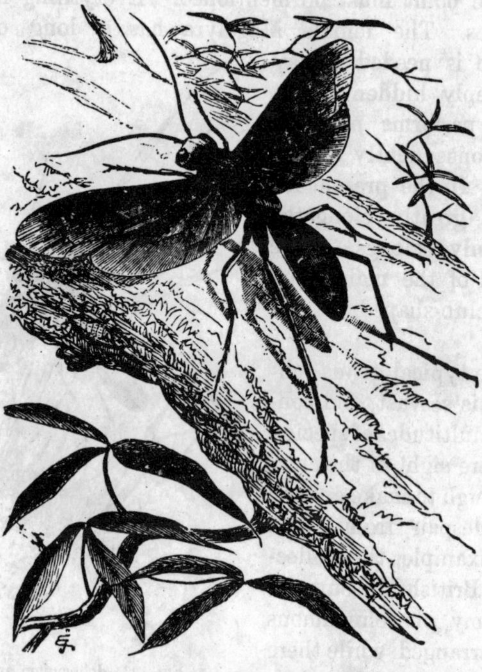

FIG. 194.—Scolobates (?).
(Black; wings glossed with purple.)

Independent of its size, which is quite gigantic for one of the Ichneumons, it is a singularly handsome insect. The head and body are black, and so is the abdomen, the latter being clothed with a coat of short, soft, dense pile, which makes it look exactly as if it had been cut out of the finest black silk velvet. The legs are black, with the exception of the tibia, which are pale brown.

The chief beauty of the insect, however, lies in the wings, which are ample, very shining, and, when viewed from above, seem to be simply brown. When, however, a strong side-light is thrown upon them, they flash out into the most brilliant purple, as if they had been made of purple mother-of-pearl. The ovipositor is exceedingly long, and much stouter than is generally the case, the two portions which form the sheath being each of them as thick as the entire ovipositor of the Megalyra.

The reader will perceive that a note of interrogation is placed after the generic name *Scolobates.* This is done because the insect has not as yet been examined and its place in nature settled. All that is known is, that it is at all events allied to the genus Scolobates, even if it does not belong to it, and it has therefore been provisionally attached to that genus.

The well-known genus Pimpla has many foreign representatives, of which the species here figured is a conspicuous example.

Fig. 195.—Pimpla intricatoria.
(Black, with yellow spots.)

It is very simple in colouring, the body and abdomen being shining black, with a few short streaks of bright yellow upon the sides of the abdomen, and some spots of the same colour on the thorax. The wings are quite translucent, except that on the top of the upper wings there are two black spots, as shown in the illustration. It inhabits Australia.

All the Ichneumonidæ are liable to great variation in point of size, and in none of them is this variation so extreme as in the genus Pimpla. Even in the present species, the variation is so great that none but an entomologist would think that insects so apparently distinct could possibly belong to the same species.

The reason for this difference is simple enough. In its larval stage the young Ichneumon feeds upon the larva of some other insect, the victim not being visible to the mother Ichneumon, and therefore permitting no choice. It may be that she happens to hit upon a large and well-fed larva, in which the young one finds ample nourishment, and is enabled to reach the fullest development of which the species admits. But she may happen to hit upon the larva of some small insect, and in that case it is evident that the amount of nourishment must be circumscribed.

Now, it always happens with insects, that even though they are stinted of food while larvæ, they are not debarred from attaining the perfect form, although in such cases they are not half as large as those which have been more fortunate. In fact, I believe that with insects, whether British or foreign, all variations in size are occasioned by the amount of food which they obtain in the larval state.

ON the next page we have another example of the Ichneumons with long ovipositors.

Even in the present species the length of that organ is very remarkable, but there are some species in which it is very much longer in proportion to the size of its owner. The most astonishing of these insects is one that has not yet been described, and which is in the collection of the British Museum. In this species the basal half of the abdomen is yellow, and the rest black. Mr. F. Smith kindly measured it, and found that while the length of the insect from the head to the end of the tail is barely one inch, that of the ovipositor is six inches and a half. I wish that I could have introduced a portrait of this most remarkable insect, but, inasmuch as the illustration must have been at least eight inches in length, of which six and a half are occupied by three hair-like lines, such an illustration would have been nothing but a waste of the space which we can so ill afford.

This insect was brought from Bogotá, and has not yet been named.

The present species has only recently found a place among the arrangements of the British Museum. It was brought from the

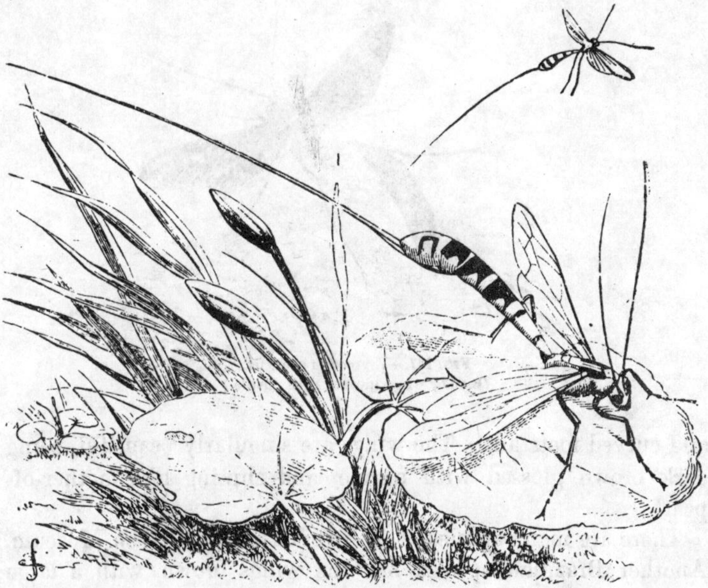

FIG. 196.—Rhyssa nobilitator.
(Black and yellow.)

Celebes by Mr. Wallace, who has done so much toward enriching our collections. Its colour is light yellow and shining black, arranged in the peculiar pattern shown in the illustration There are some species of Rhyssa inhabiting China. They much resemble the Celebes insect, except that chestnut has taken the place of black. Another species, *Rhyssa lunator*, is well known in Canada. It is about as large as *Rhyssa nobilitator*, but is paler in colour and has the ovipositor half as long again.

THE genus Thyreodon extends over a considerable portion of the globe.

The fine insect which is here shown is a native of Brazil, and is one of the largest as well as the most beautiful of the genus. The head is black, and the thorax appears at first to be of the same colour, but is in reality of the richest and deepest purple, with a velvet-like surface. The abdomen is black. It is much compressed, and is attached to the thorax by a curiously long

FIG. 197.—Thyreodon cyaneus.
(Black ; wings glossed with purple.)

and curved footstalk. The wings are singularly beautiful, being dark brown glossed with purple, and shining like mother-of-pearl.

There are many species of Thyreodon in the British Museum. Another Brazilian species has the wings brown, with a large pale yellow spot in the middle of each ; and one which inhabits China has the wings glossed with a beautiful golden yellow.

AMONG all the larger Ichneumon Flies there are none that surpass in beauty the species which is figured on the next page, and very few that even approach it.

There is nothing very remarkable about the body, which is black, as are the head and thorax. The legs are also black, except the basal half of the tibia, which is yellow. The chief beauty of the insect lies in its wings, which are coloured in a most gorgeous fashion. As is the case with so many of these insects, the wings appear to be plain brown when viewed with a direct and not very strong light; but when the light is allowed to fall upon them sideways, they flash out into all sorts of colours. So great, indeed, is the variety of colour, that it is almost impossible to fix on any one here as predominating. Perhaps a ruddy copper may be considered as the ground colour, and upon it are patches of crimson, azure, purple, and gold, each patch shifting its colour together with the direction of the light.

These colours are rendered more intense by the structure of the wings, which are not flat and smooth like those of most Ichneumons, but covered with little crumples. In fact, when viewed with a magnifying-glass, the surface of the wings presents just the same appearance as does a sheet of paper when it has been rolled into a ball and then flattened out again.

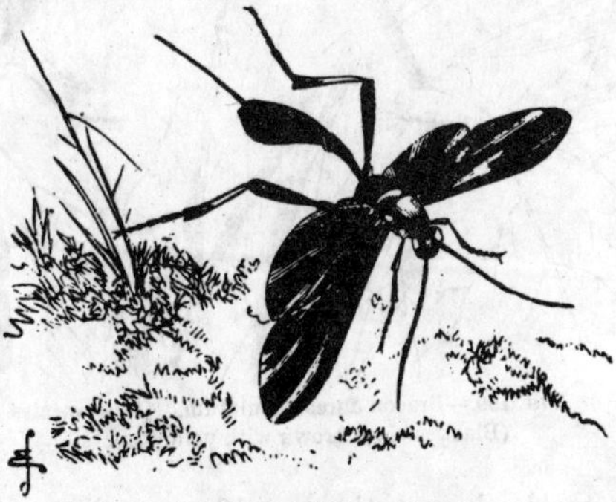

FIG. 198.—Osprynchotus objurgator.
(Black; wings many-coloured.)

This species comes from the Congo, and fortunately some of its habits are known. It is parasitic upon the solitary bee called *Eumenes tinctor*, one of the burrowing bees. In the British Museum there is a fine group of these nests, the burrows being sunk into a piece of clay. And from that group of nests was hatched the specimen whose portrait is given above.

THE remarkable insect which is shown on page 404 has not been described, although the authorities of the British Museum have placed it in its proper genus.

The body is shining black, with a few white marks on the edges of the abdomen near the base. The wings are brown, diversified with some white spots, arranged as shown in the illustration. The large spot, however, on the upper edge of the wing is not white, but rich golden yellow, for which reason

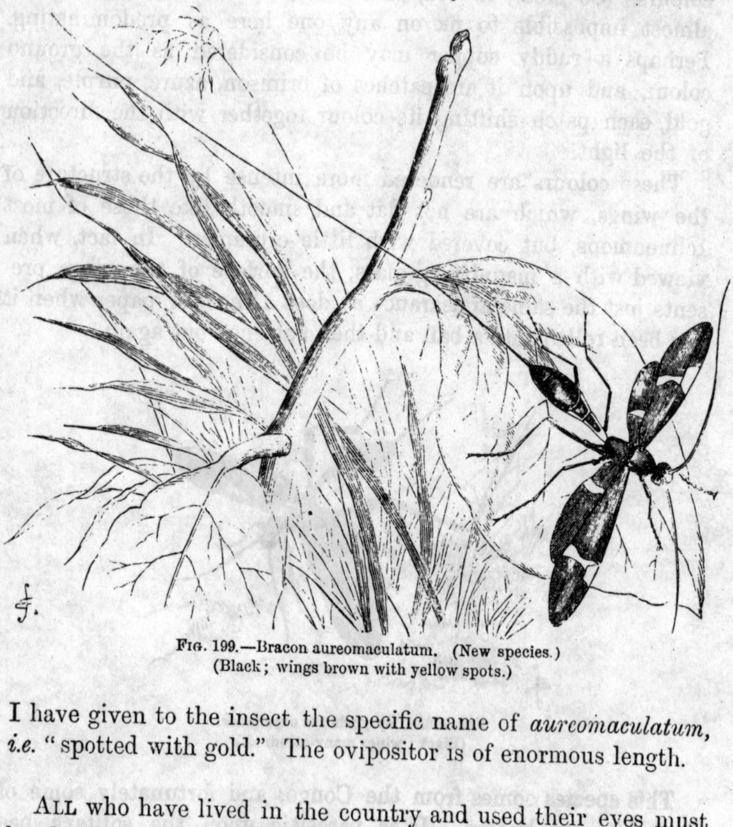

FIG. 199.—Bracon aureomaculatum. (New species.)
(Black; wings brown with yellow spots.)

I have given to the insect the specific name of *aureomaculatum*, *i.e.* "spotted with gold." The ovipositor is of enormous length.

ALL who have lived in the country and used their eyes must be familiar with the curious excrescences called galls, which appear upon the leaves, branches, and even roots of trees. These galls are produced by a group of insects called, scientifically, Cynipidæ, and popularly known as Gall Flies.

The process is almost exactly like that by which the Ichneumon Flies deposit their eggs in the bodies of other insects. The mother Gall Fly pierces with her ovipositor the leaf, twig, or bark, inserts the egg, and injects at the same time a small drop of a fluid which produces very extraordinary effects. That portion of the plant which comes in contact with the liquid is forced into an abnormal growth, and rapidly encloses the egg. Sometimes, especially on leaves, the galls are quite spherical, and of about the same consistence as a green gooseberry. Other leaf-galls are quite flat, like so many small coins stuck on the leaf; while others hang by strings like bunches of currants. Some are covered with leaf-like appendages, and look like miniature artichokes; while others, like the well-known bedeguar of the rose, are clothed with a dense mass of long, soft filaments.

In the midst of the gall lies the young larva, which feeds upon the soft centre of the gall, and by continually eating makes for itself a little cell, which increases in proportion to the size of its body. It is evident that all locomotion is denied to the larva, and that all it can do is to turn round and round in its cell. Consequently it has no legs, and is only able to move itself about by the edges of the rings or segments of its body.

As a general rule, the larva remains in the gall until it assumes the perfect form, and then gnaws its way into the open air. There are some species, however, which wriggle their way out of the gall before they become pupæ, fall to the ground, burrow in it, and there undergo their changes. Generally there is only one larva in each gall, but there are several species in which a great number are found in the same gall, each larva occupying its separate cell. The bedeguar of the rose and the oak-root gall are familiar British examples of these compound galls.

Even in England there are many species of Gall Flies, while the foreign species seem to be without number. In the collection of the British Museum, besides a vast number of species that have been named, described, and arranged, there are whole drawers full of species that have as yet received no name. They are all little insects, the species which is drawn on page 405 being one of the largest. The figure is magnified two and a half diameters. It is one of the American insects, the specimen which is figured having been taken in Massachusetts. As is the case with most of the genus, the colour is dark, being simply shining black. The wings are translucent, with the exception of the spot, which is black, fading into brown.

These insects are examples of the uses that lie hidden in Nature. Many thousands of years had the Gall Flies been making their wonderful cells before anyone discovered that the galls which disfigured the oak could be of any service to man. Yet, within the gall lay the principal element of the ink which has had as important a part to play in civilization as has the press itself, the latter depending almost wholly on the former. Scarcely larger than average-sized hazel-nuts, the galls absolutely crowd the branches of an oak which grows plentifully in the Levant, and so it is to these insignificant insects that we owe one of the most absolute necessities of modern existence. The galls are to be procured at most chemists' shops; and anyone who wishes to procure the insect can do so by selecting those galls which have no holes in them. On cutting them open, the insect will generally be found inside. Such specimens are technically

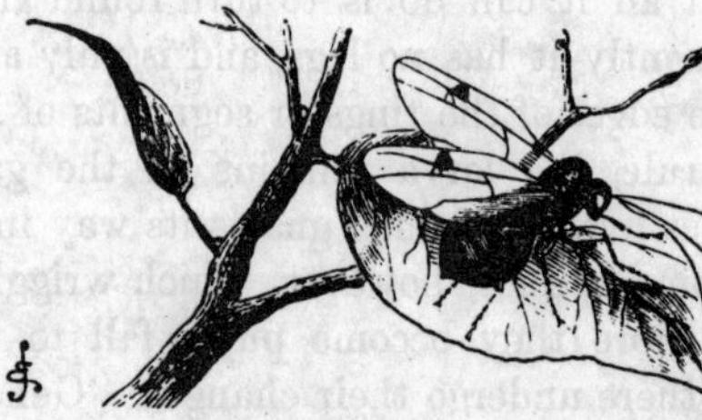

FIG. 200.—Cynips confluens. (Black.)

called "green" galls, "blue" galls, or "black" galls, and are thought to make better ink than the "white" galls, from which the insects have escaped.

As a general rule, the species which made any particular gall can be identified by keeping the specimen until the insects are hatched out. All rules, however, have exceptions, and such is the case with the galls. Sometimes, although the specimen has been kept in a box by itself, two distinct species of insects will be hatched from it, or a single species which is clearly not a Gall Fly at all. The fact is that there are certain Ichneumon Flies, called Evanias, which are parasitic upon the larvæ of the Gall Flies; and the consequence is, that in a compound gall both the true Gall Flies and Evanias are hatched, while in single galls the Evania takes the place of the Gall Fly.

THE next illustration represents an insect called *Scleroderma dux*. This genus has, until lately, been placed among the

Scoliadæ, a group of insects which will presently be described, but has now been shifted to its present position.

The whole of the species belonging to this genus, of which there are great numbers, are parasitic upon the larvæ and pupæ of moths. They are little creatures, and the present species, which is among the largest, has been magnified two diameters, so as to enable its real form to be seen. It is a native of Pará, and its colour is pale yellow. The reader will doubtless have noticed the curiously swollen thigh of the hind leg. It is armed on the lower edge with a row of short teeth, and when the curved tibia are closed upon it, the insect looks as if it were one of the jumpers.

FIG. 201.—Scleroderma dux.
(Pale yellow.)

MEMBERS of the genus Scleroderma are spread over a great portion of the world. The curious little insect which is here shown is a native of Albania. It is very small, as may be seen

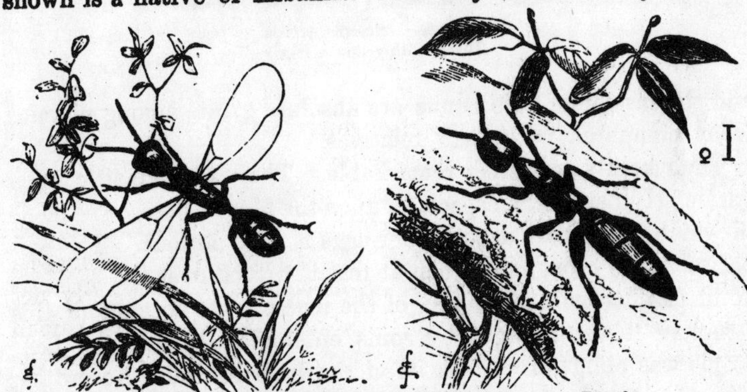

Male. FIG. 202.—Scleroderma cylindrica. Female.
(Reddish brown.)

by the line on the right of the illustration, which represents the real length of the female. The male is very much smaller than his mate—so small, indeed, that it cannot be examined without the aid of a tolerably powerful magnifying-glass. The body of an ordinary specimen is very much the same size as the letter *i*; and if an *o* be placed at either side of the *i*, they will be about as large as the wings. The generic name of *Scleroderma* is formed from two Greek words signifying "hard-skinned," and is given to these insects on account of the hardness of the integuments.

THE species which is here represented is one of a large and very interesting group of insects. There are many of them, and this particular species has been selected because it is one of the largest of the group. As a rule they are very small,

FIG. 203.—Leucospis Aruera.
(Black, with yellow marks.)

and the insects of this genus are absolute giants among pigmies when compared with their relatives.

Their habits are rather remarkable. They are parasitic upon various Hymenoptera, especially upon the Mason Bees. The mode in which the female deposits her eggs is very curious. The ovipositor is very long, and when at rest is turned over the back, its point passing over the thorax of the insect. On account of this structure it was thought by some entomologists that the Leucospis was obliged to attack its victim from behind. According, however, to an account given to Mr. Westwood by an eye-witness, this is not the case, and the insect proceeds as follows:—

Mason Bees always choose for their building-place a hole in an old wall. In this hole they deposit an egg, together with a supply of food for the young larva, and then close it up.

The Leucospis hunts over the walls until she has discovered a Mason Bee's nest, and then settles by it. Raising herself as high as possible on her tarsi, she slowly brings the ovipositor from the upper to the under side of the body, the point projecting beyond the head. She then carefully works the ovipositor into the nest until she has fairly buried it, and then, passing an egg between the blades of the instrument, leaves it in the nest. In course of time the egg is hatched, and the larva eats not only the food which was intended for the Mason Bee larva, but the larva itself. Here, then, we have another example of the difficulty which is often found in determining a species by hatching the insect out of the nest—a parasite taking the place of the rightful inhabitant.

The specimen which is given in the illustration is a male, this being known by the absence of the ovipositor and the form of the abdomen, which has only three joints, or segments, that of the female having five. Its colour is black, varied with golden patches and spots. The wings are yellowish brown. The genus has a very wide range, and in the British Museum there are specimens from Europe, Asia, and nearly the whole of America. This species inhabits Arú, whence its specific name of *Aruera*.

By referring to the illustration, the reader will see that the two preceding insects are remarkable for the thickening of the thigh of the hind legs. This thickening is carried out to a much greater extent in the remarkable insect which is here shown, and which is called *Phasganophora*, or "blade-bearer," because the thigh is modified into a broad, flat, blade-like shape.

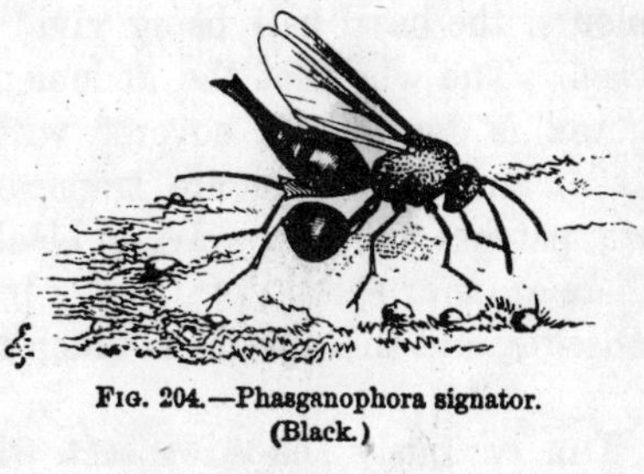

Fig. 204.—Phasganophora signator. (Black.)

In the female insect the ovipositor is very conspicuous, the instrument itself being black, and the sheaths broad, triangular, and of a bright yellow colour. This apparatus is shown just above the flattened portion of the hind leg. The wings are transparent, and the whole of the body of the insect is black, the abdomen being polished and shining, and the thorax and head dull and granulated. This species is a native of Java. In order to show the peculiar structure of the hind leg and the ovipositor, the figure has been drawn rather larger than the insect.

In the very unpretending form of *Lycisca Romandi* we have one of the most splendid insects that the earth produces. As is the case with many insects which have already been described, the colours are so exceedingly rich that they can hardly be seen except in a brilliant light. When placed in a drawer with other insects, the Lycisca might easily be passed over as one of no greater beauty than those which surround it; but when a gleam of light darts across it, the sudden flash of emerald-green and crimson at once catches the eye.

FIG. 205.—Lycisca Romandi.
(Green, crimson, and black.)

The abdomen of this species is divided boldly into two colours, the basal half being vivid crimson and the rest shining green. The whole of the abdomen has a metallic polish. The thorax is deep black, covered with bars and dots of emerald-green, and the wings are transparent, the upper pair having two patches of deep velvety black. It is a Brazilian insect. There are four species of Lycisca in the collection of the British Museum, and this species is much the largest of the four.

THE curiously shaped insect which is shown in the next illustration is a very small one—barely one-third of an inch in length, and the figure, therefore, has been magnified three diameters larger than the insect itself.

It has a singularly ant-like appearance, and to an ordinary observer is so exactly like a yellow ant with long legs, that he would probably set it down as belonging to those insects. Its colour is pale yellow.

The insect belongs to the family of the Proctotrupidæ, a group of Hymenoptera which has a very large range. The present species is a native of the Celebes Islands, but others are found spread over the greater part of the world. Even our own country produces *Gonatopus pedestris.* This little insect frequents hot, sandy places, and, where the sand is white and fine, can be captured on account of its habit of falling into deep footprints and other hollows in the sand, into which it rolls much after the same manner that the victims of the Ant Lion are caught. Mr. E. A. Smith tells me that he has often taken it at Lowestoft and Bournemouth; and Mr. Westwood mentions Yarmouth as a favourite locality for this insect.

FIG. 206.—Gonatopus Celebicus. (Pale yellow.)

The resemblance to an ant is in this species so singularly close, that none but a practised entomologist would take it for anything but a little ant running about with great speed. They are all very active insects, as indeed might be inferred from the length and structure of the legs. Some can even leap, but the generality content themselves with running and flying. Mr. Westwood remarks that some of the Proctotrupidæ have a habit of alternately raising and depressing the abdomen while resting on hot sunny banks.

The reader will have noticed that the insect which is shown in the figure has no wings. In the genus Gonatopus this peculiarity belongs to the females. It was once thought that in the wingless specimens of Proctotrupidæ the wings had been intentionally broken off, as is done by the ants. This, however, is not the case; for even where the rudiments of the wings are seen, the edges are quite smooth, and not jagged as they are when they have been broken away. In the present genus, the hind pair of wings of the male are lobed.

In all the Proctotrupidæ the wings have either very few nervures, or none at all. There is a very singular little insect belonging to this group, *Mymar pulchellus*, in which the hind pair of wings are reduced to two delicate hair-like projections, and the fore-wings are shaped just like battledores—the expanded portion being edged with hairs. The antennæ of this insect are of enormous length when compared with the body, but all things are measured by comparison; and when it is remembered that the insect, with its wings expanded, is scarcely larger than the dot over the letter *i*, the word enormous seems rather absurd. One species has been called by the specific name of *punctum*, and another by that of *atomos*, in allusion to their minute dimensions.

All the Proctotrupidæ are very small insects, some being so tiny as to be scarcely visible, while the present species, which is not the third of an inch in length, appears quite a giant among them. There are many species in England, and whenever the entomologist employs the "sweep-net" he is sure to find plenty of these tiny insects within it.

Probably on account of their very minute size, little is known of the habits of the Proctotrupidæ. As, however, those who have been successfully watched are known to be parasitic, it is inferred that all are of a similar nature. Several species are known to deposit their eggs in those of other insects, especially Lepidoptera; others live within the bodies of Aphides, and others upon those mischievous little gnat-like insects which do so much damage to the wheat, and are known by the scientific name of Cecidomyia.

Others capture small larvæ and bury them as provision for the future young; and this brings us to a peculiarity in the structure of the female Gonatopus. Not only are all the legs long and powerful, but the tarsi of the first pair of legs are armed with large double claws, aptly compared by Mr. Westwood to the claws of a lobster. This structure is supposed to be for the purpose of enabling the mother insect to capture her prey and drag it to the cell where it is to lie. The word *Gonatopus* is Greek, and literally signifies "jointed foot." The ovipositor has a very close resemblance to a sting.

Now we come to a very remarkable group of Hymenoptera called Chrysididæ. This is a Greek word signifying "gilded," and is given to the insects on account of the brilliant colours with which they are adorned. Several species of Chrysididæ are inhabitants of our own country, and are popularly known by the name of Ruby-tailed Flies.

If a female Ruby-tail be carefully examined, the abdomen will be seen to consist of only three segments, each being of considerable size. Should the specimen be dry, it will not be easy to find out what has become of the missing segments; but if it be fresh, there will be no great difficulty in finding them. If the abdomen be carefully pressed, there will issue from it a long telescopic tube, which will be found to be formed from the other segments. At the end of this tube is the ovipositor, which is very short and looks much like a sting. It can even be used for defence, and can give a tolerably sharp prick; but as there is no poison-gland connected with it, no real harm is done.

The object of this structure is evident. The insect is parasitic, the eggs being deposited in the nests of other insects, generally solitary bees. The egg of the Chrysis is hatched before that of the real owner, and in consequence the larva eats up all the food which was prepared for its unintentional host. It will be seen, therefore, that the telescopic ovipositor is needed in order to enable the Chrysis to deposit its egg at the bottom of the nest, and yet to do so without disturbing the work of the insect whose offspring is to be supplanted.

In the early spring, specimens of the Chrysis may often be found in holes which were originally intended for other insects. Near my house is a park fence which has recently been mended with a number of pine slabs, the bark being still on them. The bark has been pierced by holes, apparently those of the Sirex, and advantage has been taken of them by sundry small solitary bees. One day, while examining the fence, on which the sun was shining brightly, I caught a sudden flash of crimson in one of the holes, and, on carefully cutting away the wood. found a fine Chrysis quite perfect and ready to emerge when the year should be sufficiently advanced.

On following up the investigation I found great numbers of Ruby-tails similarly situated. They were all curled up after their peculiar fashion, so that they were as round as balls. They are enabled to assume this attitude by means of the structure of the body. In the first place, the abdomen is attached to the thorax by a short foot-stalk; and in the next, its under surface is hollowed. The insect, therefore, can bring the abdomen completely forward, when the thorax and closed legs fit into the hollow of the abdomen, and, the head being bent downwards, the Ruby-tail is rolled up as completely as a hedgehog.

There are numbers of species belonging to this splendid group, and, on account of their insect-destroying habits, many of them are extremely useful to agriculturists, as they feed not on the food laid up for the larvæ, but on the larvæ themselves. For example, we have already seen that the larvæ of certain Saw Flies pass the chief part of their larval state upon the plant on which the eggs have been laid, and then, when they are full-fed, leave the plant and burrow into the ground, where they pass through their changes into pupa and perfect insect. Such is the case with the well-known Saw Fly which infests the gooseberry; and the services rendered by the Chrysis in thinning the numbers of these troublesome insects, are thus described by M. St. Fargeau.

He remarks that after the larvæ of the Saw Fly had burrowed into the ground, he saw a female Chrysis make its way to the burrows, bend her abdomen forward, and thrust the tubular ovipositor into the holes and deposit an egg in each, the whole operation occupying barely a second of time. In the following year he witnessed a wonderful sight at the same spot. At least a hundred males as well as many females had been hatched, and were traversing in all directions the ground in which the Saw Fly larvæ had burrowed. As they ran backwards and forwards in the sunbeams, their glittering bodies flashed like jewels, and this beautiful scene was repeated for many days.

The insects always made their appearance from ten to twelve in the morning, after which time they dispersed; and M. St. Fargeau thinks that when they had once left the spot they did not return, but that those which appeared on each successive morning were merely hatched out of the cells of the Saw Flies which they had supplanted.

As is often the case with insects, the two sexes differ much in their colouring, so that the males and females of the same species have been described and catalogued as belonging to two different species. It is curious to see how analogies hold good in zoology. The Ruby-tails have been aptly compared to the Humming Birds, and the rule holds good with the insects as with the birds, namely, that the two sexes are so differently coloured that they may readily be taken for distinct species.

As our British Chrysididæ are tolerably numerous and are so brilliant in colour, it is but natural to conclude that the foreign Chrysididæ—especially those within the tropical belt—would be many in number and exceed our own species in point of beauty. This however is not the case, for there are but few exotic Chrysididæ, and scarcely any of them exceed our own lovely Ruby-tails in size or brilliancy of colour. Even in tropical America, whence come so many of the most dazzling insects in the world, scarcely any Chrysididæ have been discovered. I have, therefore, only selected two species as types of foreign Chrysididæ.

Of course there may be yet undiscovered species, for, as we have seen from M. St. Fargeau's interesting account, hundreds of Ruby-tails may be assembled within a few square feet at 10 A.M., and at noon not one will be seen on the very spot which was but a short time before a blaze of living jewels.

THE insect which is here represented belongs to the genus Stilbum. This word is formed from the Greek, and signifies "polished," or "glittering."

Just a hundred years ago Fabricius described the splendid insect which is here figured, mentioning it under the title of *Chrysis splendida*. It is an Australian insect, and is remarkable not only for its size but its beauty, which fully deserves the name of splendid. The head is emerald-green, as is the thorax, and both are washed with a tinge of azure. The abdomen is of the richest blue, glossed with green and purple; and the whole of the head, thorax, and body is covered with bold and

FIG. 207.—Stilbum splendidum. (Azure, glossed with green.)

deep punctures which increase the rich depth of colour. One specimen in the British Museum has the abdomen green. The abdomen is tipped with a horny plate cut deeply into four bold teeth.

Besides the Australian specimens there are many others from different parts of the world, such as Ceylon, China, the Eastern Archipelago, Madagascar, Brazil, Southern Africa, &c. These are smaller than the Australian specimens, and, as a rule, the abdomen is green instead of blue. The Australian specimens are much larger than any other of the Chrysididæ, and it is just possible that they may prove to be a distinct species. As to the prey of this insect, little if anything seems to be known about it. But it is always difficult to identify the particular species of insect on which any particular Chrysis is parasitic—the latter seldom restricting itself to any one species, and being at one time parasitic on a bee, and at another on a wasp. Mr. F. Smith suggests that the reason for this indifference is that the larva of the Chrysis always feeds upon some other larva, and that there is little distinction between the larva of a bee and that of a wasp.

THE insect called *Chrysis oculata* is also described by Fabricius. It is an Asiatic species, and is subject to great variation of colour—some specimens being wholly green, while others are entirely blue; and in either case the surface has a gloss of the second colour, green being glossed with blue, and blue with green. On either side of the abdomen is a single eye-like spot of glowing, ruddy gold, redder in the middle, and with an outer ring of yellow. This eye-like spot has gained for the insect the specific title of *oculata*. The abdomen is tipped with six teeth.

FIG. 208.—Chrysis oculata. (Emerald green.)

CHAPTER III.

ACULEATA.—MUTILLAS AND SCOLIAS.

IN the preceding insects the ovipositor is so formed as to serve only its primary purpose; namely, the deposition of the eggs. In those creatures, however, which will now be described, the ovipositor is used as a weapon, and is connected with a poison-gland by means of which a venomous fluid is injected into any wound which is made by the sting, as this modified ovipositor is called. In the social Hymenoptera, such as certain ants, bees, wasps, &c., there is always a great proportion of undeveloped females, called neuters, or workers. These insects do not lay eggs, but they notwithstanding possess the sting, which is employed solely as a weapon of offence. This group of insects is technically called *Aculeata*, from a Latin word signifying "a sting."

THE first group of Aculeata is called Mutillidæ, and the insects which compose it are popularly known by the name of Solitary Ants. As the latter name implies, they do not live in communities as do most of the true ants, and therefore no neuters or workers are required. There is, indeed, one genus, Dorylus, in which males and neuters have been discovered, but no females. Probably because of the existence of the neuter insect, several practical entomologists are disposed to consider that Dorylus ought by rights to be placed among the true ants, and not among the Mutillas. A species of Dorylus will be described presently. The females are wingless, and are armed with stings. No insect seems to be so venomous in proportion to its size as the female Mutilla; and in the case of one of our own species, *Mutilla Europæa*, the sting is scarcely less to be dreaded than that of the hornet itself.

One foreign species, *Mutilla coccinea*, of North America, is said to possess so venomous a sting that a person who was stung by one of these insects became insensible in a few minutes, and very nearly lost his life.

So unlike are the males and females of these insects, that the two sexes have more than once been catalogued not only as different species, but as belonging to different genera.

THE accompanying illustration represents a species from Bahia, bearing the specific name of *cerbera*, in allusion to the legendary dog which guarded the portals of Hades. As may be seen by the figure, it bears a curious resemblance to our well-known

FIG. 209.—Mutilla cerbera.
(Black and white.)

hunting spider. Its colours are very simple, being only black and white—the latter being of a peculiar dull, dead character that is very difficult to express. The insect looks indeed as if it had been originally black, and that a pattern had been drawn on it with white paint. It is thickly covered with hair, as is the case with most of the Mutillas, though in this species the hair is not so long as in many others.

THE really fine insect called *Mutilla occidentalis* belongs to North America.

This is a very hairy species, and is most splendidly coloured with black and scarlet. In the male the head and a large patch upon the thorax are scarlet. The abdomen is black, but is adorned with a number of scarlet rings, of exactly the same hue as that upon the thorax. The wings are brown. The wingless female is also black and scarlet, though the colours are differently arranged. In this sex the whole of the insect is scarlet except a single chevron-shaped bar of black across the middle of the abdomen. Seeing that the difference in colour is so great, it is really no wonder that the two sexes may have been thought to belong to separate species.

FIG. 210.—Mutilla occidentalis.
(Scarlet and black.)

There are several hundred species of Mutilla in the British Museum, many of which have not as yet been described. Among those that have received names I will briefly mention three. First is *Mutilla Klugii*, of Mexico, a very strange looking insect. Its head and thorax are black and covered with short hairs, while its abdomen is thickly covered with very long yellow hairs, so long and so thick that they make the insect look like a yellow brush with a black handle.

Mutilla cephalotes, i.e. the Big-headed Mutilla, is very rightly named. It has a head of enormous size in proportion to the body, and looking exactly as if it had been covered with black silk velvet. The thorax and abdomen are also black, but upon the middle of the latter is a large patch of orange, and beneath it the abdomen is crossed by several bright yellow bars. This insect is a native of Brazil. Another of the large-headed Mutillas is one named *Mutilla capitata*, of Mexico. This insect is coloured almost exactly like our common wasp, and might be taken for a wasp were it not for its very large head.

An idea of the general appearance presented by the large-headed Mutilla may be obtained by inspecting the accompanying illustration, which represents *Mutilla armata*, a Brazilian

Fig. 211.—Mutilla armata.
(Black and yellow.)

insect. The ground colour of this species is black, and the light-coloured marks are white, taking a greyish hue on the head and thorax.

Now comes the remarkable genus Dorylus, to which a reference has already been made. The species which is here represented comes from Java. In this genus the abdomen is long and almost cylindrical, not in the least resembling that of Mutilla.

Members of the genus Dorylus are found in various parts of the world; and in the British Museum are very many species, some from Africa, some from New Guinea, some from Ceylon, and some from Palestine. Several specimens were taken at Ramoth-gilead. None of them have any brilliancy of colouring, the usual hues being brown, black, and dull yellow.

Although one of the largest of all the genus, the present species is in no way conspicuous, and presents no attractions except to the entomologist. Its colour is brown-yellow, and the wings are transparent, but clouded with brown. The first of the two figures represents the winged male. Both in Africa and Java the male Doryli are known to be nocturnal in their habits, and, like many of our English insects, fly into houses at night; immediately making their way towards the lamp or candle which attracted them. The worker is very small in proportion to the male, as may be seen by reference to the line on the right of the illustration, which represents the average length of the worker. Its colour is nothing but brown, and

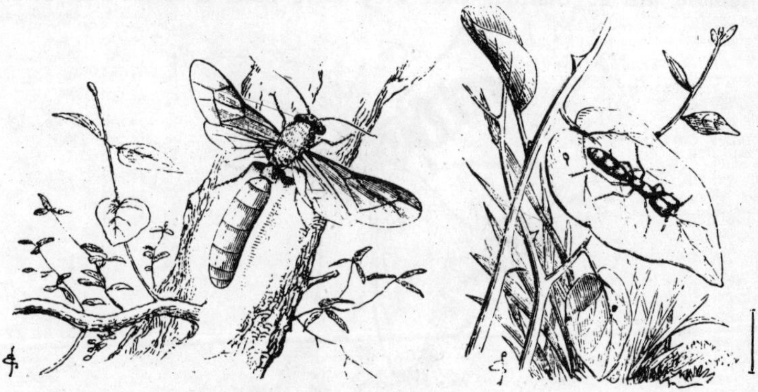

Male. FIG. 212.—Dorylus longicornis. Worker.
(Brownish yellow.)

only the peculiarly shaped head indicates its relationship to the Mutillas.

It is a very strange thing that the male should be quite a familiar insect, the worker tolerably plentiful, and not a female to be found anywhere. This difficulty probably arises from the great dissimilarity between the sexes, a phenomenon which is very common in the Mutillas. It is conjectured that the real female of this species may be an odd-looking creature which has been called *Dichthadia glaberrima.* This is a flattish, grub-like creature, about half as long again as the male insect, and having its tail curiously forked, something like the tail of a fish. Indeed, the whole creature looks very much like one of those mother-of-pearl fishes made in China and used as card-markers or counters. The name *Dichthadia,* which signifies something which is cleft or split in two, refers to this form of the tail; and the word *glaberrima*, which signifies "very smooth," is given to it on account of the glossy and polished surface of the body.

MANY systematic entomologists have formed the insects of which the *Thynnus Australis* is an example into a separate family under the name of Thynnidæ.

Why this name should be given to the insect, or indeed to any insect at all, is more than I can understand, inasmuch as the word *Thynnus* signifies the tunny fish, and ought never to have been foisted upon an insect. In this genus the male and female are so distinct that they have been described as two

FIG. 213.—Thynnus Australis. Male.
(Black and yellow.)

distinct species—the one as Thynnus, and the other as Myrmecoda. Indeed, had it not been for an opportune discovery by Mr. Lewis, the identity of the two insects would not even have been suspected. It is rather curious that another so-called Myrmecoda has turned out to be nothing but the female of a Scotæna.

The genus Thynnus appears to be exclusively Australian, and all of them have a very wasp-like look about them. The present species almost exactly resembles our common hornet, except that the dark portions are black instead of deep chestnut. They are all parasitic insects, feeding on the subterranean larvæ and pupæ of certain moths. One species, *Thynnus Wallisii*, is most curiously coloured. The male is plain yellow-brown, but the female is covered with a tracery of fine black lines exactly resembling that heraldic bearing termed "vairy."

To judge from analogy, the sting of the female Thynnus must be really terrible. There is a little British species allied to Thynnus, and known as *Methoca ichneumonoides*. Mr. F. Smith has described and figured this insect in his "British Fossorial Hymenoptera," in which a minute and detailed description may be seen. He tells me that he has taken both sexes on the sands in several parts of our southern shores. It prefers the hottest part of the day for action, and the female runs about rapidly over the sands in a very ant-like fashion. If incautiously handled she uses her sting, and the effect has been likened to a red-hot needle piercing the hand. So, if so tiny an insect can inflict real pain, the sting of the comparatively gigantic must be even dangerous to life.

FIG. 214.—Thynnus Australis. Female. (Black and yellow.)

Mr. Westwood says that when touched or alarmed, the Methoca acts after the fashion of the Chrysis, and rolls itself into a ball, the abdomen being bent upon the thorax, and the head drooping downwards. Here, again, the two sexes are so different that they have been described as separate insects, the female retaining the name of Methoca, and the male being placed in the genus Tengyra, one of the Scolia group. It is no wonder that such a mistake should have been made, for no two insects can seem more dissimilar than the wingless and ant-like female which runs about on the sand, and the male which flies above her in the air. The female has short antennæ, a pear-shaped abdomen, and the thorax formed into three knots, just as if strings had been tied round it when soft. The male, on the contrary, is slender, long-bodied, has very long antennæ, and his thorax is continuous and not broken up into knots.

Next comes a small group of Hymenoptera called Scoliidæ. These insects are chiefly found in the hottest parts of the world, and the warmer the temperature the more plentiful are the Scoliidæ. In some of the genera which belong to this group, the females are without wings, like those of the Mutillas which have just been described. Two examples of the typical genus will be briefly described.

The first of these insects is called *Scolia flavifrons*, and inhabits the warmer parts of Europe. Its colour is black, diversified with four bold yellow patches on the abdomen. The front of the head is also yellow—a fact which has gained for the insect the specific name of *flavifrons*, i.e. having a yellow forehead.

As the habits of this species are very well known, they will be described as an example of the entire genus.

Fig. 215.—Scolia flavifrons.
(Black and yellow.)

When the female is about to prepare for a future brood, she begins by seeking some dry, sandy spot, and there digging a hole which is of considerable depth. There is one species, *Scolia bicincta*, which makes a hole at least eighteen inches deep. The hole being dug, the Scolia goes off in search of prey, and soon returns with a large larva, mostly that of a lamellicorn beetle. This she places at the bottom of the hole, and then lays an egg close to it.

The egg is soon hatched, and the young larva at once begins to devour the beetle-grub which has been placed there as food. The grub is always large enough to last the Scolia larva throughout its first stage of existence. When the larva has eaten the whole of its food, it prepares for its next change by spinning an oval cocoon, in which it passes to the pupal and afterwards to the perfect state. This cocoon is a long oval in shape, tolerably alike at each end, but having at the upper end a sort of lid, which is pushed open by the newly-developed insect when it makes its way into the open air. Any of my readers who would wish to see these curious objects, can do so by visiting the Nest Room in the British Museum, where is a fine series of cocoons brought from Florence, most of them being cut open so as to show the method in which the inhabitant is packed up within them.

I believe that each species of Scolia chooses some particular insect as the food for its young, or at all events that it selects insects that are closely allied. The *Scolia bicincta,* for example, places a single large locust at the bottom of its cell; and some entomologists think that several species of this group do not dig burrows, but place their eggs in the nest of some Solitary Bee.

FIG. 216.—Scolia procera.
(Black and yellow.)

MANY of the Scoliidæ are large insects, and the species which is shown in the above illustration is one of the giants of the

Hymenoptera. Indeed, its specific name, *procera*, which signifies something which is very much elongated, refers to its great size. It is drawn of its proper dimensions.

Even independent of its size, this is a really handsome insect. The body is black, with some patches of yellow arranged as shown in the illustration, and the bold and ample wings are rich shining black, glossed with dark and almost metallic green. The body is thickly clothed with dense furry hair.

CHAPTER IV.

FORMICIDÆ, OR ANTS.

THE wonderful insects which are known by the popular name of Ants are essentially creatures of the sun, even though, as in many cases, they are unable not only to endure his direct beams, but even to bear the ordinary light of day. Wherever on the face of the earth the sun shines strongest, there are the Ants in greatest force. In fact, they form a broad belt round the earth, thickest towards the equator, and thinning gradually towards the poles.

Take, for example, the northern parts of the world, and scarcely an Ant is to be seen. Take our own country, and there we have a few species—none large, most small, and some of the very minutest dimensions. But in the tropical parts of the earth the Ants are masters of the soil, and no living creature can stand in their path. Not only do they absolutely swarm in point of numbers, but they attain no small size—many species being as large as the common English wasp, and infinitely more formidable.

As even a slight sketch of the Ant tribes would occupy several volumes, it is necessary to select those species which afford the most salient examples of this vast group. The first example is the largest of all the Ant tribe, and is appropriately called *Componotus* (or *Formica*) *gigas*.

This is an insect which has a very large range of country, the specimens in the British Museum having been brought from India, Singapore, and Borneo. As the figures which are here given are drawn from measurement, the reader will easily see that the insect is a most formidable creature. It is distributed over a considerable part of the world, the specimens in the

British Museum having been brought from India, Singapore, and Borneo.

The three illustrations represent three of the forms of the perfect insect. The first is the winged male. The thorax is black and the abdomen brown, and in this, as in the female, the legs are slender and very long in proportion to the body. The second figure represents the winged female, which is very much larger than her mate, and has a much stouter and more rounded body. As is the case with our English Ants, the winged specimens only retain their wings for a very short time, breaking them off close to the body when they are about to settle down in life.

FIG. 217.—Componotus gigas. Male. (Blackish-brown.)

The third figure represents the Soldier. This is nearly as

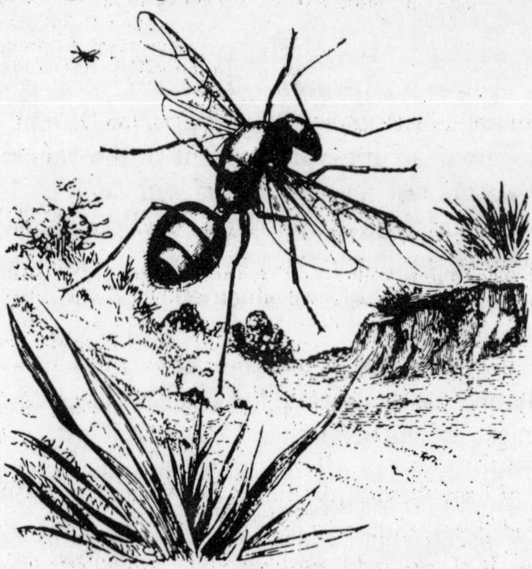

FIG. 218.—Componotus gigas. Female. (Blackish-brown.)

large as the female. The abdomen, it is true, is smaller, but this is compensated by the head, which is squared, and of enormous relative size. This development of the head is necessary in order to afford attachment to the muscles which work the formidable jaws. A good idea of these weapons can be formed by inspecting the illustration, but their real power cannot

FIG. 219.—Componotus gigas. Soldier. (Blackish-brown.)

be appreciated without the aid of a magnifying glass. They are flattened, and on their inner edge are covered with teeth, one long and sharp tooth projecting from the middle. The edges are yellow in all the sexes, and in the Soldier are exceedingly conspicuous.

THERE are many species of this genus, and all seem to possess similar habits. There is, for example, *Componotus compressus,* so called on account of the shape of the body, which is rather flattened. Respecting this insect, Mr. F. Smith gives me the following information :—

It is much smaller than the preceding species, and lives underground. It is one of the commonest of insects, and indeed is more plentiful than welcome in inhabited places. The workers act very much like those of our common Wood Ant, and are perpetually ascending and descending trees.

The soldiers are wonderfully combative in their nature, and fight so constantly and so fiercely, that an entomologist finds great difficulty in capturing a specimen which has not been more or less mutilated in battle. Indeed, it seems that two soldiers can hardly meet without having a single combat, when a certain code of rules is as strictly observed as in the prize-ring of our own country. It often happens that one of the combatants kills the other, and in that case the body is at once seized by a number of little Ants belonging to the genus Myrmica, which run in and drag the dead body to their nests. This species begins to swarm somewhere towards the end of May, and the females fly with a loud whirring sound.

ANOTHER species of Componotus has been selected because it has some claims to beauty. Its body is black, but across the middle of the abdomen runs a broad band of greyish white hairs

FIG. 220.—Componotus sericeiventris.
(Black, with white band on abdomen.)

having a peculiar silken sheen, which has earned for the insect the specific name of *sericeiventris*, or "silver-belly."

IN the various accounts of Ant life which have been narrated by observers, there is often an absolutely startling resemblance to the conduct of human beings. We have heard of Ants which make regular slave-hunting expeditions into the territory of less powerful Ants, carry off their captives, and make them their servants. We know of Ants which build walls and domed roofs, as if they had been taught by an architect. We know of Ants which have their milch kine, and which tend and guard them as carefully as any dairyman tends his cows. We know of Ants which cultivate the ground, keep it clear of weeds, sow the future crop, and, when the harvest has come to maturity, get it in, just like human beings. In the history which now follows, a new and unexpected phase of human life is found to exist among Ants; namely, funeral honours paid to the dead, and burial in the earth.

In the "Journal of the Linnæan Society," vol. v. p. 217, is a singularly interesting communication by Mrs. Lewis Hutton, of Sydney, New South Wales:—

"One very hot and cloudless day, when not a breath of air stirred the leaves, my eldest boy (four years old), coming up from the beach fatigued and hot, threw himself on a grassy mound near where I was sitting, and remained quietly enjoying the rest and the pleasure he would have in showing to his sister the pretty shells and corals he had found. I was startled by a sudden scream, such as one only gives when in terrible pain. A snake was my first thought, and in horror I went to the child, but was at once reassured by seeing him covered with 'Soldier Ants,' on whose nest he had unwittingly laid down. Some of the insects still clung on with their forceps and stung my poor boy, who roared with pain at every fresh attack, while I killed them as fast as I could, assisted by the nurse. At length all were removed, about twenty being left dead on the ground.

"Going to see the little fellow bathed with something to ease the pain, I was absent about half-an-hour, and then returned to the same place, when I saw a number of the Ants surrounding the dead ones. Being fond of natural history, and having read much concerning the instinct of Ants, I determined to watch them closely. At last, four ran off very quickly, and I followed them until I saw them enter a hillock containing an ants' nest, which we had in vain tried to get rid of on account of the annoyance caused by their close vicinity to our sitting tent.

"They remained here about five minutes, when a number more came out two by two and proceeded slowly to the place where their dead companions lay. Here they seemed to wait for something, and presently we saw coming from the other side near the creek, a number surpassing those I had followed, and halting at the same place. Then two Ants took up one of the dead ones and marched off, followed by two others as mourners; then two others entered the procession with a second dead Ant, succeeded in the same way by another pair, and so on until all the dead were taken up; a number of, I should think, two hundred bringing up the rear.

"Following the train, I found that the two empty-handed followers relieved their fellows in advance, the latter following behind in the place of those who relieved them, and thus continuing to alternate from time to time. They had now gone a considerable distance towards the seaside, when they stopped at a sandy hillock, where those who marched in the rear of the procession commenced operations by making holes; but I soon observed that only about half the number took part in this employment.

"When a sufficient number of graves had been dug, the dead bodies were laid in them, and I found that those Ants which had hitherto stood idle were deputed to cover them in. About six would not stir from their places, and on these the others fell and killed them, whereupon they made a single large pit at a distance from the other graves, into which all the six were put and duly covered up. The Ants then all paired off, and marched back to the scene of slaughter, where they remained together for a few minutes, when each company left for their own habitation.

"The observation of this curious proceeding gave me great pleasure, and I had frequent opportunities afterwards of seeing the insects act much in the same way. If one of the workers, however (who are much smaller than the rest), were killed, it was buried where it fell, and no friends attended the funeral."

THE almost human aspects of Ant life are well known to entomologists. We have seen the rules of single combat strictly observed, and the still more remarkable fact that Ants bury the bodies of their comrades and attend the funeral. Another phase of humanity is to be found among those most remarkable insects,—namely, the power of utilizing other Ants to do their work for them; in fact, keeping domestic servants. And, as is the case with primitive civilization, these servants are slaves, yet are happy and devoted to the masters who stole them from their own homes. Not that they ever saw the home which was theirs by rights, for they are captured while still in the pupal state, and therefore know no other home than that of their masters.

The latter insects depend entirely on the slaves, and are

absolutely helpless without them. Those who have observed the manners and customs of these Ants say that the relative behaviour of the two species is most curious. The masters can scarcely even feed themselves, much less go in search of food. The experiment has been made of putting into a glass case a number of the master Ants, together with a portion of the nest, with food and all needful requisites. The Ants were ludicrously helpless, running about in a purposeless sort of manner, and not having the least idea what to do. After their incapacity had been proved, a single slave was admitted, when the whole state of things was changed. The slave—a mere dwarf among giants —treated the master Ants as a nurse would treat a number of children, fed them, and then began to rebuild the damaged nest.

The accompanying illustration depicts one of these slave-making species, *Polyergus rufescens*, one of the Ants being shown as carrying in its jaws the pupa of a slave. The relative size of master and servant is thus shown, the slave being scarcely larger than our common Red Ant. It is a European species, and is common in France. The jaws of this species are very slight and feeble, so that the insect is physically incapable of doing the work which generally falls to the lot of Ants who have to make their own nest, find their own food, and nurse their own young. Mr. Darwin makes much use of this phenomenon in his well-known work on the "Origin of Species."

FIG. 221.—Polyergus rufescens. (Red-brown.)

The following account of a slave-making Ant is contributed by Mr. W. H. Dale to the "American Naturalist," and is valuable both as showing that division of labour is employed among Ants, and that the slaves can be sent from one place to another by the order of their masters :—

"It was growing rather dark in the dense thicket, and I retraced my steps towards the beach. On my way I added several other interesting birds (Momoti) to my collection, and one—a dark-coloured, sad-looking bird, which proved the greatest prize of all—being a new species, afterwards described by Mr. Lawrence as *Spermophila badiiventris.* Reaching the edge of the wood, I found a small brook between me and the sand. The banks, being low, were covered for several rods on the farther side with a succulent plant of the order Portulacacæ, with round leaves about half an inch in diameter. I noticed little well-beaten paths, about one inch wide, running all through this bed of green, and stopped to discover if possible what made them.

"Some were wider than others, and on one of these I soon discovered a foraging party of Ants. They were of two species, one being a rather small black Ant with weak jaws or nippers, and the other nearly twice the size, each bearing a formidable pair of prolonged mandibles of jaws; and as near as I could see there were no two with jaws exactly the same size or shape. The small ones were evidently slaves. They were marched between two rows of scouts, and if a slave attempted to pass the line, he was speedily seized and put back, not very gently, into his place. I watched their motions with a great deal of interest. The 'soldiers,' after searching till satisfied for a rich succulent leaf, bit it off and gave it to a slave, who immediately marched off with it in a contrary direction to the main body. Following the train for a rod or two, I came to the brook just where it had made an abrupt bend, with an eddy in it. Here the banks were rather high; a moderately brisk sea-breeze was coming from the shore, and just here a small tree about two inches in diameter had fallen across the brook. On this pole were myriads of Ants going in different directions.

"Those above, each with a leaf in his mouth, were crossing to the wooded side; those on the under-side were empty-handed (or mouthed) and were coming from the woods. Here I noticed a curious thing—the leaf, being larger by far than its bearer, acted as a sort of sail to catch the wind; and I saw many an unfortunate slave-ant, after struggling with all its might to save its precious load, finally let it go in self-defence, and immediately join the excursionists on the lower side of the pole, going back for another leaf. In the eddy before mentioned there was at least a bushel of leaves which had been blown from their bearers."

It is worthy of notice that in their slave-hunting raids the master Ants always select the pupæ of the worker slaves. The slaves are not always of the same species, for the master Ant, which has been taken as an example, takes indifferently the pupa of *Formica fusca* and *Formica cunicularia*.

THE very curious nest which is shown below is drawn of its natural size, and is the work of an insect called *Polyrachis textor*, a native of Malacca.

The nest looks exactly as if it were made of coarse hair, and is of so open a texture that the inmates may be seen through the walls. Although the workers are tolerably common, the males are hardly ever to be seen, and the females are comparatively rare. The colour of the insect is black.

FIG. 222.—Polyrachis textor.
(Black.)

There are many species of this genus in different parts of the world. The generic name *Polyrachis* signifies "many-ridged," and is given to the insects on account of the projections which appear on various parts of their bodies. Perhaps the most remarkable species in this respect is *Polyrachis bihamata*, an insect which is found both in India and Borneo. The name *bihamata* signifies "double-backed," and is very appropriate. Upon the upper surface of the thorax are set two hooks, sharply pointed, curved backwards, and sloped almost exactly like the horns of the chamois. These are long and conspicuous, but are far surpassed by two other hooks which rise from the centre of the footstalk which connects the abdomen with the thorax.

These hooks are of enormous comparative size, each of them, if straightened, being about half as long as the entire body.

There are many species of Polyrachis, nearly all of which are black. There is, however, an exception in one of the species from Sarawak, which has the thorax and abdomen banded with yellow.

UNTIL lately it was thought that the only honey-makers were the bees, and no one would have been bold enough to say that honey could be obtained from any other insects. Yet we now know that there are honey-making wasps, building cells which are as capable of holding the liquid sweets as those of the bee; and here we have an example of an Ant, which not only makes honey, but stores it in a way which I believe to be unique. The bee and the wasp store the honey in cells composed of materials which will resist its action, but the Ants actually store the honey in their own bodies. This is done in a very remarkable manner.

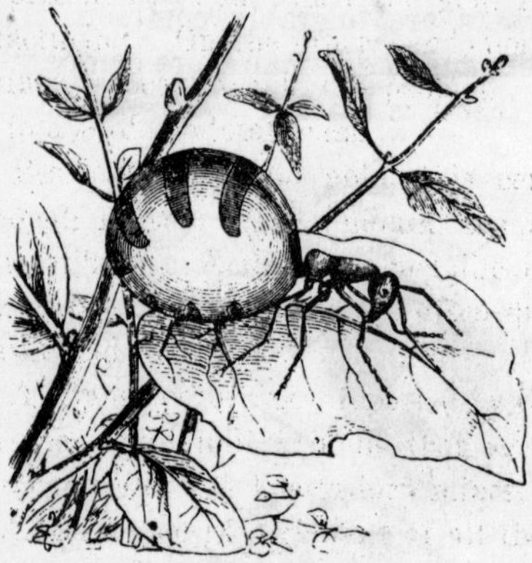

FIG. 223.—Myrmecocystus Mexicanus. (Reddish brown.)

Certain of the workers are set aside for this purpose, and are bitten at the end of the abdomen. The bite causes an inflammation, the result of which is that the passages of the body are entirely closed. These insects are then perpetually fed with honey, none of which can escape, and the result is that their bodies swell to an enormous extent, assuming the shape which is shown in the illustration. This form is caused by the distension of the membrane between the segments. How great is the distension may be seen by reference to the illustration, the dark portions representing the segments, and the remainder the membrane.

These Ants are natives of Mexico, where they are very common, being popularly known either as "hormigas miêleras," *i.e.* honey-ants, or "hormigas mochileras," *i.e.* pouch-ants. They are in great request, and are sold by measure. One of the principal uses to which they are put is the manufacture of a sort of mead, the Ants being first pressed so as to squeeze the honey out of them. There is a bottle full of these strange insects in the British Museum.

The colour is like that of the common burrowing Ant, being reddish brown on the thorax, and darker on the abdomen. The honey-pot insects have a most curious look, the membrane of the abdomen being so thin and transparent that the honey can be plainly seen within the body. The generic name *Myrmecocystus* is formed from two Greek words, the one signifying an ant, and the other a bag or pouch.

THE insect which is here shown, although not quite the largest of the Ant tribe, is among the giants of the group. It is an inhabitant of tropical America, and is tolerably common.

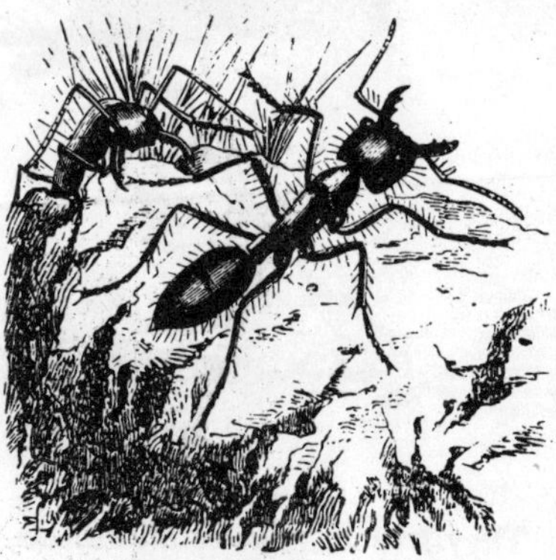

FIG. 224.—Dinoponera grandis. (Black.)

It is by no means a prepossessing insect in appearance, being of a dull, dead black in colour, and slow and sluggish in its movements. It lives in very small colonies, consisting of some six or seven individuals only, and the inhabitants of each colony do not seem to have any idea of working in concert. Their nest is generally under a stone.

Both the females and neuters possess stings, and the venom with which their weapons are armed causes such excruciating pain that the name *Dinoponera* is very appropriate. This name is formed from two Greek words, the former signifying "terrible" and the latter "wicked." In consequence of the virulent character of the poison, the Macoushie Indians employ the Ant in the manufacture of their celebrated Wourali poison. I do not believe that it has the least effect on the poison, the active part of which is purely vegetable. The body of this Ant is nearly bare, only a few short hairs being scattered over it. The description is taken from a fine specimen in my collection, presented to me by the Rev. J. H. Bernau.

An allied species, *Ponera contracta*, has been discovered in England. It is widely spread, though not very plentiful. It is a very tiny insect, but yet has many of the habits of its gigantic relative, living under stones in small communities and not working in concert. The nest, like that of the Dinoponera, is found under stones or at the roots of plants.

THE insect which is here shown belongs to a group of insects which are popularly called Foraging Ants, on account of their singular habits.

FIG. 225.—Eciton hamata.
(Reddish brown.)

They live in vast communities, and sally out in large armies in search of food. They are marshalled as regularly as if they were soldiers, and, as is the case with human soldiers, are commanded by officers. These officers are the large-headed neuters, one of which is shown in the illustration. Their legs are long and active, their bodies are slender, but their heads are of enormous comparative size, each side of the head being swollen into a semi-globular form. The jaws with which the head is armed are exceedingly formidable. Each jaw is nearly half as long as the body, is very sharply pointed, and is curved into a hook-like shape both inwards and downwards. Mr. F. Smith was kind enough to present me with a good series of these insects.

varying in size from the largest soldier to the smallest worker, which is no larger than our Red Ant.

Mr. Bates gives a very graphic account of this insect and its predatory excursions. He states that a column of Foraging Ants is of very great length. One column that he saw must have been at least a hundred yards in length, because the portion that was visible was from sixty to seventy yards in length, and neither end of the column could be seen.

"The large-headed individuals were in proportion of about five in one hundred to the small individuals, but not one of them carried anything in its mandibles; they were all trotting along outside the column, and distributed in regular proportions throughout the whole line of army, their globular white heads rendering them very conspicuous among the rest, bobbing up and down as they traversed the inequalities of the road.

"The progress of these Ants is not in one simple line when on a foraging expedition, but a line with many branches; a column is occasionally pushed out in the direction of some promising locality. I once observed one of these terminating at a decayed fallen tree. The Ants were busy about it, a few having seized some large Formicidæ, and also some soft-bodied wasps. These they tore in pieces and divided the load; the whole party then retired, and re-entered the main line. A branch column is not a party separated from the rest—there is no break in the lines of the Ants—but there is always a number passing and re-passing, keeping up the line of communication."

Mr. Bates gives also an account of another species, *Eciton prædator*:—

"This species of Eciton differs from all the others in its habits: instead of foraging in narrow columns, it hunts in dense masses of myriads of individuals. Nothing in entomology is more curious than to watch the vast compact body moving rapidly along; when they pass, all the rest of the insect world is in agitation and alarm. They stream along the ground, and climb to the summit of all the lower trees, searching every leaf to its apex. When they come to a mass of decaying vegetable matter, they cover it with a living crowd, penetrating every chink and cranny; then leave it, and rapidly move on.

"All apterous insects, especially fat spiders and larvæ of

Blattæ, which latter are excessively numerous about the fallen foliage, scamper off before the rapidly moving mass in quite a ridiculous manner. The smaller larvæ of Lepidoptera and Diptera fall an easy prey to them, as well as some of the large obese species of the genus Formica.

"The phalanx altogether, when passing over a tract of open ground, occupies a space of from six to ten square yards. On examining them closely, they are seen to move not altogether in one uniform direction, but in variously spreading dense columns, now separating a little from the general mass, now re-uniting with it. The margins of the phalanx spread out at times, like a cloud of skirmishers from the vast army."

The Ecitons do not restrict themselves to the open air, but penetrate into houses, where they exterminate every living thing. My brother has had much experience of these visitations, and the following passage is an extract from one of his letters:—

"You mention what I told you in relation to the Ants and cockroaches. The time when I wrote to you on the subject was my first experience of the Ant, but since then I have seen the same game every year since I have lived in this country. The performance always takes place just before the commencement of the rainy season, at which time the Travelling Ants commence their marches. Wherever they make their appearance, every living thing bolts (not that they are frightened, but that their business engagements carry them elsewhere in a hurry) as fast as the number of legs given them will permit.

"The first sign of the approach of the Ants is a peculiar rustling, which sounds like a few dead leaves in an eddy of wind. Then a big cockroach, in size and colour like a large date, scuttles across the floor, and about a yard behind him comes one little Ant about a sixth of an inch in length. One's first impression is that the cockroach is a great coward, but his conduct is soon explained, for from every hole and crevice on all sides of the house pour continuous streams of Ants, until the whole floor is black with them.

"Then our friend's fate is sealed. It is no avail to him that he is many hundred times bigger than his enemies; they fasten on him in a body, and in a few minutes no sign of a cockroach is visible. As a rule, these Ants go through every part of a house; and when they leave it, which is in one or two hours after their first appearance, no vermin of any description remain in the house. Rats, snakes, cockroaches, spiders, scorpions, and even fleas, all are gone, and for a month or two there is peace in the house."

These Ants not only devour the insects that go by the popular name of vermin, but attack every insect that may come in their way. They have been seen to capture the nests of the large and formidable wasp which hangs its nest from the Brazilian trees; and once Mr. Bates saw a column of Ecitons deliberately attack a nest of a great burrowing Ant, sink a shaft into it, and then pour into it by thousands. They tore out the inhabitants from their home, and were so fierce and bold that when Mr. Bates tried to catch some of the burrowing Ants for his collection, the Ecitons tried to pull them out of his fingers. This species was *Eciton legionis*, which always forms in a broad column when on the march, and not in a long narrow column.

ALTHOUGH the insect which is scientifically termed *Atta cephalotes* looks even more formidable than the Ecitons, it is not to be

FIG. 226.—Atta cephalotes.
(Reddish brown.)

dreaded as a foe. As we shall presently see, it is a most annoying insect, and often does great damage to the property of man, if not to his person. The native name of this insect is Saüba, and it is popularly known by the name of Umbrella or Parasol Ant, on account of a curious habit which it has of carrying pieces of leaves in its mouth. Whole columns of the Saüba Ant march deliberately along, each with its leaf held over its head like Malcolm's soldiers at the wood of Dunsinane. These leaves are employed in house-building, and are used after a very curious manner.

The nest of the Saüba is partly above ground, though the greatest portion of it, including all the tunnels, is below the surface of the earth. The visible part of the nest consists of a dome, seldom more than two feet in height, but often reaching forty feet in diameter. This dome is really formed of the leaves, the superincumbent earth being of slight thickness. It is a curious fact that the workers who fetch the leaves do not build with them, but merely lay them down and go off for more. In fact they are to the real nest-builders exactly what labourers are to bricklayers. Two figures of the Umbrella Ant are given in the illustration, one showing the front of the head, and the other the entire insect. The latter figure is a portrait of a specimen in the British Museum, which has preferred to die rather than loosen its hold of the leaf.

Large as the nest is, the dome forms but an inconsiderable portion of it. Vast tunnels radiate from it in all directions, and are carried to distances that seem almost incredible. The Ants work away underground, leaving no signs of their passage, and have a way of suddenly coming to the surface when least expected. My brother has sent me an account of a serious damage that was done to a gold-mine by the Travelling Ant, as he calls it. In mines where the gold is extracted from quartz-rock, the ore is obtained by driving galleries which are nearly horizontal. These galleries are supported by timber both at the sides and on the roof, and a tramway runs along the floor for the purpose of conveying the ore to the stamps. Last year (1872), during the wet season, the mine was suddenly flooded in spite of all the precautions that had been taken, a torrent of water pouring through the galleries with such force that the supporting timbers gave way, and the sides closed in so much that the cars could not pass over the tram.

On examination it was found that this misfortune was caused by the Saüba Ant, which had driven one of its tunnels completely into the gallery, and so diverted a large amount of surface drainage into the mine. A professional ant-killer was sent for from a considerable distance, and the extirpation of the nest decreed. It may seem strange that there should be such a profession, but the local circumstances make it needful.

The process of extermination is a very curious one. In the first place, the ant-killer has to find the nest itself—a task which requires the greatest knowledge of the subject. Having found the dome which has been already mentioned, he builds round it a sort of large vaulted edifice, something like the snow hut of an Esquimaux. This oven is then filled with charcoal, sulphur, capsicum, and wood, both dry and green, through an opening at the top of the dome. The oven is then finally closed, with the exception of several small apertures which are made around it.

Fire is then introduced, and a number of negroes are set to work, each with a large pair of bellows, the nozzles of which are thrust into the apertures already mentioned. They never cease from blowing night or day, and on an average the operation is not complete until they have laboured for four days and as many nights. Meanwhile, the ant-killer is on the watch for smoke escaping from the ground, and wherever he sees this he knows that he has come upon one of the galleries. The place is at once marked and the aperture stopped with clay. In the present instance the nest was found upwards of eighty yards from the mine.

After the four days' work the negroes cease their labour, the oven is taken down, and the nest opened. Guided by the marks which he has made, the ant-killer lays open the whole of the tunnels, and, after taking care that not a living creature remains in them, he fills them as well as the nest with clay, which is well stamped down and left to harden in the sun. Then, and not until then, is the place considered safe.

It will now be seen how detrimental a neighbour the Umbrella Ant may be, even though it does not attack man personally. Here is a case where a mine was thrown out of work for many days, the whole of the timbering had to be replaced at no small expense, and the ant-killer paid very highly for his trouble. I have heard of another instance where the Saüba Ant drove its tunnel through the bank of a reservoir and let out all the water.

The sizes of the insects belonging to the same nest vary greatly, some being nearly as large as our common wasp, while others are scarcely as large as the common Red Ant of our garden. There are two distinct kinds of the large-headed neuters, one with smooth and the other with hairy heads. These latter insects seldom make their appearance in the open air, and the only way to evoke them is to break a hole in the dome and push a stick down the hole as far as possible. In a few minutes a few of these creatures will come slowly up, looking, as Mr. Bates says, like Cyclops, with their big head and the eye in the middle of the forehead. Why they should make their appearance is not very evident, for they seem to have no connection with or control over the workers. Neither do they fight, for Mr. Bates found no difficulty in securing several of them with his fingers.

The general colour of the Saüba is reddish brown, the colour being brightest on the head and dullest on the abdomen, where it is obscured by a coat of dull brown hairs. The wings of the perfect male and female are very much like those of the hornet, being firm, transparent, shining, and of a reddish brown, fading to yellow towards the tips. There are very few nervures.

We are all familiar with the passage—

"Go to the ant, thou sluggard; consider her ways, and be wise: which having no guide, overseer, or ruler, provideth her meat in the summer, and gathereth her food in the harvest."—Prov. vi. 6—8.

Many a time have we heard it said that Solomon was entirely wrong, and that the Ants, being essentially carnivorous, lay up no store for the winter, but become torpid until the same weather comes round again. Now this is all very true as regards the Ants of our own climate, but it is not true of Ants belonging to other countries. At the date of this book, at least nineteen species of Harvesting Ants have been discovered, some of which inhabit Palestine. I believe that no English Ant has been known to lay up seeds. The Black Ant was once seen to carry some fresh violet seeds into the nest, but they were all ejected on the following day.

The history of the present species has been admirably given by Mr. J. T. Moggridge, and for nearly all of the information here given I am indebted to his most interesting work on Ants and Trapdoor Spiders.

This species is spread largely over the world, and is well known at Mentone. It gathers seeds of various kinds and takes them to its subterranean treasure-houses. The burrows run to a considerable depth, sometimes passing even through sandstone rock, and at intervals are placed the granaries, which are about as large as a gentleman's watch. They vary in point of depth from the surface, some being fully thirteen inches deep, and others barely two inches. Among the seeds which the Mentone Ants take into their granaries are those of the oat, nettle, speedwell, goosefoot, calaminth, chickweed, amaranth, and shepherd's purse. They even take the green seed-vessels of the last-mentioned plant, twisting them off neatly with their jaws.

Fig. 227.—Aphenogaster barbata. (Black.)

They are very fastidious as to the quality of the seeds which are brought. A worker, which was evidently but a young one, was seen to bring in some rubbish instead of the proper seed, and was at once sent back. Mr. Moggridge played a trick upon them by placing little beads in their way; at first they took them for seeds and carried them into their nests, but they soon found out their error, and never touched them again.

With regard to the condition of the seeds, Mr. Moggridge has the following remarks:—

"It is extremely rare to find other than sound and intact seeds in the granaries, and we must conclude that the Ants exercise some mysterious power over them which checks the tendency to germinate.

"Apparently, it is not that moisture or warmth or the influence of atmospheric air is denied to the seeds, for we find them in damp soil, in genial weather, and often but a trifling distance below the surface of the ground, and I have proved that the vitality of the seeds is not affected, by having raised crops of young plants, such as fumitory, pellitory, *Polygonum aviculare*, and grasses, from seeds taken out of granaries.

"I have frequently remarked that it is the seeds last collected before a fall of rain which are brought out in a sprouting condition from the nest; for I have observed that it is these which are carried out from the nest and placed to dry after a wet night. And so, in the case of a nest which I kept in captivity, when a variety of different seeds had been successively supplied to the Ants, it was the cabbage, lettuce, and chicory seeds given the day before the nest was watered, that reappeared after being carried below, and not the hemp, canary, and mixed seeds of wild plants previously strewed on the nest.

"It seems possible that the process, whatever it may be, to which the Ants submit the seeds which are to remain dormant, may require some time, and the construction of the granary chambers is doubtless a long affair; so that when unusually large supplies of grain, &c., are brought in by the workers, some part of them may not find the necessary accommodation and attention.

"When the seeds do germinate in the nests—and it is my belief that they are usually softened and made to sprout before they are consumed by the Ants—it is very curious to see how the growth is checked in its earliest stage, and how, after the rudicle or fibril—the first growing root of dicotyledonous and monocotyledonous seeds—has been gnawed off, they are brought out from the nest and placed in the sun to dry, and then, after a sufficient exposure, carried below into the nest.

"The seeds are thus in effect *malted*, the starch being changed into sugar; and I have myself witnessed the avidity with which the contents of seeds thus treated are devoured by the Ants."

It seems almost a pity that creatures possessing such excellent qualities should be thieves, but thieves they are—robbing not only the nests of other insects, but those of their own species. In the course of these raids there are always severe combats, often terminating with loss of life. The antennæ being the most sensitive portion of the Ant, each combatant uses its utmost endeavours to seize one of the antennæ of the opponent, and when that is done the enemy always succumbs. Should, however, both parties succeed in evading the fatal grasp, they fight until one or the other is killed. They are not at all particular as to their food, eating grasshoppers, flies, bees, wasps, and even lizards when they can assemble in sufficient numbers. Mr. Moggridge gives an interesting account of a struggle between the Harvesting Ants and a caterpillar :—

"I was once a witness of a singular contest between a soft-bodied, smooth, greyish caterpillar, about an inch in length, and two medium-sized *barbara* Ants. The Ants were mere pigmies in comparison with their prey, for as such I believe they regarded the caterpillar, but they gripped its body with set mandibles, showing the most savage determination not to lose their hold.

"When I first discovered the group, the war was being waged in a tuft of grass over one of the entrances to the Ants' nest, and the caterpillar was striding along the leaves, and thrusting itself between the culms in the hope to shake off or brush away its little persecutors. From time to time the caterpillar would turn viciously round and endeavour to pluck away its assailants; but though it actually succeeded in stripping, by means of fore-legs and mouth, five of the six legs of one of the Ants, which was within its reach, they never loosened their hold.

"At length, a chance movement of mine shook the grass-leaf on which they were, and Ants and caterpillars rolled together down a steep and rocky slope to about four feet distant. They tumbled over and over several times, but still the Ants gripped their prey as firmly as ever.

"The last endeavour of the giant victim was to rub off the Ants by burrowing into the soil; but on uncovering its retreat I saw that their position was still the same. After watching this struggle for twenty minutes, time failed me, and I returned home, carrying with me, however, the combatants. When on my return I opened the box in which they were imprisoned, these bull-dog Ants were clinging with mandibles locked as firmly as ever; and now as I write, in death they are clinging still, drowned in a sea of spirits of wine."

From the observations of Mr. C. Horne, it appears that an Indian species of Ant, *Podomyrma rufonigra*, has a similar habit of storing up grain, carefully removing the husks. The grain is called by the natives *jarroon*, or sweepings; and it is stored in such quantities that in time of famine the granaries of the Ants are ransacked, and both the grain and the husks ground together into a coarse meal.

THE fine Ant which is here shown was first described by Mr. F. Smith, of the British Museum, in 1858. As may be seen, it is almost equal in size to *Componotus gigas*, the wings being ample and the body thick and rounded. The head is small in proportion to the rest of the body. The colour is shining black,

FIG. 228.—Carebara dux.
(Black.)

the polish being especially conspicuous in a broad belt round the abdomen. It is a native of Southern Africa.

WE have already seen that the Ants partake of many human characteristics,—how they make war with duly officered armies, take captives, employ slaves, fight single combats by rule, gather grain and harvest it. We have now to deal with an Ant that possesses another characteristic of humanity, and that is, the power of agriculture. Scientifically the insect is known as *Myrmica barbata*, and popularly as the Agricultural Ant of Texas. The habits of this wonderful insect have been carefully watched by Dr. Lincecum, who has recorded them in a paper read before the Linnæan Society in 1861.

The insect begins by digging a hole in the ground, by way of a wicket-gate or entrance, and around this hole it raises a mound, generally about five or six inches in height, and from six to eight feet in diameter. Sometimes, if the nest be made on low ground, where there is a probability of inundation, the Ant raises the mound to a height of fifteen or twenty inches, and in any case gives the surface a slight slope from the centre to the circumference. Around this mound the Ant clears the earth from stones and weeds, so as to make a perfectly smooth belt of a foot or two in breadth.

Fig. 229.—Myrmica barbata. Male. (Yellowish brown.)

Within this space the Ants plant the seeds of a peculiar grass, and tend them as carefully as any human agriculturist could do, cutting down every weed that may make its appearance, and watching it until the seed is matured. When ripe, the grain is small, white, and very hard. The Ants then cut it down, and carry it into the subterranean galleries, where it is separated from the husks, which are thrown outside till cultivated anew. Sometimes when the rainy season has been more than usually long, the grain becomes damp, and in that case the Ants take advantage of the first fine day, carry the seed into the open air, and spread it to dry in the sunbeams. When dry it is taken back to the granaries; but those seeds which have sprouted are rejected, and thrown away among the husks.

Fig. 230.—Myrmica barbata. Female. (Yellowish brown.)

Dr. Lincecum watched these Ants for more than twelve years, and never saw them plant any seed except that which has been mentioned. He also records another curious instance of instinct, or, perhaps, of reason. At first the nests were made freely within an orchard. But after a while the orchard was opened to cattle, who naturally ate the succulent grass-grain which the Ants had planted. Finding this to be the case, the Ants abandoned the orchard, and took to making their plantation in the garden and other spots where the cattle could not disturb them. The crops generally spring up about the beginning of November.

There are many specimens of these Ants in the British Museum. Their colour is yellowish brown. The first of the illustrations represents a fully developed male on the wing. The second shows one of the fully developed females taking a flight at their swarming-time, while another is leaving the burrow. The third illustration represents the workers carrying seeds to the granary.

☿

FIG. 231.—Myrmica barbata. Workers.
(Yellowish brown.)

CHAPTER V.

POMPILIDÆ, SPHEGIDÆ, AND BEMBECIDÆ.

THE insects which are placed under the titles which are at the head of this chapter are popularly known under the general title of Sand Wasps. They are so called because the females dig holes in any earth, generally of a sandy nature, and place therein the insects on which their future young are to be fed. We have plenty of them in this country; and any observer of Nature must have seen and admired their industrious energy as they pursue the task which is the one object of their lives.

The Pompilidæ are among the very fiercest of insects, and have among them some of the largest of the Hymenoptera. I have not the least idea why this name should be given to insects, as it rightly belongs to a fish which follows ships, probably the "rudder-fish" of the sailors. The word literally signifies "an escort," whence our word "pomp," on account of the number of attendants required by a person of high rank when on a journey of state. All the Pompilidæ have the legs very long and the abdomen oval and attached to the thorax by a short footstalk.

FIG. 232.—Pompilus atrox.
(Black, with orange patch on abdomen.)

THE fine insect which is called *Pompilus atrox* has long been known to be a native of North America, but specimens have lately been discovered in Japan. The colour of the head, thorax, and abdomen is shining black, but towards the base of the abdomen there is a bold patch of orange. The wings are brown, firm, and with a highly polished surface. Formerly, this insect was called by the specific name of *tropicus*, but it is now known that this name belongs rightly to a smaller species also from North America.

IN all insects there is a very great difference between good and bad specimens, and sometimes the difference is so great that they hardly seem to belong to the same species. This is peculiarly the case with the insect which is called *Pompilus Gravesii*. A specimen in bad condition betrays no beauty of colour, but looks simply of a dull yellow brown, with a few spots of a golden hue when the light shines upon the more projecting portions. But a specimen in really good condition is a splendid insect, looking just as if it had been cut out of pure gold. Mr. F. Smith tells me that the late Mr. Cuming had some thirty specimens, and their appearance as they were massed together in the box was simply gorgeous.

FIG. 233.—Pompilus Gravesii.
(Shining gold.)

This golden lustre is given by the hairs with which the whole body, including the head, is thickly covered. The hairs lie very flat to the body and are nearly parallel, all the points being directed backwards. Even in the imperfect specimens a good magnifying glass will, with the assistance of a strong light, bring out the golden lustre which the unaided eye cannot detect. The wings are yellow, and each of the upper pair is marked with two squared black spots. This insect is exceedingly variable in form. It is never larger than the figure, but is often much smaller—some specimens scarcely exceeding the common housefly in size.

In the British Museum the insect appears under the generic name of Parapompilus, Mr. F. Smith having comprised under that title all the short-winged Pompili. The name *Gravesii* is rather an unfortunate one, because it expresses nothing of the characteristics of the insect. The name *speciosus* had been suggested, but in the meanwhile the insect had been described under the name of *Gravesii* in honour of the name of the captain of the ship in which the insects were brought to England.

BEFORE the discovery of the last-mentioned insect, *Pompilus nobilis* was by far the most beautiful of the family, and, just as that insect glitters with gold, so does this one shine with silver. A good specimen looks, indeed, just as if silver leaf had been laid upon it and rubbed smooth with a burnishing tool. This silvery gloss is produced by a coating of very fine silvery hairs, set like the pile of velvet, and therefore called "pile" to distinguish it from ordinary hair.

There is scarcely any insect which shows so plainly the distinction between a specimen in good condition and one that is damaged or has suffered by careless handling. There are several specimens in the British Museum, and of them all only one shows the silvery surface perfectly, the rest looking almost black, with a faint silvery patch here and there. It is astonishing how easily the beauty of a specimen may be marred. One very fertile source of damage is re-setting. When an insect has been badly set or not set at all, it is necessary to relax the stiffened joints by damp, and then to place the wings and limbs in their proper position. Sometimes too much moisture is used, and then the surface of an insect is often damaged. Hairy insects suffer most in this respect, as the hairs become matted together and so lose their lustre. In such an insect as this, therefore, where the whole of the silvery sheen depends upon the way in which the light is reflected by each individual hair, it is evident that the least undue amount of moisture must do very great injury, and in all probability destroy the lustre for ever. Perhaps the sheen might be restored by soaking the insect completely in spirits of wine, and then drying it by

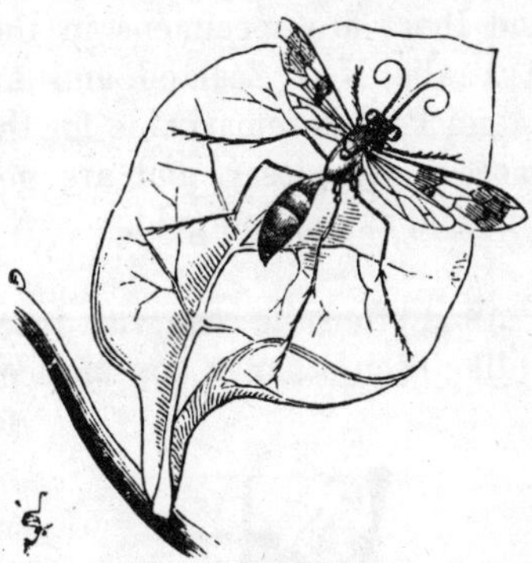

FIG. 234.—Pompilus nobilis. (Black, silver-glossed.)

means of a strong current of air directed against the set of the hairs. In this way I have succeeded in restoring the beautiful downy softness of our Goat Moth, and the furry richness of the humble-bees and similarly adorned insects. In the British Museum insects are relaxed by placing them in a closed earthenware vessel containing about half an inch in depth of damp sand; and the late Mr. Doubleday used to attain the same object by placing the insects in a large flower-pot sunk into the ground.

The wings of this species are very much like those of the Ant Lion in colour, being firm, shining, and transparent, with two patches of dark brown on the upper pair and two similar patches of very pale brown on the lower pair.

This genus is spread over a very large portion of the world, and there are specimens in the British Museum from Europe, Australia, New Zealand, and America. One species which inhabits Pará is remarkable for the beauty of its wings, which are exceedingly glossy, and are gorgeous with the most brilliant crimson, azure, and gold.

As is often the case with insects, the sexes of this genus are so unlike each other in appearance that they might easily be taken for two distinct species. The chief difference lies in the antennæ, which in the female are simple, long, and boldly curved at the ends. Those of the male, however, one of which is drawn in the illustration, are nearly straight and most elaborately formed, each joint looking very much like the head of a trident. Indeed, if we take the conventional Neptune's trident with its spear-headed point, and cut away three-fourths of the central prong, we shall have a very good idea of a single joint of Ctenocerus.

FIG. 235.—Ctenocerus ramosus.
(Black; wings yellow, edged with brown.)

Each prong, so to speak, is slightly bent downwards, and they are so arranged that when the antenna is seen sideways it looks like a flattened strip of yellow horn, covered with an embossed pattern and pierced with a double row of holes, the holes being in fact the spaces left between the successive joints, the prongs being so long that the point of one would be nearly three-fourths of the length of the one immediately above it. Both names of this insect are very appropriate. *Ctenocerus* is formed from two Greek words, and signifies "comb-horned;" while *ramosus* is Latin, and signifies "branched."

The wings of this species are shining yellow, edged with a dark brown band, which is wide at the tips, and narrows rapidly towards the base. The body and wings are quite black, and on the thorax there is a dense covering of thick black hairs. There are three species in the British Museum, and this, which comes from Southern Africa, is by far the handsomest and largest. The antennæ of the male are much yellower than those of the female.

THE fine insect which goes by the scientific name of *Mygnimia avicula* comes from Java, and is closely allied to *Mygnimia*

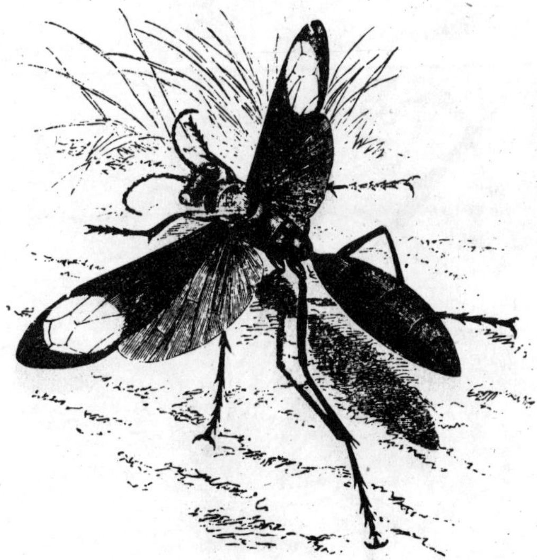

FIG. 236.—Mygnimia avicula.
(Black; wings with a silvery white spot.)

ducalis, a native of Penang and India. It is shown of the natural size, and probably derives its name of *avicula*, or "little bird," from its great size. The colour of the head, thorax, abdomen, and legs is dead black, with a slight scattering of white like hoar-frost. The wings are also black, and in the upper pair there is a large white spot with a silvery lustre when viewed by a side light. The lower wings are not of so deep a black as the upper pair, and they have no spot.

The reader will notice the structure of the claws, each of which has a bold tooth-like projection in the midst of the inner side. It has been suggested that this tooth is intended to aid the Mygnimia in catching its prey; I can, however, scarcely accept this theory, because the Pompilidæ do not seize their prey by the claws, but by clasping it in their legs, and so holding it while the sting is brought to bear. The wounded insects are also carried off in the clasped legs, and are never grasped by the claw itself, which is comparatively feeble.

ANOTHER species of the same genus, *Mygnimia aspasia,* has derived its specific title from its beauty, the name of Aspasia

FIG. 237.—Mygnimia aspasia.
(Black, glossed with blue.)

being that of the very beautiful but not at all moral lady who taught eloquence at Athens and numbered Socrates among her pupils. This species has been found in Dory, Amboyna, Aru, and one or two other localities.

Though not so large as the preceding insect, it is a handsome species, for whereas the former species is entirely black with a single spot of white on each wing, the present species is strongly glossed with blue. This effect is obtained by means of a soft, velvet-like pile, which even extends to the head. The wings are transparent and yellow, while the nervures are rust-red, becoming black at the base. There is a slight pale brown border to the wings. The legs, especially the hind pair, are armed with a number of bold tooth-like spines, thereby contrasting with those of the previous species, which are unarmed.

THE magnificent insect which is here shown is one of the largest of the Hymenoptera, and is very handsome, not only

FIG. 238.—Pepsis elevata.
(Black-green.)

on account of its size, but by reason of its splendid colouring. Like many insects, the colouring is so deep that a very strong light is required in order to bring out its beauties, and, if the light be insufficient, the whole of the tissues appear to be dull velvety black. In point of fact, the real colour of the head, thorax, abdomen, and legs is Prussian green, so deep and rich that at first sight the insect will probably be set down as a black one. The wings are shining brown, and the antennæ are black for half their length, and yellow for the remainder.

The reason for giving the name of Pepsis to these insects is to me one of the many insoluble mysteries in connection with insect nomenclature. The word *Pepsis* is Greek, and primarily signifies "digestion" or "concoction," and when used in reference to wine it signifies "fermentation." The term is familiar to most persons in forming part of the word "dyspeptic," *i.e.* difficult digestion. I very much wish that all persons who give a name to any new species, whether it be animal or vegetable, should be bound at the same time to explain that name and state their reasons for giving it; and I should like to abolish, once and for all, the custom of giving to a new species the name of any human being. Every name ought to designate some characteristic, and that can never be done under the system that is so largely followed.

On Plate IX. Fig. 1 is shown a Brazilian species, called, on account of its size and strength, *Pepsis heros.*

Like the preceding insect, it looks at first sight as if it were black, the colour being in fact the deepest blue, with a sort of velvet-like lustre. The wings are brown and glossy, and the legs black.

The insect which is here given is, I believe, a new species and hitherto undescribed. On account of the general richness of its colour, Mr. Smith has given it the specific title of *nigrescens*, *i.e.* "blackish." It is a native of Demerara. The colour of the insect is black, with a thick velvet-like fur on the head and thorax. The legs are long, and without spines. The reader will notice that the tibiæ of the hind legs are much flattened, this being a peculiarity common to the male sex throughout the whole genus. The wings are very beautiful. Their general colour is black, but they are adorned with many bold

PLATE IX.

1

2

3

streaks of steely blue, each streak having a narrow edge of purple.

FIG. 239.—Pepsis nigrescens. (New species.)
(Black; wings streaked with blue and purple.)

With this insect we end the Pompilidæ, and now proceed to the next group.

THE Sphegidæ are at once known by the shape of the abdomen. This is attached to the thorax by a long footstalk, composed of the first segment of the abdomen greatly elongated, just

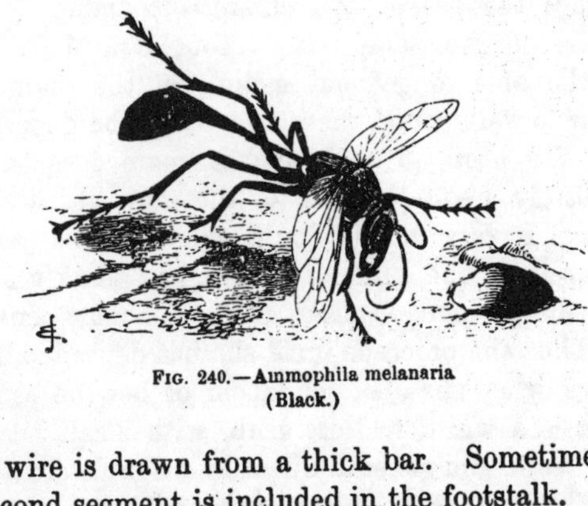

FIG. 240.—Ammophila melanaria
(Black.)

as a thin wire is drawn from a thick bar. Sometimes a portion of the second segment is included in the footstalk.

Some species have this footstalk wonderfully elongated

especially in the genus Ammophila. This word is formed from the Greek, and literally signifies "sand-lover," because the insects always select sandy spots for the purpose of forming their burrows. All the Ammophiles have similar habits, and our own familiar species, *Ammophila sabulosa,* affords a very excellent example of the manner in which insects of this genus prepare the homes for their future young. The mother insect selects a suitable spot, and then digs a tolerably deep burrow, rather narrow in diameter, except at the bottom, where it is widened into a chamber. She never drops the excavated soil near the mouth of the burrow, but carries it out between the jaws, flies to a little distance, and then, with a peculiar jerk, scatters the sand in a shower. Mr. Westwood has given a detailed account of this process in the "Transactions of the Entomological Society," vol. i.

The burrow being made, the Sand Wasp, as the creature is popularly termed, goes off in search of a spider, or caterpillar, or an insect of some kind, which is destined to serve as food for the future young. The prey is seized firmly in the grasp of the long legs, and is at once disabled by the sting, which, however, does not kill it at once, but paralyses it and prevents its escape. She then drags the disabled prey towards the burrow, her wings buzzing loudly and her whole movements full of fiery energy. Having reached the burrow, she transfers the insect to her jaws, and begins to descend the burrow backwards, dragging the insect after her.

Now comes the use of the enlarged chamber. Were the burrow to be of the same size throughout, the Sand Wasp would not be able to get out again, but the chamber allows space for her to walk round the insect, when she deposits an egg. Sometimes she goes off and fetches more insects, but this depends entirely upon the size of the prey which she at first brought in. I very much doubt whether the Ammophila restricts herself to one kind of victim, and think that she will take either spider or caterpillar, as may be most convenient at the time. Thus she proceeds until she has deposited her whole stock of eggs, when she dies, the labour of her life being over.

The larva is a white, footless grub, with small head, armed with strong teeth, and generally bent in a double curve, like the letter S. When it is full fed it spins a double cocoon, the outer one being white, and looking something like paper, while the second or inner cocoon is made of similar material, but has a dark, smooth lining.

Our first example of these insects, *Ammophila melanaria,* is a native of Brazil. The head is rather small and rounded, and the jaws are long, sharply pointed, curved in a sickle-like form, and are armed with a boldly projecting tooth in the middle of the inner margin. This structure enables the insect to grasp its prey firmly, as it drags it into the narrow tunnel. The wings are transparent, and the colour of the head, thorax, and abdomen is black, as is shown by the specific name, *melanaria,* which is formed from the Greek, and signifies "blackish." The footstalk of the abdomen is very long and slender, being, indeed, scarcely thicker than a fine pin.

FIG. 241.—Ammophila opulenta. (Black.)

OUR second species of Ammophila is a native of Pará. Like the preceding species, it is black, but its tarsi are armed with long spikes, which is not the case with its Brazilian relative. The jaws are very powerful, toothed, and remarkable for a narrow line of long curved hairs along their outer edge. There are great numbers of insects belonging to this genus in the British Museum, and it is remarkable that among that large and varied collection there is not one single specimen which is not dull-coloured.

SCARCELY any of the genus Pelopæus are known to exist except in the warmest portions of the earth. Their generic name is taken from a Greek word signifying "mud," and is given to them because they make their nests of sand ; it is very finely worked and kneaded, and then left to dry in the heated air. The nest is generally composed of a series of cells, each being closed as it is completed, and the entrance being always from beneath. The Pelopæi store their nests with various insects.

mostly caterpillars, but they often employ caterpillars, just like the Sand Wasps of our own land.

It has been said that the Pelopæus not only places a disabled insect in the cell occupied by its offspring, but continually adds fresh insects as those which are already within are devoured. Mr. Westwood, however, totally dissents from this opinion, on the ground that none but the social Hymenoptera feed the young larvæ.

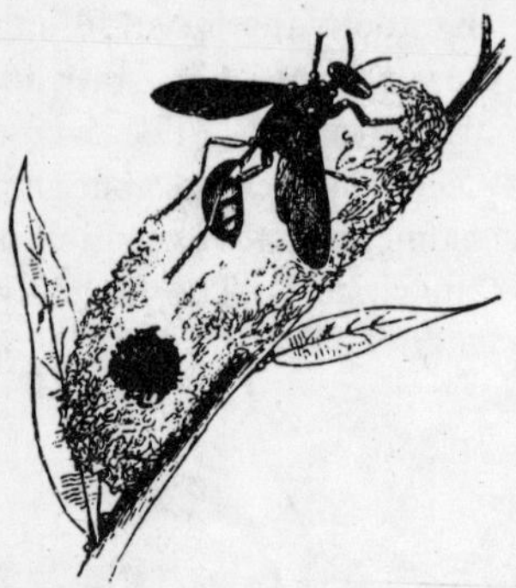

FIG. 242.—Pelopæus chalybeus. (Shining blue.)

The accompanying illustration depicts a South African species, *Pelopœus chalybeus.* The specific name, which signifies "blue," is given to it because its whole body is of a deep rich blue, very much like that of the blue-bottle fly. The whole of the head, thorax, and abdomen are thickly and deeply punctured, which gives additional richness to the colouring. The wings are dark, with a slight but decided blue gloss. The insect is shown as standing upon its mud-built nest, the aperture which serves as entrance into the last cell being seen towards the bottom.

ON Plate IX. Fig. 2 is seen the figure of an Australian species, called *Pelopœus lœtus*, flying towards the nest, which is placed on the trunk of a tree.

Although not so brilliant a species as the last, it is boldly and prettily coloured. The general hue of the body is black, as far as the end of the thorax, in the middle of which is a bold oblong patch of yellow. From the end of the thorax to the middle of the abdomen the colour is yellow. Then comes a broad band of black, and the rest of the abdomen is yellow. The antennæ are also yellow, and there is a collar of the same colour on the neck.

It has been discovered that some species of the Pelopæus are parasitic creatures, affecting the nests of a solitary bee called Eumenes. That this is the fact has been proved by finding in the nests of the Eumenes the cocoons of the Pelopæus, which are almost exactly like those of the Ammophila which have been already described.

We now come to the typical genus of the Sphegidæ, an example of which is the beautiful *Sphex argentata*, so called from the broad silvery band which encircles the middle of the abdomen. There is a peculiarity about this silvery band. It is very conspicuous, and yet, when examined closely, it disappears. This effect is produced by the very short and fine silvery pile which exists upon that part of the abdomen, and

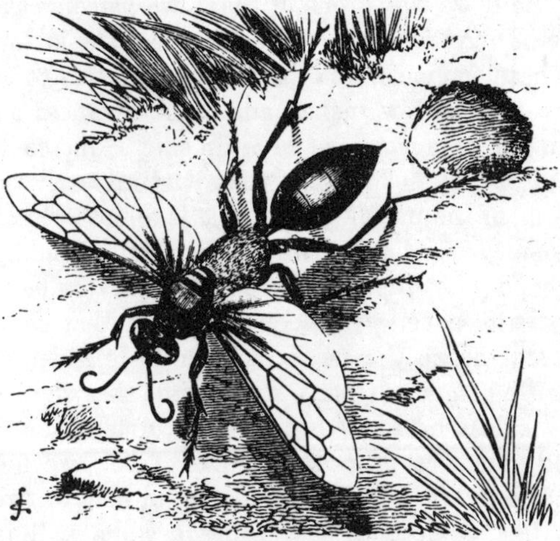

Fig. 243.—Sphex argentata.
(Black, with silver belt on abdomen.)

sometimes extends to the metathorax. The rest of the insect is black, and the wings are transparent.

Few insects have so great a range as this, specimens having been brought from India, Sumatra, Java, Celebes, Ceram, and many parts of Africa and Europe.

A very graphic account of the proceedings of a Jamaican species of Sphex is given by Mr. Gosse in his "Naturalist's Sojourn in Jamaica":—

"On the earthen floor of the building, formerly used as the boiling-house on Bluefields Estate, but now dilapidated and partially unroofed, where twine-like roots depend from the rafters, and elegant ferns spring out of the crevices of the c umbling walls, a good many large wasp-like flies may be observed in the hottest part of the day, briskly flying to and fro. It is a species of Sphex, closely allied to *S. ichneumonea*, but with the abdomen wholly rufous. On closer examination we discover numerous holes entering diagonally into the dry and dusty ground, into which some of these bright-coloured flies are crawling, and from which others are emerging.

"From some of the holes proceeds a shrill, but intermitted, buzzing; and if we watch one of these, we perceive the Sphex at work therein. At first we cannot see what she is doing, for she crawls in head foremost, and in a second or two comes out tail foremost, recedes a few inches, and then advances again, again emerges in the same manner, and again enters; and continues thus to crawl backward and forward with bustling activity, and with much flirting of the purple wings. She is almost white with dust, and is evidently very busy, if we can but comprehend her motions.

"On stooping down and bringing our face very near the scene of labour, we discover, by narrow watching, that she is digging the hole; and hence the negro children have given her the appropriate title of gravedigger. Every time that she comes forth, she brings a load of the powdery earth, much larger than her head, tightly held between the shanks of her two fore-feet, her breast, and her chin, and this she drops an inch or two from the cave's mouth. Sometimes she brings a stone still larger, and this is grasped in the jaws, and dragged to the distance of four or five inches, for fear it should roll in again. I have seen her bring two stones together, one grasped beneath the chin, the other in the jaws. Each time she has dropped the load, she never fails, as she advances, to keep the road clear by scraping with the fore shanks, throwing the dust behind her. But for this, the earth brought out would soon accumulate in a heap, and roll back. If a dry leaf or small stick happen to drop against the mouth of the hole, she seizes it with her curved jaws and carries it to a safe distance.

"I observed one filling up a hole. No doubt she had deposited her egg at the bottom, and stored sufficient provision (caterpillars or spiders, disabled but not killed, according to the custom of these interesting insects) to last the young grub, when hatched, until its maturity, 'haud ignara ac non incauta futuri.' With her tail towards the hole, she scraped back a little heap of dust; then turned, and with her head moved it about, that it might fall to the bottom. Then she turned again and did the like, repeating this procedure several times in succession. At length no more earth would go down, for the hole was full; she then rammed it two or three times with her head, and flew away, leaving still, however, the situation of the orifice obvious enough.

"These insects work very fast in the soft dusty earth, for they are indefatigable in their exertions. The bee is the recognised symbol of industry, but the labour of the bee is play compared with the efforts of the grave-digging Sphex."

THE rare and very remarkable insect which is here shown is a native of South America, and was captured by Mr. T. P. G Smith at Pernambuco. Two specimens, male and female, are in

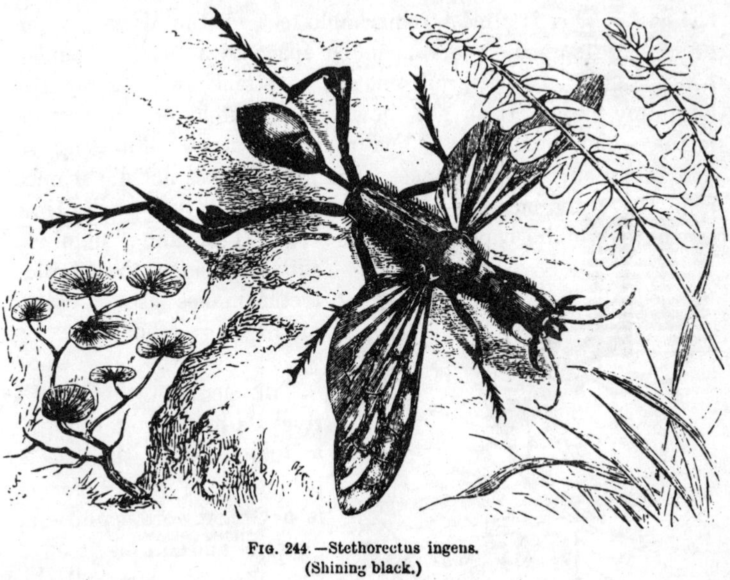

FIG. 244.—Stethorectus ingens.
(Shining black.)

the British Museum, and I believe that they are unique. The illustration represents the male. There is a full and detailed description of the insect by Mr. F. Smith, in the "Annals and Magazine of Natural History," vol. xx. p. 394.

The chief characteristic of this species is the enormous length of the thorax, which is rounded in front and cut off abruptly behind. It is covered with a moderately thick coating of long hairs. The abdomen is quite small, and is joined to the thorax by a rather short and very slender footstalk. The head is large, and carries a pair of very powerful jaws, jetty black and shining. The legs are long and spiny, and in the male the end of the thigh is thickened into a knob, which is curiously bent inwards, and armed with several strong but blunt teeth. The name *Stethorectus*, which signifies "lengthened breast," is given to the insect in consequence of the great length of the thorax. The wings are shining brown, glossed with blue, and are singularly beautiful.

The female Stethorectus feeds her young upon spiders of various kinds, and so fierce and powerful is she that she will even attack the enormous Mygale, or Bird Spider, and carry it off to her nest. This is a most remarkable feat, for the Mygale, when its legs are spread, covers as much space as a man's extended hand, and it is powerful enough to attack and destroy the humming-birds. It is not, however, a match for the Stethorectus, which darts upon it and paralyzes it with its sting, so that it can offer no resistance. The Mygale does not die at once from the sting, but lingers for five or six days, thus giving time for the egg of its captor to be hatched. If it cannot obtain a suitable spider, the Stethorectus makes use of caterpillars or grasshoppers.

Fig. 245.—Chlorion lobatum. Male. (Shining green.)

The genus Chlorion derives its name from the prevailing colour of the insects belonging to it. *Chlorion* is a Greek word, signifying "green," and shining green is the colour of nearly all the species. There are several blue species, but even in them there is a decided gloss of green.

The species which is here represented is an Asiatic insect, and is spread throughout India and China. It is a very pretty insect, the body being always polished and shining, and mostly of a brilliant emerald green. Some specimens, however, are entirely blue, sometimes the thorax is half blue and half green, and in a few specimens the colour is so vague that it is impossible to decide whether the real colour be blue or green. The wings are yellow and shining, and in most instances those of the female

FIG. 246.—Chlorion lobatum. Female. (Shining green.)

are clouded with brown at the tips. It is one of the spider-eating species, and displays great powers of perseverance in capturing and dragging its prey to the burrow.

The two sexes are very dissimilar in appearance, and both are therefore represented, the small specimen being the male, and the larger the female.

THE genus Ampulex is a very large one, and is spread over the warmer portions of the world. There are in the British Museum specimens from India, China, the Celebes, Africa, and tropical America. The present species comes from Borneo, and there is only a single specimen in the British Museum.

The commonest species is *Ampulex compressa*, a native of China. This is a very brightly coloured insect. The head, thorax, and abdomen are rich shining purple, and the wings are pale brown. The legs are bright blue, except the thighs, which are red. All the species belonging to this genus stock their burrows with large insects, preferring for this purpose the field cockroaches, one of which is shown in the illustration. In all the species the abdomen is much compressed, but in the Chinese species which has just been mentioned the abdomen looks exactly as if it had been squeezed between the finger and thumb. The reader will probably recollect that in entomological language, "compressed" signifies flattened sideways, and "depressed" flattened downwards as if by a weight. As the insects on which the Ampulex preys are large and strong, it is necessary that the jaws should be very powerful, and this is the case in every species.

FIG. 247.—Ampulex hospes (Purple.)

THE Larridæ, although rather a small family, are spread widely over the world, and in the British Museum there are examples of the genus Larrada, taken not only from Europe,

FIG. 248.—Larrada ducalis. (Black, with blue wings.)

Asia, Africa, and Australia, but both from North and South America. The present species is found in Java and the Celebes. Only two specimens are in the Museum.

This species was called *ducalis* by Mr. F. Smith, on account

of its size, which is very much greater than that of any other species. At first sight it is not a very handsome insect, but a careful inspection shows beauties, which do not appear at first. The whole of the body is black, but each segment of the abdomen is marked by a slight edging of very short silvery pile, looking as if a fine line of silver had been drawn round it. The eyes are large, and round them is drawn a line of short hairs of a rich golden lustre. There is also a patch of similar hair in the front of the face, between the eyes. The wings are brown, with a very strong blue gloss.

Of all the species, I think that *Larrada hæmorrhoidalis* of Australia is by far the handsomest. The golden pile, which in the preceding species is confined to the head, is spread over the entire body, and the effect is singularly beautiful, the play of light and shade being just like that of the richest velvet. The thorax has apparently two brown stripes, but when the light is changed the stripes become golden, and the rest of the thorax brown. The wings are shining yellow, tipped with brown.

THE name *Tachytes* is taken from a Greek word signifying "rapidity," and is given to the insects of the genus on account of their exceeding swiftness both on the ground and in the air, and their constant restlessness. There is a British species, *Tachytes unicolor*, which is so swift that it can hardly be captured.

FIG. 240.—Tachytes Sinensis. (Dark brown.)

As its name imports, the present species inhabits China. It is the largest of all the known species, and is coloured very much like our hive bee, except that a fine line of silvery pile grows on the edges of the segments of the abdomen. The wings are pale yellow. It is a very large genus, and, like Larrada, extends over all parts of the world. All the species of whose life-history anything is known have very similar habits. They make burrows in the ground, lay their eggs in them, and stock them with insects as food for the future young. They seem to prefer grasshoppers, or at all events Orthoptera, to any other insects, though they sometimes take caterpillars, if they can get nothing better. The British species, *Tachytes pompiliformis*, almost invariably stocks its nest with grasshoppers, having previously deprived them of life, or at all events of motion, by the sting. Yet, Mr. Shuckard has seen the insect engaged in the capture of green caterpillars, possibly because it could find no grasshoppers.

On Plate VIII., Fig. 2 is shown an insect that is rather insignificant in appearance, though it is very interesting in its habits. Its name is *Parapison rufipes*, and it is one of a number of insects that were brought from India by Mr. C. Horne, and described by Mr. F. Smith. Its colour is very simple, being nearly brown, with a sprinkling of silvery down. Attached to the flower-stem in the lower corner of the plate is seen a group of its curious cells, the construction of which is thus described by Mr. Horne:—

"It constructs a wall of loosely-arranged cells of earth attached to some hanging object, such as a creeper, tendril, or pendent straw, or even a curled dry leaf. The interior of the cell is strengthened by a very fine glutinous silky-looking substance, and this is the more necessary as the least damp would otherwise destroy the whole fabric.

"I believe the insect to apply some kind of gluten, while the pupa secures its safety by spinning a very slight silken web within its abode. The cells are very globular, and are filled with the smallest spiders, of which I counted eighteen in two chambers. These are generally of a pale green colour, and their plumpness is curious. Sometimes, however, it builds a wall with more or less regularity. The pellets used in construction are, comparatively with the size of the insect, very large, and loosely attached to one another: very little smoothing is effected exteriorly, and were it not for the interior binding together of the particles, the wall would apparently fall to pieces of itself.

"The earth brought is prepared by water, as is the case with all clay-building insects which I have observed; and the insect affects the vicinity of water, and hence, probably, is seldom found far from wells. It builds in September and October, and the perfect insect sometimes emerges early, though it often delays its appearance until the spring (viz. March or April) of the following year, when the heat sets in.

"A small Pemphredon, or another even smaller species, often takes possession of the cells of this insect, rendering the identification of the pupa very difficult. The chrysalis is more ovate in form than that of Pemphredon. I have no drawing of the grub." In another part of his paper Mr. Horne mentions that a hymenopterous insect belonging to another family, namely *Trypoxylon intrudens*, was hatched from cells made by the Parapison, the former insect having taken possession of the cells made by the latter.

THE next family is that of the Bembecidæ, in which the tongue is often so long that it resembles the same organ in the hive bee. The name is Greek, signifying "a humming-top," and

FIG. 250.—Bembex rostrata.
(Black, with greenish yellow bars.)

is given to the insects on account of their quick, fussy movements, and the buzzing sound which they produce when on the wing.

As far as is yet known, no species of the genus Bembex is an inhabitant of England, though this species extends throughout the greater part of Europe, and is even found in Northern Africa. It is nearly, though not quite, the largest species belonging to the genus, and is rather prettily coloured, the greenish yellow bands contrasting well with the black which forms the ground hue.

The habits of this insect are much like those which have already been mentioned. The female digs deep burrows in the sand, using her fore-feet just as a terrier scratches at a rat-hole, and working with wonderful speed and activity. She then catches flies of various kinds, and places them in the burrow for the use of the future young. She is so active that she can even catch the swift-winged Hoverer Flies (*Syrphidæ*), pouncing on them during flight, just as a falcon swoops on a partridge. Having stocked the nest with a sufficient quantity of flies, she closes the entrance with earth, and leaves the eggs to be hatched in their own time.

It is rather remarkable that so fierce and active an insect should itself be the victim of another insect, but such is the case. The gorgeous Ruby-tail Fly, called *Stilbum splendidum*, and described on page 415, haunts the burrows of the Bembex, crawls into them during the absence of the real owner, and surreptitiously deposits its eggs there. As the egg of the Stilbum is hatched before that of the Bembex, it naturally happens that the former not only eats the flies, but the Bembex larva itself.

In the generic name of the present insect there is another of those curious, not to say inexcusable, confusions in nomenclature which have been more than once mentioned. The word is Latin, and is used by Ovid to signify "a jackdaw," so that it clearly ought not to be used as a name for a genus of insects, especially as it is anticipated in the scientific name of the jackdaw, *Corvus monedula*.

FIG. 251.—Monedula heros. (Black and yellow.)

This is altogether a South American genus, and a good description of the manner in which the insects dig their burrows and stock them with flies may be found in Mr. Bates' well-known book on the Amazons River.

This is one of the largest of the genus, and is a really fine insect. The colour of the head, thorax, and abdomen is velvety black, while on each side are five patches of brilliant yellow. There are also some yellow marks on the thorax, as shown in the illustration. The legs are black, covered with a greyish down.

The two colours of black and yellow run through the genus, and it is on account of their pied appearance that the name of Monedula has been given to the insects. The colour is, however, very differently arranged in the various species. One of them, *Monedula magnifica*, of Brazil, has the ground colour velvet-black, while at each side of the base of the abdomen there is a large patch of deep orange, and an interrupted band about the middle. Perhaps the most curiously marked species is one in which the body is shining black, and has on the abdomen four rows of circular greenish yellow spots arranged with curious regularity.

THE family of the Nyssonidæ, which comes next in order, derives its name from a Greek word signifying "something that pricks or goads," and is given to the insects on account of the power of their stings. In none of those insects is the abdomen attached to the thorax by a foot-stalk.

FIG. 252.—Stizus speciosus. Male.
(Black and yellow.)

The name *Stizus* is taken from the Greek, and signifies "a point," in allusion to the sharp points which arm the end of the abdomen in the male. The colour of *Stizus speciosus* is nearly the same as that of the Monedula. The abdomen is shining black, diversified with patches of bright yellow, arranged as shown in the illustration. The shape and size of these marks are somewhat variable. The thorax is round, with a beautifully rich pile like dark brown velvet.

Mr. Walsh gives a curious account of this insect, which is a North American species. It usually stocks its burrows with grasshoppers, and is called by the name of the Digger Wasp. A correspondent, however, who sent him specimens of the Digger Wasp, states that the insect is known in Texas as the Horse Guard, because it is always flying about the horses,

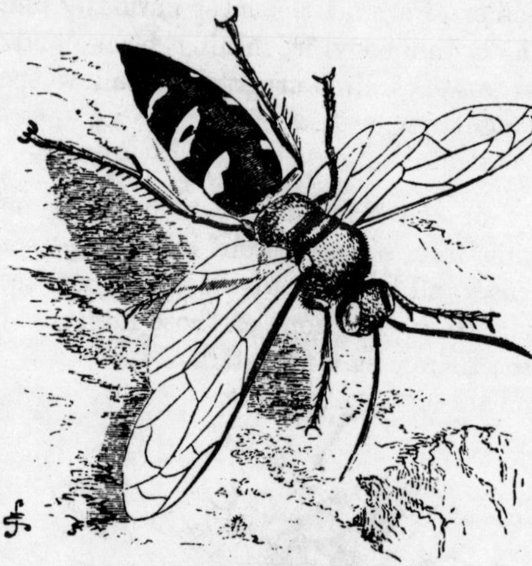

FIG. 253.—Stizus speciosus. Female. (Black and yellow.)

seizing upon the flies that annoy them, and carrying them off to the burrow. Mr. Walsh thinks that there may be some error in this account, and that the insect which really does catch and store up the horse-flies is a species of Bembex which much resembles the Stizus.

Six species of Stizus are found in America, one of which, *Stizus grandis*, stocks its burrows with Cicadæ instead of grasshoppers.

OUR last example of the Nyssonidæ is *Exeirus lateritus*, a fine insect from Australia. This was first described by Mr. Shuckard in 1836, and the whole account may be found in the Transactions of the Entomological Society for that year. The general colour of the insect is black, but the head is yellowish red, sprinkled with silvery down. The thorax is black and very hairy, and the middle of the abdomen is red. The legs are black, except the tibiæ, which are light red. They are of great proportionate length, and have given rise to the generic name *Exeirus*, which is formed from a Greek word signifying to "stretch out," or "elongate."

There is considerable difference in the sexes. The male is smaller than the female, and the end of the abdomen, instead of

Fig. 254.—Exeirus lateritus.
(Black and red.)

being long and pointed, is short, blunt, and rounded. Moreover, the male has one more joint in the antennæ than the female, he having thirteen joints, and she only twelve.

Of the Crabronidæ we have many examples in our own country, there being some forty species of the one genus Crabro. They are all burrowers, most of our own species preferring decayed wood for that purpose. It has been remarked by Mr. Shuckard that there is a difference in the mode in which the various burrowing wasps carry their prey. Oxybelus conveys it by means of the hind legs, Pompilus and Ammophila seize it in their jaws and drag it backwards; while all, if not nearly all the others grasp it in their jaws, hold it with their fore-legs, and so laden fly to their nests.

Mr. Westwood has successfully watched the development of several species of Crabro, and has noticed that while burrowing in wood the insect bites off small splinters with its teeth, passes them under its body by the first and second pairs of legs, and then kicks them out of the burrow with the hind pair. The strong spines with which the tibiæ of the hind legs are armed assist the insect in propelling the fragments well out of the burrow. The burrow is stocked with insects, varying according to the species of Crabro, and when the larva is full fed it spins for itself a silken cocoon of a reddish brown colour. As the silken threads of which the cocoon is formed are of a viscid nature when first spun, the wings and other *débris* of the flies on which the larva had fed are sure to adhere to the exterior and so give the cocoon a very singular aspect.

FIG. 255.—Crabro subterraneus. (Black and yellow.)

The species which is given as our example of this genus is an inhabitant of Southern Europe, and is rather prettily coloured, the general hue being black, and the abdomen marked with interrupted bands of greenish yellow, arranged as shown in the illustration.

ON Plate VIII. Fig. 1 is shown a pretty insect of Northern India, called *Trypoxylon rejector.*

The generic name is formed from two Greek words, and signifies "a wood-borer." As may be inferred from that name the generality of the insects belonging to this genus bore holes in wood. Several species of Trypoxylon inhabit England, and have been noticed to enter the burrows of other insects. Mr. Westwood, having seen this done several times, naturally thought that the insect was a parasitic one. Afterwards, however, he found that the only object was to save itself trouble, and that the Trypoxylon merely enlarged the burrows and then lined them with sand. One species makes a number of successive cells

PLATE VIII.

3

4

2

1

in each burrow, placing a single egg in every cell, and accompanying it with spiders, more or less in number according to their size.

One small species, *Trypoxylon alternatum*, may often be found in the dead and broken stems of roses and brambles, the insect boring away the soft pith and constructing a series of cells, each separated from its neighbour by a wall of sand. The cells are stocked with small spiders, and if the stem be carefully cut open, the cocoons may be seen all in a row, each cocoon filling as exactly as possible the cell in which the larva has been reared.

Whatever may be the case with the British species, it is evident that some of the foreign Trypoxylons are parasitic upon other insects, or at all events that they take possession of their nests in order to avoid the trouble of making burrows for themselves. The reader will remember that in the account of *Parapison rufipes* Mr. Horne mentioned that he had bred from it specimens of *Trypoxylon intrudens.* The same observer states that although *Trypoxylon rejector* builds cells of its own, it is in the habit of appropriating those of other insects. In Plate VIII. the elongated cells in the nests of the illustration are those of the Trypoxylon. This is Mr. Horne's account of the insect as given in the Transactions of the Zoological Society, vol. vii. part 3:—

"This curious little insect, when first hatched from the delicate little Serpularia-like cells, was taken by me for some parasite allied to the Ichneumonidæ, in consequence of my having often observed it hovering at the mouths of the cells of the smaller cell-building insects in my verandah. I found, however, that it brought mud and worked for itself, as well as appropriated the cells of other insects which it found ready to its hand.

"I have nowhere found recorded its habits; but I think I have seen it carrying minute green spiders wherewith to fill its cells. It certainly does not feed its young, but stores food; for it closes its cells directly they are ready, which none of the Vespidæ do.

"The construction of these is very curious; and the pellets of earth used appear of a sandy character, which gives to the structure great delicacy and fragility. At the same time the interior of the cell is lined with some glutinous ejection which binds it together.

"The specimens of cells figured (the originals of which are now all in England) show how strongly this cementing fluid acts.

"The nests are extremely difficult to find, being small, and many straws hanging in the places where they are usually constructed, such as under a thatch of coarse grass.

"As might have been expected, they remain a very short time in the pupa state; and the month of September is their favourite season of construction, although they continue to build in October.

"I have often watched them as I sat in my thatched summerhouse at Mainpurí; and the rapidity with which they came and went was surprising. I know of no other special peculiarity which calls for remark, excepting that all the cells I have found have been under cover."

The general colour of this insect is black, but the second and third segments of the abdomen are red.

SOME systematic entomologists have formed a family called Philanthidæ, but there seems to be no need for it, the Crabronidæ being quite comprehensive enough One species, *Philanthus triangulum*, is tolerably common on the Continent, but very rare in England. Mr. Shuckard predicted, some years ago, that when its metropolis was discovered, it would prove to be plentiful though very local, and therefore rare except in its own peculiar home. Mr. F. Smith discovered the metropolis of this insect at Sandown, Isle of Wight, and so Mr. Shuckard's prophecy was fulfilled.

FIG. 256.—Philanthus coronatus. (Black and yellow.)

The insects were in considerable numbers, burrowing into the sand, and flying about with great activity. Their strength and boldness may be inferred from the fact that they provision their nests with the hive bee, an insect nearly twice as large as the Philanthus, and armed with a sting which even man fears to meet. Some preyed upon Andrena bees, and Mr. Smith tells me that the choice of prey seemed to depend very much on locality, the Andrena being preferred where it was plentiful, and the hive bee taken when Andrenas are scarce. On the Continent this Philanthus is said to do great harm to apiarians, each female making on an average five cells, and depositing a bee in each.

Although so bold, strong, and active, and possessing a sting which is venomous enough to disable even the hive bee, the Philanthus is curiously averse to using its sting except for the purpose of securing its prey. Mr. Smith found that he absolutely could not provoke the insects to use their stings, even though he held them in the bare hand.

The species which is represented in the illustration is a native of Southern Europe. Its colour is black, with yellow marks on the abdomen and thorax, as shown in the illustration. Round the head there is a radiating fringe of yellow hair, which has earned for the species the name of *coronata*, or "crowned." The name *Philanthus* is formed from two words signifying "a lover of flowers," and is given to the insects because they are fond of haunting the wild flowers when they are not forced by resistless instinct to dig their burrows and search for prey. In order to show the peculiar markings, the figure is enlarged about one-third.

We now come to a great group of Hymenoptera in which the wings are folded longitudinally throughout their length when at rest. Anyone can see this peculiar structure by looking at a common wasp. Both sexes have wings, and so have the neuters.

The first family in this group is the Eumenidæ, which comprise the solitary species, and which may be known at once by their double claws. We have in England one species of the typical genus, *Eumenes coarctata*, which is a local insect, but tolerably common in those districts which suit it. Sandy ground well covered with heather seems to be its favourite locality. It makes a curious vase-shaped nest, forming it of sand, fastening it to a heather spray, and then provisioning it with little caterpillars after it has deposited an egg. I may here mention that the name Eumenidæ has been appropriately, if somewhat fancifully, given to these insects on account of the havoc which they work among sundry larvæ, spiders, &c. The Eumenides were the furies of the Greek classics, the ministers of vengeance appointed by the greater gods to inflict punishment on offending mankind.

The present species derives its name of *xanthura*, or "yellow tail," from its colour. The head and abdomen are black, except that a considerable portion of the end of the abdomen is ruddy chestnut. The thorax is also chestnut, but on its upper surface is a large patch of deep brown. The abdomen has a soft velvet look, on account of the deep punctures with which it is perfectly covered. The wings are shining, and yellowish in colour. It is an Indian insect. Closely allied to it is another Indian species, *Eumenes petiolata*, which very much resembles it in form, but may be distinguished by a single broad bar of yellow across the middle of the abdomen. This insect makes a large nest of mud, about the size of a pigeon's egg, and affixes it under some projection, probably for the sake of sheltering it from the rain. An egg is placed in each nest, which is then well stored with caterpillars. Sometimes, in a favourable position, a whole row of these nests may be seen, set side by side. The insect builds them in all kinds of places; and in a paper in the Transactions of the Entomological Society it is stated that in one case a keyhole was chosen as a locality for the nest, and in another, the interior of a disused flute.

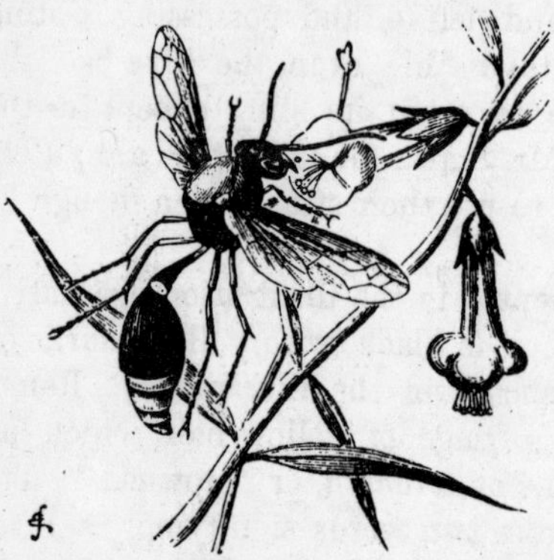

FIG. 257.—Eumenes xanthura. (Black and yellow.)

ON Plate VIII. Fig. 3 is drawn a beautiful species from Northern India, called *Eumenes esuriens.* In his paper on the Indian Hymenoptera, Mr. Horne observes that the insect has a habit of choosing doors and posts as localities for its nest, which, like that of any Eumenes, is always made with an opening having a recurved lip. As a rule, the insect manages to preserve the spherical form of its nest, no matter what may be the exigencies of the locality. The nest is stocked with caterpillars, mostly belonging to the Geometridæ, and almost invariably green in colour.

As is often the case with solitary wasps and bees, the Eumenes is liable to the attacks of parasites, of which the ubiquitous Ruby-tail (*Chrysis*) is sure to be one. Mr. Horne mentions one very remarkable instance of parasitic development. From a single cell of *Eumenes esuriens* the insect was hatched in due course of time. But there was also hatched a beetle belonging to the genus Emanadia. This insect is allied to our *Sitaris muralis*, which is so well known to entomologists as being parasitic on various solitary bees. Besides this, a fly, apparently belonging to the genus Anthrax, was hatched from the same nest. Now, the wonder is, how all these insects contrived to obtain sufficient food when packed within so narrow a compass, especially as the fly is not a small one, and the beetle is fully three-quarters of an inch in length. Had the beetle or the fly appeared instead of the Eumenes, there would have been nothing strange; but that all these should appear, and be fully developed, is an absolute mystery.

The Anthrax, by the way, is a very troublesome insect to the Eumenes, as well as to other solitary Hymenoptera. Generally, after a cell is closed it is tolerably safe, but the Anthrax contrives to pierce through the covering of the cell, and so to deposit an egg. The reader will therefore understand how difficult is the task of identifying the builder of a nest when, instead of an Eumenes or Pelopæus, an Anthrax, a Chrysis, or an Emanadia may emerge, and sometimes two or three at once.

Mr. Horne further remarks that it is very rare to find a nest from which the Eumenes has escaped, unless it be perfectly empty and affording no clue as to the habits of the occupant. This is due to the ants, who swarm in India and are ever restless in search of food. As long as the mud-nest of the Eumenes is closed, the ants cannot touch it, but no sooner does the newly developed Eumenes leave its nest, than the ants pour into it and carry off everything in it, not only the unconsumed caterpillars if there should be any, but the skins of those that have been eaten by the Eumenes larva, and the cast larval and pupal skins of the Eumenes itself. Just below the figure of the insect on Plate VIII. is shown a small group of the nests.

Another species, *Eumenes conica,* builds a very delicate cell, always using a wall or beam for one side of it, so that the most skilful workman can scarcely remove the nest without breaking it. Owing to the thinness of the cell-wall, the larva is very liable to be attacked by parasites, Mr. Horne having found that out of five cells only two produced the rightful Eumenes. The colour of the insect is rather curious. The head and thorax are nearly black, but the footstalk and the basal portion of the abdomen are orange. Then comes an interrupted black bar, and beyond this bar the abdomen is pale yellow and highly polished.

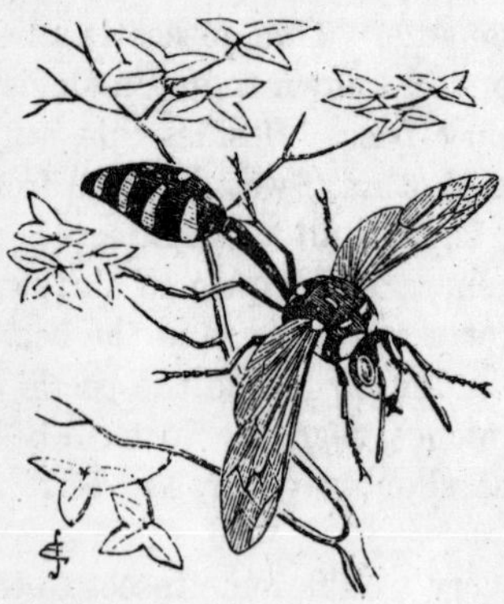

FIG. 258.—Eumenes arcuata. (Black and yellow.)

THE preceding insects being Indian, we have here a species from Australia, called *Eumenes arcuata.* The latter name signifies something that is bent like a bow, and refers to the outline of the insect when seen in profile. The wings are pale yellow and polished, and the body is black, smooth, and shining, the black being relieved by sundry spots, streaks, and patches of vivid yellow, arranged as seen in the illustration.

HERE is a strange being indeed! A hymenopterous insect with jaws just like those of a stag beetle! Had the insect been unknown, no entomologist would have dared to say that such a form could be possible.

This is the most striking of a large genus of Hymenoptera, in all of which the males have exceptionally large jaws. In none, however, is the jaw so enormously developed as in the present species.

As is the case with many insects (for example, our own stag beetle), the jaws of the female are comparatively small, and show no signs of the enormous development which is found in the male. The use of these jaws is at present problematical, for the male Synagris does not use them for labour, the whole of that business devolving on the female. Neither would they serve the purpose of weapons. Even the male stag beetles, who really do fight when urged by jealousy, do very little harm to each other, the result of a battle being very much like that of a duel between two ironclads, neither of which can penetrate the armour of the other. Some entomologists think that they are used in detaining the female in case she should prove coy, but as the greater bulk of male insects have feeble jaws, and many have no jaws at all, this theory cannot be maintained. Perhaps, when we know the use of a man's beard, a lion's mane, or a turkey's wattles, we shall learn the object of these enormous jaws.

As to the name Synagris, it is utterly absurd when applied to an insect. It is a name employed by Aristotle in his "History

FIG. 259 —Synagris cornuta
(Brownish yellow.)

of Animals" to designate some marine fish, and why it should now be transferred to a terrestrial insect is more than I can understand.

This species is a native of Southern Africa, which is the great home of these curious insects. Its general colour is black, but the thorax is yellowish brown, with the exception of a large black patch in the centre; and its wings are also brown, with a decided glossy surface. The enormous jaws of the male are yellow in colour, and not only are they very large, sickle-shaped, and sharply pointed, but they each throw out a large horn or tooth near the base, the horn being large enough to make half a dozen ordinary jaws. There is also a blunt tooth on the outer edge of each jaw, placed about midway between the base and the tip. When the jaws are closed, the points cross each other boldly, while the two lower teeth are pressed tightly together.

There are many African species of this extraordinary genus. *Synagris mirabilis* is a native of Abyssinia, and is a really handsome insect, its body being black, the end of the abdomen white, and the wings glossed with a shining blue. *Synagris analis* would look exactly like the preceding insect if drawn in plain black and white, but in this species the end of the abdomen is red, and not white. In all these insects the head is large and squared, this structure being needful in order to give support to the powerful muscles which move the enormous jaws.

THE next genus, Monobia, is so called on account of the solitary habit of the insects. The name is formed from two Greek words which signify "living alone."

This genus is in reality little more than a division of the great and intricate genus Odynerus, the systematic entomologists having found that genus becoming unwieldy and capable of subdivision. In all probability, then, the Monobia act as does the Odynerus, *i.e.*, the female digs holes, lays her eggs in them, and stores them with caterpillars.

FIG. 260.– Monobia quadridens. (Black and yellow.)

The species is a North American one, and is rather striking to the eye. The head and thorax are black and profusely punctated, and the abdomen is also black, but of a velvety texture, owing to the short and thick pile with which it is covered. On the base of the abdomen there is a broad band of bright yellow, and some streaks of the same colour are seen on the thorax. The wings are yellow and shining.

ON Plate VIII. Fig. 4 is shown the figure of an insect called *Rhynchium nitidulum*. Like the last insect, this is one of the many that were formerly included in the genus Odynerus.

Several species of these insects inhabit India, and Mr. Horne has described the habits of three of them, showing that there are considerable differences in their modes of building. One of them, *Rhynchium carnaticum*, inhabits the interior of small hollow bamboos. A nest which Mr. Horne found was constructed in a very singular manner, the insect having taken possession of a bamboo which had been previously occupied by one of the solitary bees, *Megachile lanata*, and in which two cells had already been formed. The Rhynchium did not try to eject the original occupant, but simply built it in.

"It first built over the cells of the Megachile a floor, which was constructed of mud, very finely worked, stout at the edges and thinner in the middle. It then left a space empty and made another floor, after which it commenced its breeding cells. In these it stored caterpillars of many colours, and it finished off with an empty spare cell, which it covered with a heavy mass of pellets. The clay is kneaded very finely, and, although there are no sides to be made to the cell, the cap is most carefully constructed."

There seems to be more than instinct in this proceeding. As the Rhynchium is much slower than the Megachile in undergoing its changes, the latter would be developed first, and so break through all the cells of the former in trying to make its escape. So, first the Rhynchium begins by shutting off the Megachile with a strong clay wall, and then, in order to guard against the possibility of one of the insects breaking through this wall, it takes the precaution to leave a clear space, and then to build a second wall, before it proceeds to form its cells. I have noticed that all insects which have to break through obstacles before they reach the open air have sufficient strength to do so, and a little to spare besides. But the amount of strength is not much in excess of the work to be done with it, and there is no insect with which I am acquainted which would not perish before it could break through two obstacles of equal strength.

I should much like to present the reader with an illustration of this remarkable nest, but as the nest, or rather the series of cells, is half as long again as the page, and would not bear reduction, it cannot be done. The colour of the insect is ruddy brown.

Then there is *Rhynchium brunneum*, which is capable of boring holes for itself, though it prefers to take possession of those that are ready made. Mr. Horne remarks of this species, that its body is so flexible that it is almost impossible to hold the insect without being stung by it.

Lastly comes the species which is figured in the plate. In colour it is very simple, being merely greyish black. Mr. Horne's account is as follows:—

"This extremely interesting insect constructs cells of exceeding strength, mostly upon timber. The clay is very finely worked with water and some kind of gum—not only viscid ejection being employed, but also the juices of the 'Peepul' (*Ficus religiosa*), birdlime in fact, and the gum of the acacia, catechu, and other trees. Hence there is no need of thickness, and we accordingly find the walls of the chambers very thin, whilst their tenacity is so great that the portion of the hard wood on which the series of cells was fixed I have cut out with a chisel and hammer without in any way injuring the structure. One pair of insects does not usually make more than three cells; but it must be remembered that they take a much longer time in making them than does the rapid, rough-working Megachile.

"The food stored consists of caterpillars; and I have not yet succeeded in hatching a parasite from one of their nests, which are strong enough to resist all ordinary attacks. Until completed, either one or the other of the insects appears to remain at home; and hence parasites have no opportunity of effecting an entrance before the cell is closed over. The covering, though thin, is very tough, so tough that I doubt the power of a parasite to pierce it. In the figure it will be observed that six cells have been built one on another, only *one* being affixed to the door. This one was attached to a smoothly plane surface of 'Sal wood' (*Shorea robusta*), so that the cementing gum must have possessed great strength to allow me to cut it out with a hammer and chisel, as before alluded to.

"These insects build on roof-beams, so that their nests generally escape notice; besides which they are far from common. They are externally of a rich brown colour, glistening with gum."

In the plate, the nests of this species are seen just above the insect.

THE very fine insect which is here represented belongs to Australia. The colour of the species is principally black, and of a beautiful velvet-like richness. The rest of the insect is bright yellow, also soft and velvety, and the arrangement of the colours

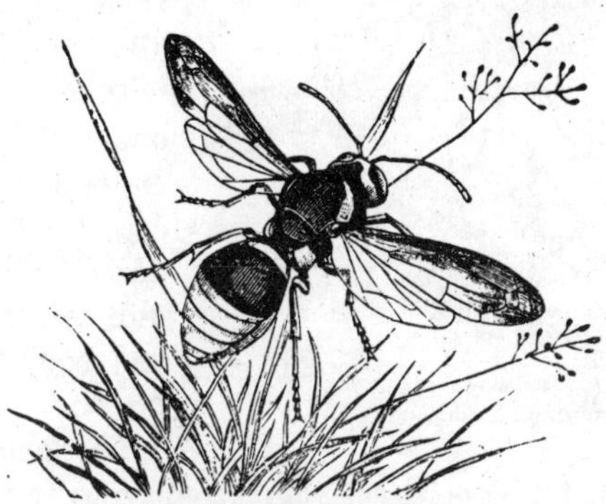

FIG. 261.—Abispa splendida.
(Velvety black and yellow.)

can easily be seen by reference to the illustration, the dark portions being black, and the light portions yellow. The genus to which this insect belongs is an offshoot of the great genus Odynerus, and shares in the habits of its relatives.

THE Wasps which have hitherto been described are of the solitary kind, and there are, in consequence, no neuters. We now come to those Wasps which construct more than one cell, and, when the number is considerable, the greater part of the architecture is performed by neuters. Our common Wasp or Hornet affords a perfect example of the Social Wasps. In England we have but few examples of the Social Wasps, and their nests are of three kinds, *i.e.*, pensile, such as that of the Tree Wasp; subterranean, like that of the common Wasp; or made under shelter of some kind, such as that of the Hornet. Abroad, however, there is a vast variety of Social Wasps, and the modes in which they form their nests are wonderfully varied, the same species often constructing its nest in different ways according to surrounding conditions.

The insect which is here given is a native of Africa, the specimens in the British Museum having been brought both from Congo and Abyssinia. Its general colour is brown, but the whole of the body is covered with a short ashen pile, which makes it look in some lights as if it were grey instead of brown. There is a slight reddish tinge upon the head. In the British Museum there are eight species, all of which are African with the exception of one which comes from India, and is accordingly called *Belonogaster Indicus.* They are all dull coloured, the wings and body being equally brown.

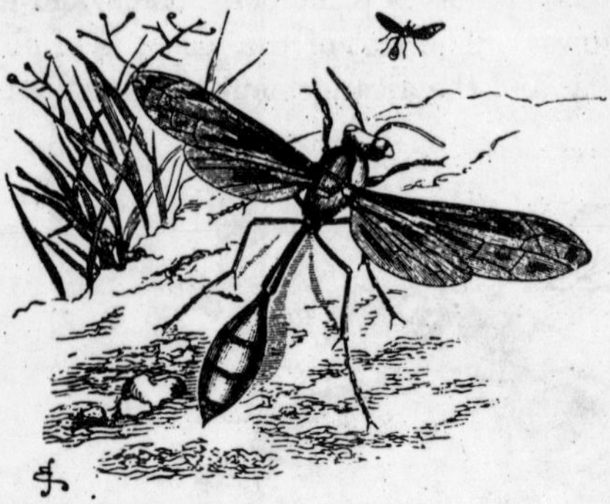

FIG. 262.—Belonogaster junceus.
(Brown, with ashen pile.)

The name *Belonogaster* is constructed from two Greek words signifying "a pointed belly," and is given to the insects because the abdomen terminates in a sharp point.

IN general form the *Mischocyttarus labiatus* bears a close resemblance to the preceding insect, and is coloured in almost exactly the same manner, being brown covered with grey down. It is a Brazilian insect.

The reader will see that the structure of the nest is very different from that of any nest or cell which we have hitherto seen. It is constructed of vegetable fibre torn off and masticated by the wasp, so as to form a sort of coarse paper. In fact, the wasps are the earliest paper-makers in the world, and utilize for that purpose a great variety of material, so long as it be a vegetable fibre.

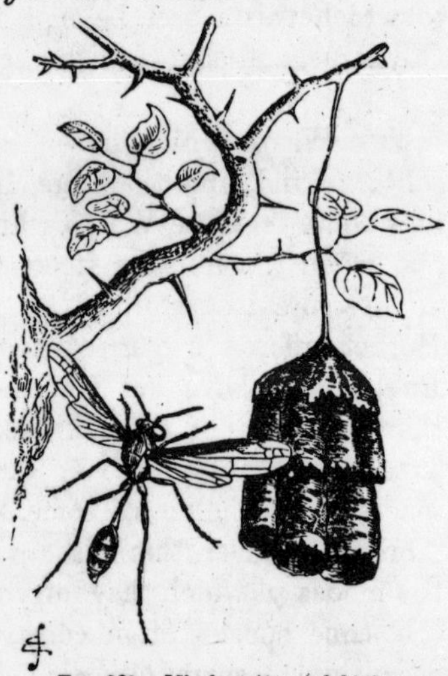

FIG. 263.—Mischocyttarus labiatus
(Brown, with grey pile.)

This nest consists of three distinct portions. First there is the cell-group, all the cells having their mouths downwards. Above the cells comes the pent-house, by which the rain or any falling substance is warded off the cells; and, lastly, comes the footstalk, by which the entire nest is suspended. The footstalk itself is very hard and tough, but is notwithstanding composed of the same material as the cells, except that the fibres are closely pressed together, instead of being spread out in flakes. The reader may find examples of such footstalks in any English wasp's nest, the successive layers of cells being supported, or rather suspended, by a number of short footstalks constructed in exactly the same manner.

This long and slender footstalk gives the name to the genus. The name *Mischocyttarus* is formed from two Greek words, the first of which signifies a stem or stalk, and the latter a cell.

The form of nest which is here given is that which is usually found, but there are cases where the insect has built two, or even three layers of cells, one above another, and all hanging by the same stalk. Whenever this is the case, the central layer always seems to be the largest.

It is not very easy to describe the insect which is here shown, so exceedingly variable is it. In fact, out of the six specimens in the British Museum, although the colours are the same, no two have them arranged in the same manner. The specimen which has been selected for the illustration is black, with a rust-red belt round the centre of the abdomen; while another has this colouring exactly reversed, and the others have the black and red distributed in various modes. The specific name, *ferruginea*, i.e. "made of iron," refers to the rust-red of the body.

FIG. 264—Icaria ferruginea. (Black and rust-red.)

As may be seen by the illustration, the cell-group, like that of the *Mischocyttarus*, hangs by a single footstalk, but the cells are very differently arranged. In the former case they are placed somewhat symmetrically around the first cell, but in this case the second cell is fastened to one side of the first, and so in a series of pairs until the group is completed.

Wherever the Icarias take a fancy to some spot, the nests are very numerous. There is a very curious example in the British Museum, where a number of nests have been fixed to the footstalk of a leaf, and a number more to the mid-rib of the same leaf.

The genus extends through all the warmer parts of the globe; and there are in the British Museum specimens from Africa and Madagascar, the Celebes, New Guinea and Australia, India, China, Burmah, Borneo, the Philippines, &c.

The habits of the Icarias are well shown by Mr. Horne in his essay upon the Hymenoptera of North-western India:—

"This pretty little insect lives in small communities, and builds an elegant nest of paper prepared by itself, which is very tough, and attached to leaves, stalks, &c., by thin but strong pedicles. It frequents flowers, and appears to feed on pollen. The posterior segments of the body are very retractile, causing the abdomen to assume a curious truncated appearance. In the example figured on a stalk, the cell-mouths are all upwards, which is strange, as the young grubs, the mouths of whose cells are open to the weather, must need some protection. The same was in a great measure the case with the cells on the mango leaf.

"The cells are beautifully regular, being perfect hexagons; and the strength with which the footstalk is fastened is surprising. There appears to be used for this portion of the work some kind of gum, with which they cover their plaster; and this much resembles varnish in appearance. It is probably derived from the babool or mango tree, both of which abound near Benares, where these nests were found.

"On one occasion I found a group of these little series of cells hanging in a covered tomb; they were attached to a stone slab, and all, of course, face downwards. Unfortunately they were old nests and quite empty. They consisted of a series of combs, and the number of cells in each averaged sixteen only. In this case shelter had evidently been sought, and in the two cases formerly noted, the insects were in a measure shielded from the direct influence of the rain by the thickness of the foliage of the mango tree above them; for the habit of this Icaria is, as a rule, to build under shelter.

"In their disposition like the rest of the Vespidæ, they fly with one accord to attack the intruder; although their sting was not very sharp, and nearly resembled the prick of a fine pin, and was in a great measure deficient in the burning feeling experienced when stung by their brethren the Polistidæ."

The reader will doubtless notice the remark made in the second paragraph, namely, that the cells are beautifully regular, being perfect hexagons. This one fact entirely disposes of two theories which at one time were generally entertained respecting the hexagonal form of the bee-cell. One theory was, that the cells were originally cylindrical and became hexagonal by mutual pressure; and the other, that they were made nearly solid at first, and were scooped out so as to assume the hexagonal form. In the case of the Icaria, however, neither mutual pressure nor scooping is possible, and yet we find the cells as perfect hexagons as those of the bee, or the common wasp, or the hornet.

Regarding the species which is represented in the illustration, Mr. Horne writes as follows:—

"This insect in its habits resembles *Icaria variegata.* It feeds its larvæ with ejected juices; hence one never finds anything but the egg slightly attached to the bottom of the cell, or the more matured grub, which spins itself a silken cocoon over its cell with which to change to a perfect insect. It associates in very large parties, and is extremely vicious when disturbed, and flies at the party interfering with it, hardly ever failing to sting him. The pain of the sting resembles burning, and in one case of my taking a nest, when I was severely stung, the pain lasted for four days. I mention this, as it is curious to observe the different degree of virulence of the poison of the various small insects of this class.

"The cells extend in masses of great size, and are placed in the midst and amongst the twigs of thick garden bushes. I also believe, from what I have seen, that the comb of one season is *not* used in another; perhaps it becomes weather-worn and incapable of proper repair. This insect also has, like the *Icaria variegata,* a retractile body, and its cells are beautifully regular hexagons. It is much molested by a small class of moths (Tineidæ), and also by an Anthrax. In fact, the nest lies very open to the attacks of parasites, who, as a rule, care nothing for the sharpest stings.

"The grubs, which I found in abundance and in all stages of growth in October, have rather a singular shape—being almost conical. The perfect insects are much plagued with a species of Stylops, the females of which lie under the scales of the abdomen. I found one piece of comb nearly one foot across each way; but generally the combs are only one-half or two-thirds of this size."

THE great genus Polistes well deserves its name, which is Greek, and signifies "the builder of a city." Species belonging

FIG. 265.—Polistes Tasmaniensis. (Rust-red.)

to this genus are found in various parts of the world; and in the British Museum there are specimens from Australia, North and South America, and Vancouver's Island. They are all dull coloured, *Polistes Tasmaniensis* being one of the brightest. The thorax is chestnut, the abdomen is rust-red, and the wings are pale brown. One species, *Polistes gallica,* affords some exception to the general rule, being banded with black and yellow, and looking like a very little wasp.

The nests of the Polistes are exceedingly variable in shape. That of the present species is very much like the nest of the common tree wasp of England without its cover, though the material is stronger and of closer texture than that of the wasp. The nests of other species are, however, arranged very differently, as may be seen by the accompanying illustration, which is taken from my "Homes without Hands." On the right hand is the pendent nest of *Polistes aterrima*, the latter name being given to the insect on account of its black colour. On the left is a triple nest group, made by a Polistes whose species is not yet identified. It is suspended by a single footstalk like that of the Icaria, but the cells, instead of being arranged side by side, are placed in a tolerably straight line and set alternately, the mouth of each being rather lower than that of its predecessor. In order to suit the exigencies of space, the figure is very much

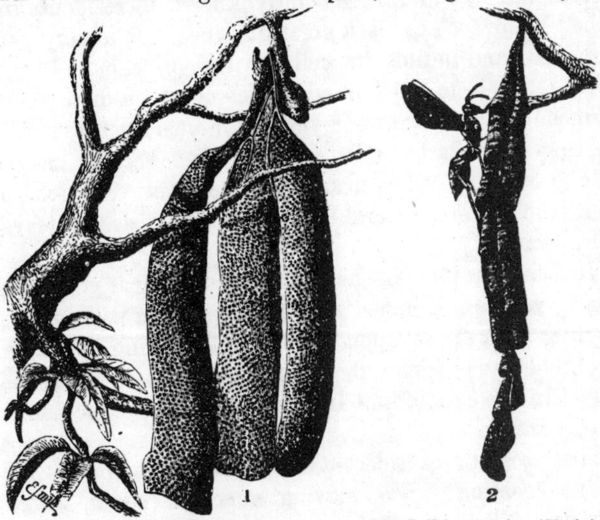

FIG. 266.—(1) Polistes (?) (2) Polistes aterrima (Black.)

reduced, the cells being nearly as large as those of *Polistes aterrima*. Strength combined with lightness is obtained by the way in which the upper part of the nest is formed into folds very much like corrugated iron.

Sometimes a totally different structure is employed, the insect seeking for shelter. In the British Museum there is a piece of wood, apparently a part of a tamarind tree, in which a large tunnel has been driven by one of the great wood-boring bees called Xylocopa. A species of Polistes, however, has taken possession of the tunnel, and has made its nest therein.

Although the Polistes is essentially an exotic genus, specimens have been taken in England, and in every case they were close to shipping. One was taken in a house at Penzance, and traced to a ship which had just come from Brazil. The captain said that great numbers of the "flies" had appeared on board, and annoyed the sailors by their stings. Another specimen was taken in the docks at Liverpool, and all the specimens were sent to Mr. F. Smith, in whose collection they now are. This species is *Polistes biguttatus.*

The following account of an Indian species, *Polistes Hebrœus,* is given by Mr. Horne:—

"This insect, which is generally known to residents in India as the 'Yellow Wasp,' is a great nuisance. It is very partial to verandahs, and builds its cells on a roof-beam. More often, however, it selects trees near houses, and, if not disturbed, builds enormous nests, continuing year after year in the same place, deserting great parts of its comb as they become useless from age, and building others near to the old ones. The food of this insect is of a very general character, and it dearly loves sugar in any form.

"It has an unpleasant habit of either flying at you if irritated, stinging you as it touches, and then flying on without stopping, or falling from above upon you and performing the same trick. I am told by a friend that the English hornet does the same thing. In the case of the Indian Polistes, however, the sting is not very severe.

"They sometimes select the oddest places for their combs. On one occasion I was moving some tin boxes, when about thirty flew out of one of them at me; and I found their comb in a corner *inside.* They had obtained access through the open window of the store-room. I have often observed the commencement of a comb.

"In the month of November the females newly hatched sit out on sunny days on the tops of venetian doors and similar situations, and buzz for males. Nor do they wait long; for at this season the whole verandah swarms with these Polistes, and I have had thousands of them killed in a morning. Having met with a suitable partner, the ova appear to be impregnated; and not long after, the queen, fully prepared, sets to and builds a single cell on a stout footstalk, lays an egg in it, and proceeds to build three or four more around it, in each of which she lays an egg.

"The young grow very fast, especially at first, when so few have to be fed; and thus in a short time there is a well-peopled colony, in which there will be a few males and workers of every size.

"The tops of the cells of the queen wasps are much elongated with silk; and these insects use some species of gluten wherewith to temper the paper of which the cells are constructed, as well as to solidify the silken cell coverings.

"They are in the habit of seizing insects and sucking out their juices, wherewith they again feed the voracious young grubs, who are always clamouring for food with open mouths.

"They are extremely troubled with Stylops—every fifth or sixth taken having a female of one under one of the segments of the abdomen; and I have sometimes seen two or three on one specimen. I have often tried to breed these Stylops, but invariably failed, the male Stylops being very scarce, and the female, Mr. Smith tells me, never leaving the body of the Polistes.

"This species is so well known that I do not think any further remarks are needed, excepting a short account of the method by which these troublesome insects are easily got rid of:—

"There is a yellow ant (*Œcophylla smaragdina*) which lives a social life chiefly upon trees, drawing leaves together in a curious manner with silk, and making in this manner large nests in the mango trees. These insects sting severely, and they seem to have a great antipathy to the Polistes, who are very fond of feeding on their poorly-protected juicy young grubs. If, therefore, you cut off a bough with a nest of these ants upon it, tie it to a long bamboo, and put it very near to the nest of the Polistes, there will be a general attack by the former upon the latter. An ant will seize upon a wasp and bite and sting him, others also coming up to help. They will together fall to the ground, when the Polistes dies, and the ant (*Œcophylla smaragdina*), having taken a sip of his blood and juices, runs up again to his nest by a string always left hanging down from the bamboo near to the nest for this purpose. They will also attack hornets. Their native name is "Mātā," and they are used by all classes for this purpose.

"No heat is too great for the Polistes, and in the hottest

weather they may be found sitting in large parties by water, evidently enjoying the season."

It has been already mentioned that the name *Polistes* signifies "a builder of a city," and has been given to a genus of insects in allusion to the character of their nests. For a similar reason the name *Apoica*, which signifies a "colony," has been given to another genus of nest-builders, one of which, together with a cell-group, is here shown. The specific name of *pallida* has been given to it on account of the very pale yellow brown which constitutes its only colouring. The only attempt at variation of colour is in a narrow stripe of rather darker brown, which is drawn upon the outer edge of the upper wings. The usual shape of the nest is given in the illustration, and it is impossible to look at one of these nests without being reminded of the remarkable compound nests built by the sociable weaver-bird of Africa.

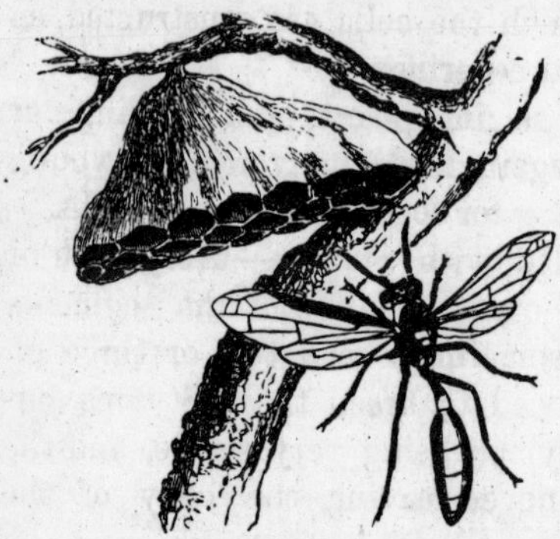

Fig. 267.—Apoica pallida. (Very pale yellow.)

In the British Museum there are a number of nests made by this species, which are not only curious, but really valuable in an entomological point of view. Not only are the cells themselves hexagonal, but the nest masses themselves are hexagons, the six sides being as regular, and the angles as true, as if they had been drawn with rule and compass. How this result is attained is at present an absolute mystery, and it is evident that neither the sculpture nor the mutual pressure theory can be brought to bear on these nests. These nests are of various sizes, so that the insects have evidently started with the idea of making the structure hexagonal, and have adhered to the same principle throughout. The hexagonal form is not adhered to in all instances, for some nests are entirely circular, while in others the hexagonal idea is but slightly indicated. These nests sometimes attain a diameter of eleven or twelve inches. A number of these nests are shown in my "Homes without Hands," p. 585.

THE insect which is here shown is called *Trigonalys compressus*, and is a native of tropical America. The following account of its mode of development is given by Mr. F. Smith:—

"John Macgillivray, Esq., Naturalist to her Majesty's ship *Rattlesnake*, lately presented to the British Museum the nest of a South American species of Polistes, which he says is very abundant at St. Salvador, where even in the street it attaches its nest under the eaves of houses; this species is the *Polistes lanio* of Fabricius, and in all probability the *Vespa Canadensis* of Linnæus; a specimen of the species is preserved in the Banksian Cabinet.

"On examining the nest, I found it consisted as usual of a single comb of cells, having in the centre, at the back, a small footstalk, by which the nests are attached in their position; the

FIG. 263.—Trigonalys compressus. (Black.)

comb contained sixty-five cells, the outer ones being in an unfinished state, whilst twenty-two of the central ones had remains of exuviæ in them, and one or two closed ones contained perfect insects in them ready to emerge. About half a dozen of the wasps had the anterior portion of their bodies buried in the cells, in the manner in which these insects are said to repose.

"In one cell I observed the head of an insect evidently of a different species, it being black and shining. On extricating it I discovered it to be a species of Trigonalys; I subsequently carefully expanded the insect, and it proved to be the *Trigonalys bipustulatus*, described by myself in the "Ann. and Mag. of Natural History," vol. vii., Second Series, 1851, from a specimen captured at Pará by Mr. Bates, now in the possession of William Wilson Saunders, Esq. The insect was not enveloped in any pellicle, nor had the cell been closed in any way; the wings were crumpled at its side, as is usual in Hymenopterous insects which have not expanded them, proving satisfactorily that it had never quitted the cell, and that Trigonalys is the parasite of Polistes.

"This discovery is one of much interest, proving the relationship of the insect to be amongst the pupivora—to which family it had been previously assigned by Mr. Westwood. (See vol. iii. Ent. Trans., p. 270.) The specimen is seven lines in length, entirely black, the head shining, the thorax and abdomen opaque, and having two white maculæ touching the apical margin of the basal segment above; the wings are smoky, the antennæ broken off. Of one of them I found subsequently seventeen joints—the perfect insect in the possession of Mr. Saunders having twenty joints."

The specific name of *bipustulatus*, or "two-spotted," has been given to the insect on account of the two white spots on the base of the abdomen, but its original name of *compressus*, as given to it by De Geer, is now allowed to stand.

THE figure which is here given represents the neuter of the splendid Chinese Wasp, which is appropriately called *Vespa*

FIG. 269.—Vespa mandarinia.
(Orange and dark brown.)

mandarinia. The female is shown on Plate IX., Fig. 3. This fine insect is found throughout China and Japan. It is coloured very much like our common hornet, but is much richer in appearance, owing to the very broad and ample head, and the amount of bright yellow upon it. The colours are rich dark brown, banded, striped, and marked profusely with "king's" yellow. The jaws are enormously powerful. The wings are yellow, darker at the base, and becoming lighter towards the tips.

THE species which is represented in the accompanying illustration is a native of Asia, and is spread over a very large tract

FIG. 270.—Vespa cincta.
(Dark brown and yellow.)

of country. There are several Asiatic species of Vespa which are almost exactly similar in their habits, and this may safely be taken as the typical species. The head and thorax of *Vespa cincta* are dark brown, covered with a moderately thick grey down, and the abdomen is very dark brown, crossed with a bold band of bright yellow, whence is derived the specific name of *cincta*, or "banded."

In the accompanying illustration, the upper and smaller figure represents the male, and the lower figure the perfect female. The single figure represents the neuter, or worker wasp.

The habits of this wasp are admirably described by Mr. Horne in the essay to which reference has so often been made. In this account Mr. Horne seems to have some doubt as to the truth of the report that horses have been stung to death by these wasps. I think it very likely to be true. Some years ago I saw, only a few miles from my house, a wasp's nest, the inmates of which had actually killed a carriage-horse on the preceding day.

FIG. 271.—Vespa cincta.
(Dark brown and yellow.)

"They build their nests of prepared earth, strongly impregnated with some viscid substance, probably derived from the gums of trees.

"In confirmation of the above, I may remark that I have often seen them sitting, apparently eating the gum of the Acacia (*Catechu*), and also the flowing juice of the Peepul-tree (*Ficus Indica*), and as they are in general carnivorous, it must have been for some such purpose. At the same time there appears to be some woody, or at least vegetable fibre, mixed with the earth.

"The cells are regular hexagons, and built from an hexagonal *ground-plan*—a fact which confirms Mr. Smith's observations to the same effect—and the whole structure often assumes a large size. One found by me was 10″ × 9″ × 9″, in the centre of a wall composed of sunburnt bricks, in a hollow which had been originally excavated by Termites, and afterwards enlarged by the 'hornets,' as they are popularly called.

"I have often seen these insects pounce on a sitting fly, just as a hawk would do on a small bird; and they are also very fond of ripe fruit, such as peaches, grapes, and apples. The *Vespa velutina* also indulges in these luxuries, and is especially fond of the hill apricot.

"The stings of four or five of these insects are said to be sufficiently powerful to kill a child, but, as in all such cases, much must depend on the circumstances.

"The outside of the nests is, as is usual with wasps, covered with a coating of loose paper.

"It is highly dangerous to disturb a colony of these insects; and, as they work in gangs at night, it is somewhat hazardous even then to take their nests. As, however, they greatly affect outhouses, it is most necessary to destroy them, as horses have been said to have been stung to death by them; but for this I cannot vouch.

"I will here quote *in extenso* from my note-book, the notes which refer to Indian 'hornets,' by which term both *Vespa cincta* and *Vespa Orientalis* are designated.

"'*August* 15, 1863.—These insects are very abundant at Benares, but not generally spiteful. One may see hundreds of them flying about the sweetmeat stalls, like wasps in the fruit-shops in England; and the vendor drives them away with a whisk—a piece of palm-leaf in a cloth—and is very rarely stung. If one, however, be incautiously touched, the sting is very suddenly given and very sharp; its pain is intense, and it induces considerable inflammation. They make their nests in the mud walls, and the form of these is just like that of the English hornet.

"'Yesterday I was drying some sugar in the sun, and this attracted a large number of them. My man killed many, throwing down their bodies on the spot, when the ants appeared to carry off the carcases; but not only did the ants so employ themselves, for the hornets also alighted and carried off their dead brethren as food. The ants (*Œcophylla smaragdina*) appear to be naturally very destructive to these insects. These ants live both in the ground and in nests made of leaves of trees drawn together.

"'I have seen the hornets trying to carry off their tiny tormentors. Again and again have they darted at them; but it invariably ended either in the hornet quietly sitting down among his enemies to be bitten or stung to death, and then carried off in triumph to be eaten by them, or in his falling to the ground with two or three ants hanging on, when his fate was equally certain.

"'One of these insects stung me on the thumb, but by sucking the place for about a quarter of an hour, I drew out the poison, and the pain and swelling were afterwards very slight.'

"'*August* 20, 1863.—This evening, having prepared two large squibs filled with damp gunpowder, I proceeded to take two nests, one of *Vespa Orientalis* and one of *Vespa cincta*, both in similar situations. Having lighted the touch-paper, the end was placed at the mouth of the hole, and wet clay was plastered around. The dense smoke and intense heat thus killed every perfect insect in the nest, which I shortly dug out for the purpose of examination. One nest was buried forthwith in a hole previously prepared, and the one taken to be set up was that of *Vespa Orientalis*, to which all the succeeding remarks will refer.

"'Both nests were constructed of earth tempered with water, and I could trace no sign of gluten of any kind in them. In the nest prepared by me were seven ranges of cells, and at the time of taking it from 400 to 500 hornets were at home. Although I took out every perfect insect, there were from forty to fifty nearly hatched by 5 A.M. next morning, showing with what enormous rapidity they increase. The nest was placed under a large wire dish-cover, and a nest of the Yellow Ant before referred to was placed with them, so that every young hornet was destroyed as soon as born.

"'*July* 1, 1864. Benares.—As a boy, when in England, I have watched a hornet carry off a fly sitting on a door-handle, and to-day I saw one pounce on a small honey-bee deep in the pollen of a flower, and, taking him off, sit down and eat him quietly, and, from the number hovering about flowers, this would seem to be a favourite food.'

"'*July* 19, 1864. Benares.—Watched hornets catching and eating the workers of Termites, whose galleries I had just destroyed on the bark of a tree, when, in consequence, the blind insects were running wildly about.'

"'*August* 19, 1864.—Watched them more narrowly and carefully. Saw that one caught at least ten Termites, one after the other, and made them all up into a ball with its jaws, when the said ball was taken away, evidently to feed the young larvæ with a rich and juicy morsel, which, however, would be strongly tinctured with acid.'"

This very interesting history requires, in order to make it thoroughly intelligible, the account of the Yellow Ant (*Œcophylla smaragdina*), to which several allusions have been made, and whose exploits will be remembered in connection with the fiercely-stinging Polistes.

LIKE the generic name of *Polistes* and *Apoica*, that of *Synœca* is given on account of the mode of nest-building. The term is composed of two Greek words, and literally signifies an assemblage of persons living under the same roof.

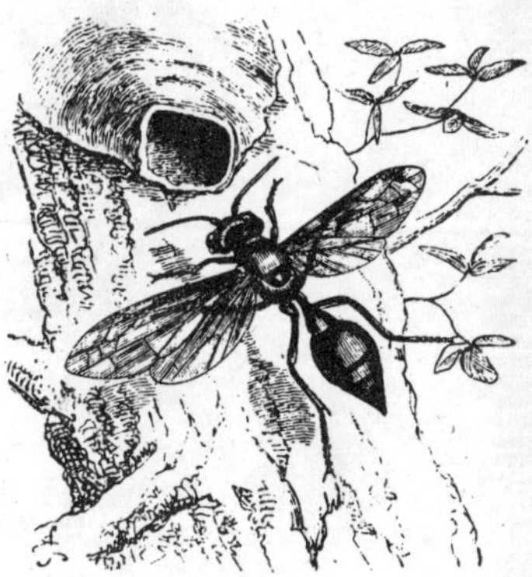

FIG. 272.—Synœca cœrulea. (Blue.)

There is rather a peculiarity about the nests of the Synœcas. They are not suspended by footstalks, but are affixed throughout their whole length to a branch, a tree-trunk, or similar object, and have the entrance below. The mouth of one of these nests is shown in the illustration.

The outer shell, or covering of the nests, is exceedingly thin —scarcely thicker indeed than the paper on which this account is printed, and yet is quite strong enough to resist the weather. Within the nest the combs are placed in regular layers, like those of the common wasp, and the shell is so thin that the edges of each successive layer is distinctly marked on the exterior. In consequence of this peculiar surface, added to the dark brown of the paper covering, the nest bears so close a resemblance to the bark of the tree or branch to which it is fastened, that a very quick eye is needed in order to discover it. As is the case with most of the Social Wasps, the nest is begun on a small scale, and gradually enlarged in order to accommodate the increasing population. There are many specimens of Synœca nests in the British Museum, the largest of which is rather more than two feet in length.

The colour of the present species is blue, even the head having a slight gloss of the same colour. The wings are brown. The handsomest of all the species is perhaps *Synœca cyanea,* in which the blue is exceedingly vivid. All the Synœcas are Brazilian insects.

THE last of the Wasp tribe which will be described is that which is represented in the accompanying illustration. It is

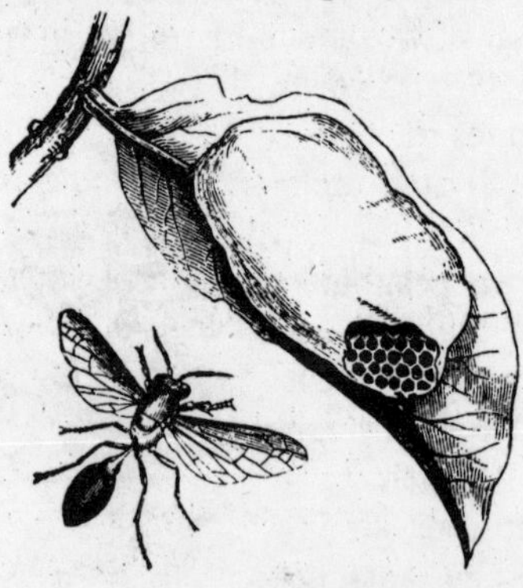

FIG. 273.—Polybia sericea.
(Reddish brown.)

called *Polybia sericea,* both of which names are appropriate. The generic name, *Polybia,* signifies "sociality," and the specific term, *sericea,* or "silken," is applied to the insect in consequence of the silken down which is spread profusely over the thorax. Most of the Polybias are South American insects, though there are some which come from the Celebes, and a few from New Guinea and Borneo.

The mode in which these insects make their nests is very remarkable. Choosing a tolerably flat surface, mostly that of a leaf, the little wasp begins by laying the foundation of a number of hexagonal cells, sometimes as many as thirty or forty in number. She then deposits an egg in each cell, and proceeds to make some more. As the larvæ are hatched and increase in size, the Wasp builds up the walls of the cells, so as to accommodate them, and then places over them a covering of thin paper. Scarcely has she done this than she proceeds to place another layer of cells upon the cover, and, as the worker wasps are hatched, they build cells at such a rate that layer after layer may be seen in one nest, each being placed on the cover of the preceding layer.

The Polybia does not seem to be very particular as to the material on which it supports its nest, though a large leaf is generally a favourite locality. There are numbers of these curious habitations in the "Nest Room" of the British Museum, and very variable they are. One of them looks just like a huge brown sausage, round which a series of strings had been tied about an inch apart. These represent the layers of combs which are placed regularly inside the protecting cover. It is remarkable, by the way, that some of the large wasps called *Chartergus*, which hang their nests to the branches of trees, act in a very similar manner.

CHAPTER VI.

SOLITARY AND SOCIAL BEES.

THE next great group of the Hymenoptera may be summed up in the words which head this chapter. Just as there are Solitary and Social Wasps, so there are Solitary and Social Bees. The habits of these creatures are curiously similar, the Solitary Bees placing their eggs in burrows which they stock with food for the future young, and the Social Bees forming a number of cells in which the young larvæ are hatched, and tending them until they are full-fed. The chief distinction is that, whereas the Solitary Wasps store their burrows with insects as food for the future young, the Solitary Bees empty the pollen of various plants. Most of them, as well as the Social Bees, procure the pollen for themselves, and for this purpose are furnished with a development of the hind-legs, technically called the "basket." Some species, however, do not possess the basket, and are therefore unable to carry the pollen. Consequently, they are forced to make use of the stores collected by other bees, and treat them exactly as do the parasitic wasps which have already been described. In the different genera of pollen-carrying bees there is great variety of form in the structure of the basket, but the general principle is the same in all.

The Solitary Bees begin with the great family of Andrenidæ, which are spread over all the insect-producing parts of the world. There are many species in England, so that their habits can be easily watched. Putting aside those that are parasitic, the habits of all the species are tolerably alike. They make burrows, mostly in the ground, and deposit therein a quantity of pollen mixed with honey, technically called "bee-bread." Upon this they place an egg, and thus protect it with a cover. Upon this first cell a second is made, and so the bee proceeds, until it has nearly filled the burrow with its cells. Having thus completed its labours, the bee closes the burrow with a stout cover of earth.

Of the genus to which *Halictus quadristrigatus* belongs, there are many English species, Mr. F. Smith having described twenty-six species, one of which is the smallest species of bee that is found in this country. As the habits of all the British species are alike, it may be inferred that the life history of the genus is tolerably similar all over the world. The present species inhabits the warmer parts of Europe, but has never been seen in England.

Fig. 274.—Halictus quadristrigatus. (Black and yellow.)

Mr. Smith found that in the spring the females appeared, and abounded until midsummer, not a single male being seen. In the autumn the males began to appear, and a week or two afterwards a second brood of females succeeded the males, immediately setting about their tunnels. Each burrow had several others running into it, all being reached by the one common entrance. In each of these burrows was placed a little ball of pollen and a single egg, and the larva was full-fed in some ten or twelve days.

The colour of this species is black, and there are four narrow bands of yellow on the abdomen. The specific name *quadristrigatus*, or four-striped, refers to this colouring.

The history of the genus *Andrena* is a very remarkable one, not so much on account of the labours of the bee, but of the persecution which it endures from other insects. In his Catalogue of British Bees, Mr. F. Smith has worked out this branch of the subject exhaustively, though briefly. After remarking upon the various hymenopterous parasites which attack the Andrenas, he refers to the extraordinary parasitic beetle called *Stylops*, which was first discovered by Mr. Kirby upon an

Andrena bee. Mr. Smith's description of these singular parasites is very interesting:—

"These insects are diminutive in size, the largest known species not exceeding a quarter of an inch in length. We are now speaking of the winged males, the females being apterous, grub-like insects, which never leave the bodies of the bees. If the abdomens of a number of Andrenidæ be examined, it is most probable that the female of Stylops will be found. Her presence is known by the protrusion of her head, and a portion of the thorax between the abdominal segments on their superior surface resembling the point of a small bud of a brown colour, or rather, a flattened scale.

FIG. 275.—Andrena holomelana.
(Shining black.)

"I have several times bred the larvæ of the Stylops in the following manner:—On finding a bee infested as described, place her in a box five or six inches square, cover it with gauze, and supply the bee with fresh flowers such as the Andrenidæ frequent. Examine the bee every day, and it is most likely that in eight or ten days she will appear as if her abdomen were covered with dust. Examine it, and in all probability she will be found to be covered with an innumerable quantity of exceedingly minute animals; these are the larvæ of Stylops.

"By the aid of a magnifying-glass they may be seen to issue from the transverse aperture on the thorax. When the bee re-enters the cell, or settles upon flowers, these diminutive creatures will of course be deposited, and by these means, when other bees visit the flowers, they attach themselves to them, and are carried to their nests.

"Judging from the multitude of larvæ produced by each female Stylops, amounting to many hundreds in each case, and the rarity of the perfect insect, the majority must perish, probably in their larval condition. From the fact of seldom more than two Stylops being found to infest the same bee, we may suppose that to be the largest number which infests one larva of an Andrena. They undergo their changes in the body of the bee, the male on its final transformation becoming an active winged insect, the female remaining a mere apod, attached for life to the bee which nourished it."

Besides the Stylops, there are several other parasites which infest this much-enduring bee, the curious little orange-coloured larva of the Meloë being perhaps the most remarkable. A full description of this larva and its development is given in my "Insects at Home," p. 154.

The specific name *Holomelana* is formed from two Greek words signifying "wholly black," and is given to the species because its colour is entirely shining black.

THE strange-looking bee which is shown in the illustration has been selected on account of its beauty. It is an European species, but has never been found in England, where only one representative of the genus is known, namely, *Dasypoda hirtipes*, which Mr. Smith describes as being perhaps the most beautiful bee found in this country.

FIG. 276.—Dasypoda plumipes.
(Black, with golden hair.)

In all the species belonging to this genus the hind-legs are clothed with very long downy hair. Both names refer to this peculiarity, the generic name being taken from the Greek, and signifying "hairy-footed," while the specific name is Latin, and signifies "plumed-foot."

This is a very beautiful bee. The original colour is black, but the thorax is covered with a thick coat of silken hair, shining as if spun from gold. The long hairs which fringe the legs are bright yellow, and the abdomen is black, and deeply fringed with golden hair. As is the case with many of the bee-tribe, this beautiful adornment can only be seen in perfection when the insect has been newly developed, for the beautiful plumage cannot endure rough work, and suffers so much from contact with the world, that a bee of a day old and one which has lived for three or four weeks would hardly be recognized as the same species, even though they may have issued from the same nest. Seven species of this genus are in the British Museum.

All entomologists are aware of the singular resemblances that occur between certain lepidoptera and hymenoptera, the "clear-wing" moths of our own country being excellent examples. Curious as is the shape of this bee, it is exactly imitated by a beautiful Assamese moth, called *Trochilium Ashtaroth.* The colours are different, but the resemblance of form is so perfect, that if the outline of either were drawn, it would not be easy to determine the insect which it was meant to represent; even the deeply-plumed hind-legs are represented in the moth.

Of all the Solitary Bees, the genus *Osmia* is the most interesting, on account of the singular variety of its architecture. Some ten species are known to inhabit England. However the different species of Osmia may vary in detail of architecture, they all agree in the habit of making cells and stocking them with food for the future young. Several species make their cells in the dead stems of the blackberry, the rose, and similar shrubs, digging out the pith, and so making a series of cells, end to end. They are, however, very much given to saving themselves needless labour, and are in the habit of taking advantage of any tubes that they may find. The straws of thatched roofs are favourite localities with some species, but they will sometimes make use of the most singular and unexpected objects as dwelling-places.

Fig. 277.—Osmia bicolor. (Black, barred with orange.)

Any hole or empty tube serves to be adapted to the purposes

of the Osmia, which will even enter into houses in search of a suitable locality. Some years ago I was at a sale at Lee, and purchased for a very small sum a band-box full of miscellaneous articles. Among them was a flute, which was quite choked up, apparently as if some mischievous child had been stuffing it with paper. On unscrewing the flute, I found it to be occupied with the cells of the Osmia, the insect having evidently entered by the mouth-hole and gradually filled the instrument with its cells. The mother-bee must have found its way into the disused rooms in which the band-box had been lying, and so contrived to discover the flute. The flute is now in the British Museum.

Empty snail-shells are favourite localities with the Osmias, and in the British Museum is a very curious specimen. The shell happened to be a very large one, so that several cells could be made in it. The bee began as usual by making a single cell far within the shell. She then placed two more cells horizontally side by side, and then, the shell being very much wider, built two more cells, also side by side, but transversely; thus showing that she possessed no small reasoning powers.

The present species is an inhabitant of Southern Europe, and has been found in England, though it is very local. Kent seems to be its favourite county. It is a very pretty insect, the colour being black, banded with orange. Generally, it does not reach half an inch in length, but a few specimens have been taken which were three-quarters of an inch in length.

One species of Osmia does not build in tubes, but makes its simple nest under the shelter of flat stones and in similar localities. This is a northern species, and its name is *Osmia parietana.* Instead of boring tunnels, or making cocoons in tubes, it merely selects the under surface of some flat stone, and to it attaches a number of balls of pollen, each ball accompanied by an egg. After the larva is full-fed, it spins a cocoon, which it affixes to the stone in the same place which the pollen-ball previously occupied. The number of these cocoons is something great. On a piece of stone only ten inches by six, no less than two hundred and thirty cocoons were found. These were placed in the hands of Mr. F. Smith, who found that the insects were developed in three distinct batches, one in 1849, another in 1850, and the third in 1851.

THE insect which is here represented is an European species, but at present is not known to be British.

There is a considerable difference in appearance, as well as size, between the sexes. The female, which is drawn in the illustration, is very black, and her wings are brown. The male is a much smaller, but handsomer insect, being covered with a dense coating of long silken hairs, either golden or pale yellow. The generic name, which is formed from a Greek word, signifying "brass," is given to it on account of this peculiarity. Hair of a similar character is to be found in the males of most species, but it is not seen unless the specimen is in the very best order.

FIG. 278.—Chalicodoma muraria. (Black.)

This insect is very liable to the attacks of a species of Clerus, a parasitic genus which infests not only the nests of the wild bees, but even the hives of the domestic bee. All the species are brightly coloured, and, were they large, they would rank among the handsomest of their order.

THE generic name of *Megachile* is formed from two Greek words, which literally signify "large-muzzled," and is given to certain bees in consequence of their large jaws. The species which is taken as an example of the genus has been selected principally because it well shows the generic peculiarity. It is a native of Australia, and is beautifully coloured, the greater part of the body being of the richest purple very deeply punctured, and relieved by a quantity of snowy white down, arranged as shown in the illustration. The wings are brown, and have a purple gloss.

This genus is spread all over the world, and has long been celebrated for the beautiful nests which are made by the different species. Nine British species are known, and are popularly called "Leaf-cutter Bees," because they cut up leaves for the purpose of forming their singular nests. The rose is the plant which is generally employed, though the leaves of several other plants are also brought into requisition.

Even the same species is very variable in the position of its nest. Mr. F. Smith remarks that our best known species, *Megachile centuncularis*, sometimes burrows in decaying wood, sometimes in the soft mortar of an old wall, and sometimes in the ground. Within these burrows it makes its cells, which are formed from the cut leaves, and look very much like a number of green thimbles stuck into each other. There is now before me a specimen which was not made in a tunnel at all, the bee having made its way into an outhouse, and placed its nest on a high shelf. It has generally been supposed that the cells were made by bending the leaves and allowing them to press by their own elasticity against the side of the burrow. But the existence of this nest shows that the bee can make its cells independently

FIG. 279.—Megachile monstrosus.
(Deep purple and white.)

of the burrow, and that it can bend and fasten together the leaves by its own unaided efforts.

In Mr. Horne's paper on the Indian hymenoptera, there is a very interesting account of the manner in which various species of this genus build their nests. One species, *Megachile fasciculata*, consrtucted its leaf-cells in the hollow handle of a large garden vase, a number of the nests being built closely together. Another species, *Megachile disjuncta*, uses mud instead of leaves, and makes two earthen tubes, side by side, sometimes giving each of them a curious twist in the middle. *Megachile lanata* is also a mud-builder, and works in a variety of ways. The following is Mr. Horne's account of this insect:—

"This insect is found in almost every house in the North-

West Provinces, and, next to the black and yellow *Pelopœus* (*madraspatanus*) is the one which attracts most notice.

"The season in which it builds its cells is from March to November; but July and August (*i.e.* during the rainy season) are its favourite months. These cells are placed in every conceivable situation; and it is curious, when sitting quietly writing, to watch the insect coming and going with his material. He or she is so deeply interested in the work that all fear is forgotten, and they will work within a foot of your writing-desk. The mud is carried, so to speak, under the head, and in part supported by the fore-legs, and it is not so finely worked up as that of the *Pelopœus;* hence we find the work much rougher exteriorly, although the inside of the cell is carefully smoothed. I have had a newspaper lying on the table and heard them working inside the folds; in short, there is no position too strange for the nest.

"The following are a few of the positions in which I have found them:—

"1. Between folds of paper; 2. in the back of a book which had been left lying open; 3. on the handle of a tea-cup; 4. in the key-hole of a door; 5. in the barrel of a gun; 6. under a fan on the table; 7. in the hollow of a bolt of a window, where three times the whole structure was crushed by the use of the said bolt in the absence of the insect; 8. on a signet-ring from which the stone had fallen out; 9. on the frill of a large fan or punka, which was kept in motion ten or twelve hours out of the twenty-four.

"I will now proceed with the method of working. Both sexes appear to labour; for I have sometimes caught a worker, and found that the work was immediately continued, which was not the case with the *Pelopœus.* They come and go incessantly, with a loud buzzing; and whilst they are tempering the clay they keep up the motion, thereby advertising the locality where they are working, although often the *exact* spot is even then difficult to find. The tenacity with which the clay adheres to substances is very curious (although the cells of the insects of the genus *Rhynchium* afford a better instance); and I believe that when the clay, having been first prepared at the water, is brought into use, it is inspissated by some glutinous substance ejected by the insect. It is certainly very carefully kneaded again by many of the clay-cell-builders. The cells are built side by side with very little cohesion, and are stocked with bee-bread and closed by three or four pellets of mud, united in such a manner as to leave thin edges next to the lips or upper edges, and thus enable the insect easily to escape. The outside is in general rough, and adapted to the situation in which it is built. It is scarcely ever truly circular on the outside, even if built free from obstruction.

"Amongst the figures will be observed a solitary cell built in a signet-ring. The power of instinct shown here is very great; for to keep the cell secure the clay has been made larger at the base, where it projects interiorly in the ring.

"This insect is very annoying from the manner it chokes up small openings, such as barrels of fire-arms and locks of drawers, in the latter case entering by the key-hole.

"I watched the construction of four cells in June 1863; and the perfect insects were matured August 12, 14, 15, and 16 respectively. This would show, what is really the case, that the cells take about a day each to construct. In fact, in one case noted by me, a cell was commenced, finished, stored with food, and closed, certainly within ten hours, which is quite possible if both sexes work, as I believe to be the case.

"Sometimes, however, a hollow bamboo is the situation selected by this insect. If it be tolerably thick there is room for several cells; and they are built from the bottom of the hollow upwards, either in a straight line or spirally. In either case I believe the single series to be constructed, and the second series commenced from the very bottom on the completion of the first. In some cases there are as many as eight or ten cells in each hive; and probably more than one pair of insects are concerned in this double series."

THE bees belonging to the genus *Anthidium* are remarkable for two peculiarities. In the first place, they exactly reverse the usual structure of bees, the male being very much larger and stronger than the female.

Their matrimonial customs are very curious, and quite unlike those of insects in general. Both sexes are fond of hovering over flowers, a habit which has earned for them the generic name of *Anthidium, i.e.* "a creature that frequents flowers."

The females remain on or close to the flowers, while the more powerful male hovers above, like a hawk watching its prey. Mr. F. Smith tells me that he has seen the male of our only English species, *Anthidium manicatum*, suddenly swoop down, just as a hawk stoops upon its quarry, pounce on one of the females and carry her off.

The second peculiarity in these bees is the method in which they construct their nests. Although they build in holes, it is believed that they do not burrow, but that they usually make use of any convenient hole that can be found, mostly in a burrow made by some large wood-boring insect. Having selected a suitable burrow, the mother-bee goes off in search of some woolly plant, from which she strips the hair, running along the stem and shaving off the down as she goes. The well-known "White of Selborne" was the first to notice this habit in the English species, and he compares the action of the bee to that of a hoop-shaver. The garden campion was the plant frequented by the bees which he watched. There are some foreign species which do not build in burrows, but make their nests in the pure air, placing them on branches.

FIG. 280.—Anthidium Florentinum. (Black and yellow.)

The present species inhabits Southern Europe, and has a curiously waspish aspect.

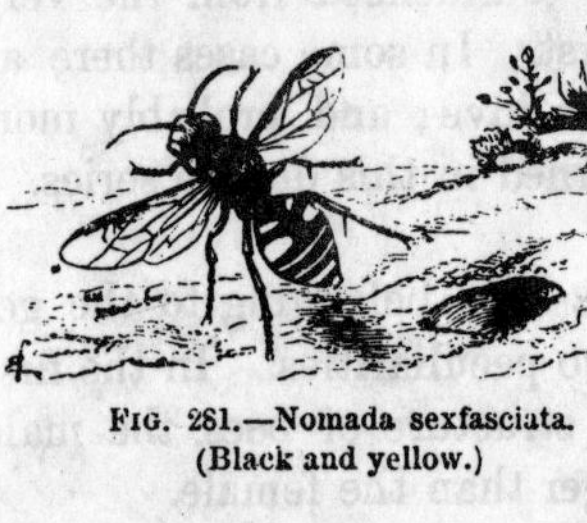

FIG. 281.—Nomada sexfasciata. (Black and yellow.)

IN the *Nomada sexfasciata* we have a good example of the group of insects called Wasp Bees, because, though they are really bees, they bear a very strong external resemblance to wasps.

They are all parasitic, preying upon the nests of other bees.

This species is known to be parasitic upon *Eucera longicornis*, Mr. F. Smith having had specimens from the nests of that insect. He believes that although this species is rare, it may be found wherever the *Eucera* makes its nest.

As its name imports, its black abdomen is marked with six bands of yellow, the three next the tip extending completely across the body, and those towards the base only about half way. This insect is spread over a very large portion of the globe.

THE generic name of the insect which is here figured is formed from two Greek words, signifying "sharp-belly," and is given to the insects because the abdomen narrows rapidly

FIG. 282.—Cœlioxys Ducalis.
(Black.)

towards the end, especially in the female. The abdomen of the male is toothed at the extremity. It is a parasitic genus, and in England has been bred from the nest of the active and beautiful Megachile and Saropoda.

The present species is African, and is extremely rare. Mr. F. Smith was indebted for his specimen to Mr. W. W. L. Walcott, who brought it from Africa. The colour of the abdomen is black, and the thorax is thickly covered with warm dun-coloured hair. The wings have a decided purple gloss when viewed by a side light.

Mr. Smith remarks concerning the bees of this genus, that the species are exceedingly difficult of identification, owing to the variety of form which prevails. "We must not forget that a species is not, as it were, cast in a mould, but admits a degree of variety, still, however, retaining intact the broad and distinguishing characteristics." If this maxim had been more generally appreciated by systematic zoologists, we should have been spared much of the confused nomenclature under which we at present suffer.

PLATE X. represents a group of Brazilian bees, the first of which is called *Chrysantheda frontalis*. It is marked No. 1, and is the upper of the two insects which are shown as inserting their long tongues into the blossom. The singularly beautiful flower which is depicted is the *Passiflora kermesiana*.

This is one of the parasitic bees, and is supposed to infest the dwellings of the great wood-boring bee, which is seen immediately above it. It is a very beautiful insect, its body being shining green, very thickly punctured, and its wings brown, with a decided blue gloss. The hind legs are furnished on the inside with a coating of thick brown hair, but on the outside are of the same shining green as the body.

ANOTHER of these beautiful parasitic bees is shown in the

FIG. 283.—Aglaë cærulea.
(Shining blue.)

accompanying illustration. Its colour is shining blue, with a gloss of green in a side light. The wings are brown.

PLATE X.

2

1

4

3

On Plate X., Fig. 3, is shown a very handsome Brazilian bee, named *Centris denudans.*

The abdomen of this insect is velvet black, and the thorax is covered with dense orange hair. The wings are glossed with blue, and the hind legs are clothed with very long black hair. There is a British genus named *Melecta*, which is closely allied to Centris. The *Melecta* is a parasite insect, and Mr. F. Smith has bred numbers of them from the nests of the well-known Anthophora.

Another species of the same genus, *Centris flavopicta*, is

Fig. 284.—Centris flavopicta. (Brown and yellow.) Euglossa dimidiata. (Black and white.)

shown in the accompanying illustration. The abdomen is yellow, crossed with bars of dark brown, and the thorax is dark brown, relieved by a greyish white pile. The brushes of the hind pair of legs are yellow.

The name *Xylocopa* literally signifies a "wood-cutter," and is given to a genus of bees in consequence of their power of burrowing into wood. They are spread over all the warmer portions of the earth, but no species has as yet been found to inhabit England. The present example is a native of Southern Africa, and, as is often the case among insects, the colours of the two sexes are very different. The male is covered with yellowish orange hair, and has transparent wings, while the female is black, varied with whitish grey hair, and her wings are black, with a blue gloss. In the illustration the upper figure represents the male, and the lower the female.

FIG. 285.—Xylocopa nigrita.
(Male, orange; Female, black.)

Between the two specimens is seen the entrance to the tunnel which these insects make. By means of their very powerful jaws, which look much like wire-nippers, a large hole is made in the side of a tree, and carried on horizontally for a few inches. It then turns almost at an angle, so as to follow the grain of the wood. A vast number of chips are of course made, and, instead of being thrown away, are stored up in a safe place until wanted.

The burrow being completed, the insect places a quantity of pollen at the extremity of the tunnel, and deposits an egg upon it. She then goes off to her store of wooden chips, and with them constructs a flat ceiling over the pollen, so as to form a cell. The ceiling is quite flat, and is made in concentric rings, just like a slice cut through the middle of an onion. More pollen and another egg are then deposited on this ceiling, which becomes the floor of a second cell, and so the insect proceeds until it has filled the burrow with its cells.

In the Nest Room of the British Museum there are many specimens of *Xylocopa* burrows, in which the whole process is easily to be seen. One of the largest is *Xylocopa trepida*, a singularly fine insect, with blue-glossed wings. The nest of this bee, is also in the Museum. One of the handsomest species is *Xylocopa caffra,* which is, as its name imports, an inhabitant of Southern Africa. The male is entirely greenish yellow, while the female is black, with a broad band of golden hair at the junction of the thorax and abdomen. The front of the thorax is black and blue.

Another fine species, *Xylocopa morio,* is seen—Plate X., Fig. 2. It is a Brazilian insect. It is shining black, with a fringe of black hair upon the abdomen. The wings are brown.

On the same plate, Fig. 4, is shown another of the parasitic bee, named *Euglossa romandi,* which is shown as inserting its long tongue in the flower of the *Passiflora.*

It is a very handsome insect, the abdomen being green, with the exception of the base, which is purple. The thorax is also purple, and the head green like the abdomen. The green has always a gloss of gold, and in some specimens it extends over the whole of the abdomen, the purple band being wanting. As may be seen by reference to the illustration, the tongue is of very great length, and in one specimen in the collection of the British Museum it is separated into its several parts. The name *Euglossa,* or "beautiful tongue," refers to the length of the proboscis.

Another species of the same genus, called *Euglossa dimidiata,* is drawn on the same block as the *Centris flavopicta,* page 519. It is a Brazilian insect.

It is handsomely coloured. The ground colour of the abdomen is black, and across it are drawn several bands of light-coloured hair, the two upper bands being either white or pale yellow, and the remainder deep orange, so that the whole insect has very much the appearance of a humble bee. The wings are nearly brown, but become transparent towards their tips. It is remarkable that there is a large dipterous insect belonging to the genus *Asilus*, which so closely resembles this Euglossa, that when the two are placed side by side, they look like two specimens of the same insect.

THE two insects which are shown in the next illustration belong to the same genus as our familiar Humble Bees.

The general habits of all the species are very similar, though they may vary somewhat in detail. They are social insects, living together in nests constructed either in or on the ground. Their cells are made of a very coarse brown wax, and are oval in shape, so that they cannot be arranged with the beautiful accuracy which distinguishes the cells of the hive bee, or even those of the common wasp. Indeed, except that they stand tolerably upright, they seem to be tossed about very much at random, the bees having apparently made the cells wherever they could find room.

Contrary to the custom of the hive bee, males, females, and neuters live socially together, the females taking part in cell-making and honey-collecting, and there being no single queen who will allow no rival to the throne. The males, however, when once they have left their nests, seldom return to them. They are all big-bodied, heavy-flying insects, and, when on the wing, they emit a deep humming sound, which has earned for them the popular title of Humble, *i.e.* Humming Bees.

There are few insects in which such variation of colour exists, as among the Humble Bees. In the first place, every species is liable to very great variation; and in the next place the colours of the long hairy clothing are so evanescent, that after a few days' exposure to light and air, they fade into the very shadows of their former beauty. With these insects, as with the Andrenas, the only mode of preserving them in their full beauty is by taking them almost as soon as they have issued from their cocoons, and then keeping them in a perfectly dark drawer.

As is the case with the wasp, the greater number of Humble

Bees perish during the cold months, only a few females surviving. These insects hide themselves in some convenient spot until the following year; and it is a remarkable fact, that instead of availing themselves of the nest in which they had lived, they invariably desert it and go to some sheltered crevice, where they spend the winter alone.

As a rule, the Humble Bees favour the more northern parts of the world; and, as Mr. F. Smith remarks, New Zealand and

FIG. 286.—Bombus cajanensis. (Black and yellow.) Bombus eximius. (Black, with ruddy belts.)

Australia seem to be without them. The two insects which are represented in the accompanying illustration have been selected as examples of southern Humble Bees. The figure on the left represents *Bombus cajanensis*, which is, as its name implies, a native of Cayenne. Its colours are very simple, being merely black, banded with bright yellow. The other figure represents *Bombus eximius*, a native of Silhet. It is covered with long, dense, black, velvet-like hair, and the segments of the abdomen are edged with fringes of long, ruddy chestnut hair.

Passing by the common Hive Bee, we take an insect which according to Mr. Bates, is in tropical America the representative of our well-known Hive Bee. As Mr. Gorse and Mr. Bates have both given public descriptions of the Melipona and its habits, I cannot do better than allow them to speak for themselves.

In his work on Jamaican Natural History, the former author writes as follows:—

"I was exceedingly interested this afternoon by the sight of two hives of indigenous Bees, shown to me by Mr. Garriques, at Shelton Pen, on the banks of the Rio Cobre. The one hive, in the hollow of a calabash tree, had an entrance about half an inch

Fig. 287.—Melipona fasciculata. (Brown.)

wide at midway up the trunk, the cavity being supposed to descend some four feet down. The other was in a cordia cherry tree, and was laid bare by a considerable portion of the tree being cut away. The cutting just disclosed the uppermost of the broad cells, but nothing of the sacklets that contained the honey. I take our Bees to be similar to, if not the same with, the Bee of Mexico, a Melipona or Trigona, called by the Spaniards *Angelitos* (*i.e.* little angels), from having no stings. They settled upon us, and we handled them; but they did no injury to us, though it was perceptible that they were excited, for they pursued the hand, and clustered on it, when portions of the brood cells were taken up.

"The black ants that infest forest trees had tracked the hive in the calabash tree, and had congregated around the entrance-hole, making an effort to gain access. A sentinel Bee, which was every now and then relieved from his guard, stood in a state of restless watchfulness, assisted at his post by two Bees behind. The Bees behind stood reversed, head downward; and, clinging to the upper arch of the entrance, they gazed upward, and watched several ants clustered above, in some two or three little groups within the crevices of the bark, prepared to rush in if the sentinels remitted their vigilance for one moment. The active ants paced upward and downward in lines, but found no opportunity of gaining a nearer access than a rapid reconnoitering of the doorway.

"The entrance, when occupied by the three sentinel Bees, admitted of no access by comers and goers of the hive, except by the centre Bee, that guarded the hole in front, momentarily stepping aside. This movement he performed with surprising quickness, as often as a Bee came in or went out. The wax of these Bees is very unctuous and dark-coloured, but susceptible of being whitened somewhat by bleaching. The honey is stored in clusters of cups, about the size of pigeons' eggs, at the bottom of the hive, and away from the brood cells. The brood cells are hexagonal, they are not deep, and the young ones, when ready to burst their cerement, just fill the whole cavity. The Mother Bee is lighter in colour than the other Bees, and elongated at the abdomen to double their length."

Mr. Bates's account of the habits of this and other Meliponæ is exceedingly interesting. It is given in his well-known work on the Amazon River:—

"But the most numerous and interesting of the clay-artificers are the workers of a species of social Bee, the *Melipona fasciculata*. The Meliponæ in tropical America take the place of the true Apides, to which the European Hive Bee belongs, and which are here unknown; they are generally much smaller insects than the Hive Bee, and have no sting. The *M. fasciculata* is about a third shorter than the *Apis mellifica:* its colonies are composed of an immense number of individuals; the workers are generally seen collecting pollen in the same way as other bees, but great numbers are employed in gathering clay.

"The rapidity and precision of their movements while thus

engaged are wonderful. They first scrape the clay with their mandibles; the small portions gathered are then cleared by the anterior paws and passed to the second pair of feet, which in their turn convey them to the large foliated expansions of the hind shanks which are adapted normally in Bees, as everyone knows, for the collection of pollen. The middle feet put the growing pellets of mortar on the hind legs to keep them in a compact shape as the particles are successively added. The little hodsmen soon have as much as they can carry, and they then fly off.

"I was for some time puzzled to know what the Bees did with the clay; but I had afterwards plenty of opportunity for ascertaining. They construct their combs in any suitable crevice in trunks of trees or perpendicular banks, and the clay is required to build up a wall so as to close the gap, with the exception of a small orifice for their own entrance and exit. Most kinds of Melipona are in this respect masons, as well as workers in wax and pollen-gatherers. One little species (undescribed) not more than two lines long, builds a neat tubular gallery of clay, kneaded with some viscid substance, outside the entrance to its hive, besides blocking up the crevice in which it is situated. The mouth of the tube is trumpet-shaped, and at the entrance a number of the pigmy Bees are always stationed, apparently acting as sentinels.

"It is remarkable that none of the American Bees have attained that high degree of architectural skill in the construction of their cells which is shown by the European Hive Bee. The wax cells of the Meliponæ are generally oblong, showing only an approximation to the hexagonal shape in places where several of them are built in contact. It would appear that the Old World has produced in Bees, as well as in other families of animals, far more advanced forms than the tropics of the New World. A hive of the *Melipona fasciculata,* which I saw opened, contained about two quarts of pleasantly-tasted liquid honey. The Bees, as already remarked, have no sting, but they bite furiously when their colonies are disturbed. The Indian who plundered the hive was completely covered by them; they took a particular fancy to the hair of his head, and fastened on it by hundreds.

"I found forty-five species of these Bees in different parts of the country; the largest was half an inch in size, the smallest were extremely minute, some kinds being not more than one-twelfth of an inch in size. These tiny fellows are often very troublesome on account of their familiarity; they settle on one's face and hands, and in crawling about get into the eyes and mouth, or up the nostrils."

We see from this history that the title of "Angelitos" is not so very well deserved, for the insects do mischief to the extent of their ability. Being venomless, they cannot sting, but they can at all events bite, and, as we have seen, do so very fiercely.

THE last of the Bees which will be described in this work belong to the genus *Trigona*. The following account of an

FIG. 288.—Trigona ruficrus.
(Shining black, with red thighs.)

Indian species of *Trigona* is taken from Mr. Horne's monograph:—

"This is one of the smallest Honey-bees I have ever met with, and its habits are curious. I noticed it under the following circumstances, and I never again met with its nest, although the natives all know it. One evening at Benares (April 4th, 1863) as I was standing at my door, I saw a swarm of from 400 to 500 of what I took to be midges, rapidly flying about in a mazy kind of dance, occupying a space of five or six feet, and being about ten feet from the ground. I brought out my insect-net and caught about a hundred in one sweep, when, to my surprise, they proved to be Bees. On watching them, I observed that they went in and out of a little hole in the wall close by under a beam where there was a hollow, and that many of their thighs were laden with pollen.

"The insects seemed quite harmless, walking about my hand and not attempting to sting. Digging out some bricks with care, I came on a portion of their nest. The space it occupied appeared to have been originally eaten out by Termites. It was coated on all sides with a layer of black wax, and in it was stored their honey. The waxen cells were of a dark brown colour, and very globular, pendent side by side from the roof, and not, as far as I could see, arranged hexagonally.

"The honey was very dark in colour, but excellent in flavour; and I was told by the natives that it possessed medicinal qualities. It had a slight astringency; and, considering the size of the insect, the quantity stored was very large. I was also told that these insects commonly use hollow trees, in which they store astonishing quantities of honey, which is diligently sought for and prized. They call them "Bhonga," which appears to me to be a generic name for *all* Bees in the North-west Provinces. Large bricks prevented my digging further, so that I cannot describe their breeding-cells.

"The Bees continued to fly in the manner before described till dark, and did not desert their nest."

The species which is figured in the illustration is a Brazilian insect. Its colour is shining black, with the exception of the thighs of the hind pair of legs, which are bright red. It is a very common insect, and is generally to be found in sandbanks in the virgin forest.

I HAVE had some doubt as to the place in which I should treat of the insect which will presently be described; and, after consideration, have determined to place them at the end of the Hymenoptera, and not among the Ichneumon Flies.

If there be in the world insects which look like anything but insects, such are the extraordinary beings, one of which is shown in the accompanying illustration. So strange are they that although a practised entomologist would at once detect them to be insects, he would need careful investigation before he could even determine the order to which they belonged. They are found in the middle of a wild fig, called *Ficus terragena*, the fruit of which is unfit for food.

That certain insects frequented the fig, and perhaps exercised some influence on the fertility of the fruit, was well known to the old naturalists, who designated their office by the name of "caprification." This belief is mentioned by Mouffet in his work on insects: "It is called *Culex ficarius*, i.e. *Fig-gnat*, not because it comes indeed of the fig-tree, but because it is fed and sustained by its fruit. For it is sprung of a certain worm that breeds in the Figs, which when Nature cannot make her perfect work upon, nor bring to the sweetness and perfection of other Figs, lest she should make something in vain, by a certain quickening vertue, out of the grains of them, being rotten and putrified, she produceth these Gnats.

"Yet not so as that the Gnat is the *parergon*, as besides the intentions of Nature (so Scaliger hath learnedly observed); or if it be, the truth is, the work by the bye is of more dignity than the main. Nature did propose to itself the perfection of a wilde Fig, a thing not so much to be esteemed of: this she not being able to bring to passe, turns herself from so common a work to an enterprise of greater weight and produceth a *Gnat*, which she effecteth.

"Concerning these Gnats, *Pliny* hath these words: the wilde Fig-tree brings forth Gnats, these being defrauded of the nourishment they should have received from their mother, being turned to rottenness they go to the neighbouring Fig-tree, and with the often biting of the same Fig-tree and greedily feeding upon it, they let in the sun withall and set free a door for plenty of air to enter in at. Anon after they destroy the milky moisture and infancy of the fruit, which is done very easily, and as it were of its own accord: and for that cause the wild fig-tree is alwaies set before the fig-trees, that the wind, when the Gnats fly out of them may carry them among the fig-trees, who, as soon as they come into them, the figs swell and, ripening of a sudden, grow very big and full.

"But what time these Gnats pass from the wilde fig to the fig-tree, they do it in such haste that many of them leave either a foot or a wing behind them. Now that they generated of the grains of the unripe fig may be evident in that the wilde fig is left void of grains."

That the ancient entomologists had detected these remarkable beings in the interior of the wild fig is very clear, though the inferences which they drew are not correct.

According to Mr. Walker, these insects are Hymenoptera, belonging to the family Agaonidæ, in the great group of Chalcidicæ, several species of which are the "gnats" which have been used for caprification.

They were found in the Mauritius, and in company with them were great numbers of another species, which he termed *Chalcis* or *Idarnes explorator*, from their habit of flitting constantly about the figs, and seeming to explore them. Whether or not they are parasites upon the insects within the fig is a matter of doubt.

As for these latter insects, they always live in darkness, and, needing no eyes, have none. Not only are they devoid of eyes, but they have no ocelli (*i.e.* the little simple eyes possessed by Hymenoptera), no palpi, and no maxillæ. Mandibles, or principal jaws, they do possess, and these of considerable size in proportion to the dimensions of the insect. Perhaps the fact that these darkling creatures are able to do without maxillæ or palpi may throw some light on the real office of those organs. When removed from the interior of the fruit, or when merely disturbed by the laying open of the figs, the insects make no attempt at escape, but roll themselves up and lie motionless.

Many other allied insects are now known to be dwellers in figs, but the complete history of these wonderful beings is yet to be written.

In the notice of these Hymenoptera in the *Entomologist*, from which part of this description is condensed, the editor makes the following suggestive remarks:—"It seems almost impossible to overrate the interest which attaches to this subject of fig-dwellers. The circumstance that these creatures are without the means of vision or locomotion does not, indeed, seem extraordinary, seeing they are condemned to perpetual darkness and perpetual imprisonment. Of what use would eyes or wings be to them? Then, again, of what sex are they? Is there any relationship—I mean consanguinity—between the prisoners and the winged atoms flying from fig to fig? And there are females, invariably females, with long ovipositors, that could communicate with the imprisoned. We have winged males and apterous females in Lepidoptera. Can we have winged females and apterous males in Hymenoptera?"

The name *Apocrypta* s ignifies "hidden," and is given to the insects in allusion to their custom of lying concealed within the fruit. Another genus of Fig-gnats is called *Sycocrypta,* which signifies "something that is hidden in figs." Several species are known, all differing greatly in shape, but the present species is a good example of their general aspect. They are very tiny, the length of this insect being about equal to that of the letter "l." There is a full description of them in the *Entomologist* for October 1871.

Apocrypta paradoxa.

LEPIDOPTERA;

OR,

BUTTERFLIES AND MOTHS.

LEPIDOPTERA;

OR,

BUTTERFLIES AND MOTHS.

CHAPTER I.

PAPILIONIDÆ.

THE great order of insects which now comes before us is easily to be distinguished from any other. A beetle may be mistaken for a Heteropterous insect, or a Hymenopterous insect for one of the Diptera. But there is no such likelihood of mistake with regard to the Lepidoptera, or scale-wing insects, the feathery scales with which their wings are covered being a distinction that is at once recognized.

These scales are arranged just like the slates on the roof of a house, and as there are many species in which the scales are squared at the ends, the resemblance is curiously exact. They vary very greatly in form and size, some being rounded at the ends, some deeply toothed in notches, some short and square, and some long and almost hair-like. If placed under the microscope, their surface is seen to be adorned with exquisite sculpturings and markings, so that each scale is quite as worthy of examination as the insect it adorns. Minute as are the scales, the microscope shows that they are composed of three distinct layers, and nothing is more common than to see the upper or under layer torn, and the ragged piece looking just like a "snuff-box" torn in a dress.

The mouths of the Lepidoptera are made for suction, the mandibles, or outer jaws, being very minute and practically needless, and the maxillæ lengthened into the organ which is scientifically known as the proboscis, and popularly as the trunk. The females are generally larger than the males, but are duller in hue, and in many cases the two sexes are so different in appearance that they have been described as distinct species. Even Linnæus fell into the error of confounding the sexes, and actually placed the male in one section and the female in another.

Their transformations from the egg to the perfect insect are known better than those of any other of the insect race, and many practical entomologists are in the habit of rearing their best specimens from the egg. As to the eggs themselves, there is more diversity in them than in those of the birds. The latter eggs, however they may differ in colour, are tolerably alike in shape, whereas the variety of form among Lepidopterous eggs is quite wonderful, and is so marked that a good entomologist on seeing an egg can be tolerably sure of naming the insect which laid it. Unfortunately their shape cannot well be preserved, as they are nearly sure to collapse after a time, even if they be not hatched, and broken by the young larva.

Many of these eggs, even of our own British species, are so exceedingly beautiful in their outlines, that they would serve as exquisitely beautiful models for jugs and vases. Indeed, some years ago I happened to deliver a lecture on the transformation of insects, and a porcelain manufacturer who was present was so struck with the drawing of an egg that he asked for a copy of it, and made a number of jars in exact imitation of it.

The larvæ of the Lepidoptera are as different as the perfect insects, both in appearance and habits. Most of them live on trees and plants, but there are many which pass almost, if not all, their larval existence beneath the surface of the earth. At present, no Lepidopterous larva is known to inhabit the water.

WITHOUT going more into scientific details, we will proceed to the examination of the foreign Butterflies.

The reader will remember that some English groups of insects are quite as numerous, as large, and as handsome as their foreign relatives. This is not the case with the Butterflies, which are comparatively few and insignificant in England. For example, of the first group, the Papilionidæ, we have but one representative, the well-known Swallow-tail, and this is quite a rarity except in one or two very limited spots.

The genus Papilio (which is the Latin for Butterfly) has all the legs fit for walking, short palpi, the club of the antennæ elongated and never hooked, and the "discoidal cell" closed. This, by the way, is the cell formed in the middle of the wing by the juncture of the principal nervures. All the insects of this genus are extremely handsome, and, with very few exceptions, can be accepted as the most beautiful of all the Butterflies. Linnæus was so struck with their splendour, that he called them by the classical name of *Equites*, or "knights," dividing them into two sections, Trojans and Greeks. To each insect he gave the name of some personage mentioned either by Homer or Virgil.

Some systematic entomologists form a number of these insects into a group called Ornithoptera, *i.e.* "bird-winged," because their wings are so large and ample that they somewhat resemble birds when flying. The larvæ of these insects are very odd-looking creatures, each segment being furnished with a number of thick, fleshy spikes that radiate in all directions. In common with other members of the group, the larva has at the neck a curious apparatus, consisting of a double tentacle that can be projected or withdrawn at will through a small aperture. This tentacle can easily be seen in the larva of our Swallow-tail Butterfly. It gives out a powerful odour, which in one species resembles that of fennel.

The pupa has some remnants of the fleshy spikes, they of course existing in the segments near the tail. The pupa is oddly shaped, being curved almost like the letter S. It is suspended by the tail, and kept from swinging about by a couple of short and stout silken cables. In our country we have many pupæ which support themselves by means of a cable which completely surrounds them, but in the present case there are two distinct cables, each being fastened to one side of the body.

We will now proceed to the various species of this group.

THE fine insect which is here represented is a native of Queensland. It is a large species, the expanse of wing being nearly two inches and a half. The longitudinal bands seen on the upper wings are green, with a coppery gloss in certain lights, which gloss also extends over the whole of the lower wings. On the under surface of the upper wings there is a row of large, rounded, black spots.

FIG. 259.—Ornithoptera Cassandra
(Black, green, and yellow.)

The thorax is covered with dense hair of a jetty black, relieved by some spots of bright crimson at the junction of the wings. The abdomen is deep yellow.

A brief reference has already been made to the larvæ of the Ornithoptera. A figure of one of these remarkable larvæ is here given, and was drawn from a specimen in the East India Museum. The pupa is also drawn, so as to show the method by which it

FIG. 290.—Larva and pupa of Ornithoptera.

attaches itself to plants by means of a tuft of silken cords at the tail and a pair of bands at the sides.

THE three figures which here follow represent one species, *Papilio pronomus,* and serve to show the great difference that exists between the sexes. The first illustration shows the upper surface of the male insect. The upper pair of wings are velvet black and emerald green, the colours being disposed as shown in the illustration. The green is more or less speckled with black, which appearance is shown by the microscope to be due to missing scales. The ornithological reader will probably remember that the black spots which are so often found on the breasts of humming-birds are produced in a similar manner, the feather being either altogether missing or tucked under its neighbours. The lower wings are mostly green, with a decided golden gloss, and on the inner edge they have a fringe of very long, pale brown, soft hairs, which are, in fact, nothing but lengthened scales.

The under surface, as shown in the second illustration, is also green and black, the former colour taking a blue tint in the middle of the wing. The abdomen is bright "king's" yellow, looking just as if it had been painted in body colour. The thorax

FIG. 291.—Papilio pronomus. Male. Upper side. (Black and green.)

is velvet black, but upon each shoulder there is a large tuft of brilliant crimson hairs, that produce a wonderfully fine contrast with the black and green of the wings.

The third figure represents the under surface of the female, and the reader can easily see how the two sexes can be mistaken for different species. The female is very much larger than her mate, and coloured after a totally different fashion. The wings are mostly black, but not of the rich velvet-like hue which distinguishes the male, and the light-coloured marks upon the upper wings are white. The lower pair of wings are also dull black, relieved by large yellow marks, which are apt to fade into yellowish grey. The abdomen is yellow, but not nearly so bright as in the male. Almost the only point of resemblance between

FIG. 292.—Papilio pronomus. Male. Under side.
(Black, green, and crimson.)

the two sexes is the crimson tuft on the shoulders, which is as brilliant in the female as in the male.

Even from this single instance the reader will see that there was much excuse for the mistakes which Linnæus made when arranging these insects. Two of them are rather remarkable, on account of a phenomenon which sometimes occurs to insects, and is well known to practical entomologists. It sometimes happens that one side of an insect is male and the other side female. Thus Linnæus had described *Papilio Polycaōn* as a Greek and *Papilio Laodocus* as a Trojan. Yet a specimen was found which had on the right the wings of *Polycaōn* and on the left that of *Laodocus*, thus proving that they were both the two sexes of one species. A similar occurrence took place with *Ulysses* and *Diomedes,* both being, as their names denote, Greeks.

The present species is a native of Northern Australia.

FIG. 293.—Papilio pronomus. Female. Under side.
(Black, yellow, and white.)

As is often the case with Butterflies, the under surface of *Papilio Emathion* gives no indication of the colours which adorn the lower surface.

Above, the wings are black, with narrow lines of grey following the nervures, and widening gradually towards the edges. The under surface of the upper pair of wings is coloured much after the same manner, but that of the lower pair is almost startlingly different from the plain black and grey of the upper surface. The greater part of the wing is velvet black, and round

PLATE XI.

1

2

its edges are some large markings of brilliant scarlet. A patch of scarlet also exists at the base, and extends partially over the

FIG. 294.—Papilio Emathion.
(Black and scarlet.)

base of the upper pair. The body is black, striped and spotted with yellow.

This beautiful Butterfly inhabits the Philippine Islands.

Two more of the Ornithoptera are seen on Plate XI.

The upper figure represents *Papilio Brookeanus.* This, as its specific name implies, is a Bornean insect, and has been named after the late Rajah Brooke of Sarâwak. As the full size of the insect is six inches and a half in spread of wing, it has been found necessary to diminish the figure.

This is a most magnificent insect. The upper surface of the wings is velvet black, and upon them are drawn a number of pointed stripes of golden green. Both in shape and colour these stripes so closely resemble the plumage of the trogon, that the Butterfly was named *Papilio trogon.* This is a much better name than that which is now given to it, but as the latter name was found to have precedence in point of time, it must be retained. Beneath, the wings are black and green, changing towards the base into a deep, rich blue when viewed by a side light. The thorax is entirely crimson above, and of the same colour below, but barred with black.

"This species," writes Mr. Wallace, who discovered it in 1855, "which was then quite new, and which I named after Sir J. Brooke, was very rare. It was seen occasionally flying swiftly in the clearings, and now and then settling for an instant at puddles and muddy places, so that I only succeeded in capturing two or three specimens.

"In some other parts of the country I was assured it was abundant, and a good many specimens have been sent to England, but as yet all have been males, and we are quite unable to conjecture what the female may be like, owing to the extreme isolation of the species, and its want of close affinity to any other known insect."

THE second figure represents *Papilio Panthöus*, a species which inhabits Amboyna and Ceram.

The figure represents the male, and is slightly reduced on account of the exigency of space. The female is very much larger, her extended wings sometimes measuring more than eight inches from tip to tip.

The upper surface of the wings is shining black with grey streaks, and the under surface of the upper pair of wings is coloured in much the same manner, except that the black and the grey are both dull. The lower wings are brilliantly coloured. A stripe of black begins at the base and runs round two-thirds of the wing. It is very broad at the base, and narrows with the anal angle, where it terminates. On the stripe there are six large yellow marks, arranged as shown in the illustration, those towards the base of the wing being orange and the other golden yellow. The centre of the wing is pearly white in the male, and duller in the female, with several large oval black spots.

The thorax is velvety black, and the abdomen is of the same colour, but adorned with several large spots of orange.

One fine species of the Ornithoptera inhabits Darnley Island, and is put to a singular use by the natives. They catch several Butterflies, and, attaching one end of a very delicate fibre to the insects and the other to their hair, allow the Butterflies to flutter about their heads. The name of the insect is *Papilio Poseidon*, and it is a most magnificent creature, measuring seven inches across, and having velvet-black and brilliant green wings, a golden body, and crimson breast. The Ornithoptera are mostly confined to the islands of the Indian Archipelago, the Moluccas and Philippines being their principal strongholds.

About the two insects which will now be described there has been some difficulty. Some entomologists consider them as two distinct species, and others as merely varieties of a single species. The controversy is not yet decided, and I shall therefore accept

Fig. 295.—Papilio patros.
(Black and red.)

that opinion which is at present more generally acknowledged. The insect is found at Ega, and is one of the many species which were brought home by Mr. Bates after his travels in the region of the Amazons. On the upper surface the wings are dark, blackish brown at the base, becoming paler towards the tip. The lower pair are velvet black, relieved by three large oblong spots near the middle. These are, in fact, one very large spot divided by the black nervures which run through it.

THE two next illustrations represent the male and female of *Papilio caudius.* The latter of these names is formed from a Latin word signifying "a tail," and is given to the insect on account of the long, narrow appendages to the lower wings.

FIG. 296.—Papilio caudius.—Male.
(Black, white, and red.)

There is much technical information respecting this insect in Mr. Horsfield's "Catalogue of the Lepidopterous Insects belonging to the East India Company." In that work some excellent advice is given to entomologists who wish to trace the transformations. Whenever a new larva was found, it was placed in a separate cage, to which a number was attached. It was then carefully drawn in colours, and its food-plants noted, a similar number being affixed to the drawing. When it underwent its first change the pupa was drawn, also in colours, and the same when the perfect insect appeared; all the drawings having the same number as that which was affixed to the cage in which the larva was bred. This system being stringently carried out, mistakes were evidently impossible, and thus a vast number of indisputable facts were added to our stores of Natural History.

In addition to the instructions thus given, I should be disposed to add a further suggestion. No provision is here made for preserving the insect for dissection. So, if several specimens of a larva could be found, I should suggest that a larva, pupa, perfect insect, and if possible some of the eggs, should be placed in spirits for the use of dissectors, the bottles being of course numbered like the drawings.

FIG. 297.—Papilio caudius. Female.
(Black, white, and red.)

The insect now before us is a native of Java. The upper surface of the wings is black, and upon them is a large white spot, flanked on either side by a grey spot. The lower wings are marked with red very much like those of *Papilio patros.*

The female is coloured much like the male, though she is not so bright, and there are slight differences of marking. The under surface of the upper pair of wings is entirely brown, but the lower wings are decorated with two large oval spots, set side by side and surrounded by five smaller spots. These marks are very prettily coloured, being pink round their edges and white in the middle, so as to give them a sort of eye-like appearance.

THE beautiful insect which is here shown is a native of Mexico.

The reader will observe that the "tail" of the lower wings is not rounded at the end as is generally the case, but is very

FIG. 298.—Papilio aconophos.
(Black, white, and crimson.)

long, and narrows to a point. On account of this structure, the insect has received the specific name of *aconophos*, which is formed from a Greek word signifying a javelin or spike.

Above, the colour is deep blackish brown, fading to pale brown at the tips. The lower wings are velvet-black, and on each of them are six brick-red marks of a somewhat crescentic or arched shape. Below, the upper wings are of a glossy sepia, without any marks. The lower wings are of the same hue, but have a number of marks upon their edges, disposed as shown in the illustration. Those towards the outer edge are white, but those of the inner edge are white above and bright crimson below. There are also some small patches of crimson on the base of the wing, and a very narrow crimson streak runs along its outer edge. The long narrow tail is quite black.

THE fashion which Linnæus set of employing classical nomenclature as specific names for the genus Papilio has been followed as far as possible by his successors. Owing, however, to the rapidly increasing number of species, it was impossible to find

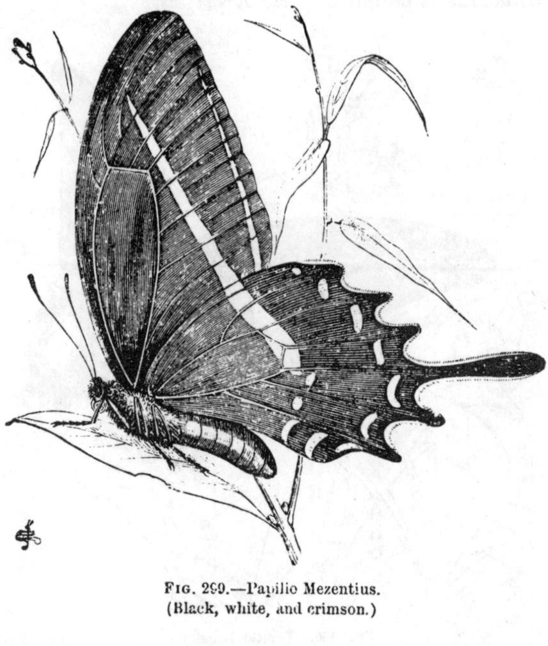

FIG. 299.—Papilio Mezentius.
(Black, white, and crimson.)

names in the Iliad and the Æneid, and it was necessary therefore to draw upon the large stock of names furnished by classic writers in general. One of these names is Mezentius, the celebrated king of the Tyrrhenians, who was accustomed to torture men to death by binding them to dead corpses and so leaving them.

This is a rare species from the western coast of America, and at present there is but one specimen in the British Museum. It is remarkable for having almost the same colouring on both sides of its wings—a very rare phenomenon among Butterflies, especially when the colours are dark and boldly contrasted. The upper surface of the upper wings is black, across which is drawn a single bold white band. The lower wings are also black, but have a number of bright crimson marks along their edges, arranged as shown in the illustration.

The under surface of the wings is almost exactly like that of the upper, the chief distinction being that a second bar of white, but very narrow, runs nearly parallel with the edge.

ANOTHER of the beautiful Butterflies which haunt the district of the Amazons is called *Papilio Ergeteles.*

FIG. 300.—Papilio Ergeteles.
(Black and scarlet.)

Above, the upper wings are black, darkest at the base, and have a large scarlet spot near the middle. The lower wings are also black, and have a large crimson spot, which is divided by black nervures into four oblong marks. Beneath, the colours are very similar, except that the spots are pale pink instead of scarlet or crimson. On each shoulder there is a large tuft of long scarlet hairs, forming a fine contrast to the jetty black plumage which surrounds it. There is only a single specimen in the British Museum.

Another species, *Papilio Æneas,* inhabiting Demerara, so closely resembles the Ergeteles that the two species can only be distinguished by practised eyes.

ALTHOUGH not so large, or at first sight so imposing, as many of the species which have been described, *Papilio Hierocles* is

FIG. 301.—Papilio Hierocles.
(Purple and crimson.)

really one of the most splendid of the Butterflies. Its beauties, however, cannot be seen unless it be exposed to a strong light and turned in all manner of ways.

The upper wings are black on the upper surface, with the exception of a patch in the middle, which is green in the male and whitish in the female. The illustration is drawn from a male specimen. Its chief beauty lies in the upper surface of the lower wings. Even when the insect is in a cabinet, and partly sheltered from the light by the sides of the drawer, it is a very handsome creature, the lower wings looking as if they were velvet black, crossed by a row of vivid crimson spots. If, however, it be removed from the drawer, placed in a strong light, and turned slowly round, its real splendour shows itself. The crimson spots retain their colour, but the apparent black background glows with the richest imaginable purple, which merges gradually at the base into deep azure, this colour passing over the wing as the insect is turned about. About the middle of the wing, and just above the crimson spots, the blue takes a decided green gloss. The best view of this species is obtained when the head is turned towards the light.

So much for the upper surface. Below, the upper pair of wings are sooty black, with one white spot. The under wings are also black, but have a row of crimson spots across the centre. The body is black, adorned with spots of the same crimson as that of the wings. This splendid insect is a native of Pará.

IN the case of the insect which is next shown no classical appellation has been given, but the specific name is expressive

FIG. 302.—Papilio Erythalion.
(Black, crimson, and white.)

of its appearance. The name *Erythalion* is formed from two Greek words, one signifying "red," and the other "a blossom." This name has been given because the broad crimson band that crosses the under wings of the male looks somewhat like the petals of a crimson flower.

There is considerable difference in the colour of the sexes. The upper wings are black above, and on them there is a light-coloured mark. In the male this mark takes the form of a pale triangle, in which are two white spots, whereas in the female it is wholly white. The under wings are also black, crossed in the male by a broad belt of deep crimson, and in the female by a similarly shaped band of pink, darker at the edges than in the centre. The illustration is taken from a female specimen. In both sexes the bar is crossed by several black nervures, so as to divide it into a number of parallel markings.

The body and abdomen are black, diversified with scarlet spots, more vivid than the hue on the bars of the lower wings. The insect was taken at Santa Fé de Bogotá.

To describe the splendid insect which is known as *Papilio Krishna* is a very difficult task, owing to the variety and com-

FIG. 303.—Papilio Krishua.)
(Black and green.)

plication of the colours. The two specimens in the British Museum came from Bhotan, in India, and the name of *Krishna* has been given to it as a recognition of its Indian origin. As this is a large insect, the female measuring fully five inches in spread of wing, the figure has been necessarily diminished nearly one-half.

Above, the upper wings are deep black, speckled profusely with gold-green dots that look just as if emerald-dust had been sprinkled regularly over them. The magnifying glass soon shows that each of these green specks is a single green scale. Across the middle of the wing runs a narrow golden yellow bar, interrupted by the nervures, which retain their black hue, and break up the bar into a succession of contiguous yellow spots.

The under wings are much more complicated in colouring. At the base is a large triangular patch of the same green-speckled black as that of the upper wings, and just below the black is an irregularly shaped patch which is entirely emerald-green, being composed of the same scales as those which have been mentioned as sprinkled over the black. In certain lights the green is seen to be glossed with purple and blue. Below the green, the speckled black again makes its appearance, and at the anal angle there is a large eye-like spot of purple with a black centre.

Beneath, the upper wings, are black, sprinkled with white instead of green specks, and is crossed by a broad white bar. The under wings are curiously coloured. At the edge runs a row of white crescentic marks, edged above with dun. Then comes a black space, and then is a crescent of purple. Another black space intervenes, and above the purple is a white crescent, speckled with black.

THE fine insect which is here shown bears at first sight a curious resemblance to our own Swallow-tail Butterfly, and almost looks like an exceptionally fine specimen of that insect. Above, the whole of the surface of the upper wings is yellow, with a slight orange tinge, and diversified with black markings as shown in the illustration. The yellow has rather a coarse aspect, the microscope showing this effect to be produced by the large size of the scales, which are squared at their tips.

The under wings are also yellow, but have a series of red crescent-shaped marks running round the margin. Near the inner edge is a small semilunar mark of red, above which is a patch of tiny blue specks that look something like a nebula when seen through a telescope, and above the blue specks is another red mark. The body is bright yellow, but along the upper surface of the abdomen is drawn a bold black streak,

FIG. 304.—Papilio Œbalus.
(Black and yellow.)

rather wide in the middle, and diminishing to a point at either end.

Below, the under wings have a row of six narrow blue crescents, and above each of these is a semilunar mark of brick-red. This insect is a native of Mexico.

In the insect which is depicted on page 556 we have an example of the effects which can be produced by the arrangement of only two colours. There are few handsomer Butterflies than *Papilio Palinurus*, in which black and green are the only colours on the upper surface.

Taking the upper wings first, the basal third is occupied with a large triangular patch of velvety black, profusely powdered with green specks, and very much like those of the Krishna Butterfly of India, which has been already described. Next comes a broad belt of verditer green, and the rest of the wing is velvet-black, sprinkled with green towards its edge.

FIG. 305.—Papilio Palinurus
(Black and green.)

The under wings are somewhat similarly marked, but with additions. At the base there is a similar black patch sprinkled with green, and then comes the green verditer band, which in the lower wings is very glossy, and has a pearly sort of surface. The black border also is on the edge of the lower wings, but near the margin are six crescentic marks of a brilliant metallic green, that sparkle so as to be visible at a considerable distance.

PLATE XII.

1

2

As is often the case with insects, the metallic splendour of these marks is not perceptible except by a strong light.

The reader will probably have remarked that the colours are so arranged that when the wings are spread they show a pattern extending over both pairs. The name *Palinurus* is that of the well-known pilot of Æneas' ship. I rather think that the name was given in consequence of the broad pearly-green band across the wings, which bears some fanciful resemblance to a wave of the sea.

The under surface presents an almost startling contrast to the upper. The place of the speckled black mark at the base of the wings is taken by a sepia-coloured patch sprinkled with pale green, the general colour much resembling that of the English moth known by the popular name of "Old Lady." There are four ruddy, eye-like spots, much resembling those of the common English Buff-tip Moth. Mr. A. Butler is of opinion that this dulness of colour is intended for the purpose of protection, the hues being very much like those of a withered leaf. Our own familiar "Red Admiral" and "Peacock" Butterflies are often indebted for safety to the dull colouring of the under surface.

A SINGULARLY handsome Butterfly is shown in the accompanying illustration, and is known by the name of *Papilio Ulysses.* Its upper surface has nearly the same colours as those of the preceding insect, but they are disposed in a very different manner. In the male insect the tips and edges of the wings are black, very slightly sprinkled with green. The whole of the centre is the richest azure in some lights, and green in others. In the female the colour is much paler, and has a faded look.

Below, the basal half of the upper wings is blackish brown, and the rest grey-brown. The lower wings are also grey-brown, and round their edges are seven rather large eye-like spots. The lower half of each spot is buff, then comes a curved streak of black, and the upper edge is white. The insect is a native of Amboyna.

ON Plate XII. Fig. 1 is seen an insect which very much resembles the preceding species, but was shown by Mr. A. Butler to be perfectly distinct. Its name is *Papilio Joësa,* and it is a native of Queensland. The black margins on the upper surface of the wings are not so deeply toothed, and on the under surface the eye-like spots are much paler.

Another species, *Papilio Philippus*, which was brought by Mr. Wallace from Sumatra, is coloured after a similar fashion, except that the centre of the wings is green instead of blue, and each spot has upon it a streak of metallic green-blue.

FIG. 306.—Papilio Ulysses.
(Black and green.)

ON the same Plate, at Fig. 2, is drawn a New Guinea Butterfly, called *Papilio Euchenor*. The figure is considerably reduced, as the insect itself measures five inches and a half across the outspread wings. It is, however, so conspicuous an insect that it cannot be omitted from the present work.

It is one of the very few Butterflies that have the upper and under surfaces of the wing almost alike. The aid of colour is not so much needed in this as in many other insects, because, if the reader will imagine that all the light portions of the insect are bright yellow, and the dark portions are jetty black, he can exactly appreciate its real appearance. As has already been stated, the under surface of the wings is very similar to the upper. The yellow, however, is paler, and occupies more of the wing. There are also some orange spots near the margins of the lower wings.

THE insect which is here represented is a native of Northern China, and its rather peculiar characteristics are well shown in

FIG. 307.—Papilio Mencius.
(Brown and crimson.)

the illustration. One of the remarkable points in this insect is the really grand outline presented by the wings, whether they be open or closed; the bold curves of the lower wings, and their long, broad tails, being in singular contrast with the firm and almost unbroken outline of the upper pair. As may be seen by the form of the abdomen, the specimen whose portrait is here given was a female.

Above, the colour of both pairs of wings is brown, each of the lower wings having five ruddy crescents along the margin. If held up to the light, the upper wings are seen to be almost transparent. Below, the upper wings are brown, and the lower pair are velvet-black, their opacity being thus accounted for. The light-coloured marks along the margin are crimson. The male is similar to the female, but is smaller, and is darker coloured.

THE general outline of the wings in *Papilio Jophon* is very similar to that of the preceding species. The colouring, however, is wholly different.

FIG. 308.—Papilio Jophon.
(Black and scarlet.)

The upper surface of the wings is sooty black, the nervures being accompanied with stripes of silvery grey. Beneath, the colours are still black grey, but on the margin of the lower wings there are seven crescent-shaped spots of bright vermilion-scarlet. The abdomen is black, diversified with scarlet spots and patches, very much resembling the colours of our own Cinnabar Moth. The insect is a native of Ceylon.

THE two illustrations which now follow represent a Butterfly called *Papilio Memnon*. It has a very wide range of habitat, being found in Borneo, Penang, Java, China, and India.

FIG. 309.—Papilio Memnon. Male.
(Black, white, and buff.)

This is a strangely variable insect, no less than ten distinct varieties being described in Dr. Horsfield's Catalogue. The general colouring is as follows:—The upper surface is velvet-black, streaked and speckled with green, and in some specimens there is a narrow scarlet line on the outer edge of the upper wings. Beneath, it is sooty black, with a large scarlet spot on the base of the upper wings, and three similar but smaller spots at the base of the lower wings.

The second figure represents a "tailed" female of the same insect. It is a most singular fact that the female should be so

FIG. 310.—Papilio Memnon. Female.
(Black, white, and buff.)

very different from the male, especially in so important a point as the appendages to the lower wings. It is, however, a fact that the females sometimes have tails, as is here shown, and sometimes have the hind wings merely rounded, like those of the male. Respecting this peculiarity, Mr. Wallace, in his "Eastern Archipelago," makes the following remarks:—

"The first is the handsome *Papilio Memnon*, a splendid Butterfly of a deep black colour, dotted over with lines and groups of scales of a clear ashy blue. Its wings are five inches in expanse, and the hind wings are rounded, with scalloped edges. This applies to the males; but the females are very different, and vary so much that they were once supposed to form several distinct species. They may be divided into two groups—those which resemble the male in shape, and those which differ entirely from him in the outline of the wings.

"The first vary much in colour, being often nearly white, with dusky yellow and red markings; but such differences often occur in Butterflies. The second group are much more extraordinary, and would never be supposed to be the same insect, since the hind wings are lengthened out into large spoon-shaped tails, no rudiment of which is ever to be perceived in the males or in the ordinary form of females. These tailed females are never of the dark and blue-glossed tints which prevail in the male and often occur in the females of the same form, but are invariably ornamented with stripes and patches of white or buff, occupying the larger part of the surface of the hind wings. This peculiarity of colouring led me to discover that this extraordinary female closely resembles (when flying) another Butterfly of the same genus but of a different group (*Papilio Coön*), and that we have here a case of mimicry similar to those so well illustrated and explained by Mr. Bates.

"That the resemblance is not accidental is sufficiently proved by the fact that in the North of India, where *Papilio Coön* is replaced by an allied form (*Papilio Doubledayi*) having red spots in place of yellow, a closely allied species or variety of *Papilio Memnon* (*P. androgeus*) has the tailed female also red spotted. The use and reason of this resemblance appears to be that the Butterflies imitated belong to a section of the genus Papilio, which, from some cause or other, are not attacked by birds, and by so closely resembling these in form and colour, the female of Memnon and its ally also escape persecution. Two other species of this same section (*Papilio Antiphus* and *Papilio Polyphontes*) are so closely imitated by two female forms of *Papilio Theseus* (which comes in the same section with Memnon) that they completely deceived the Dutch entomologist De Haan, and he accordingly classed them as the same species!

"But the most curious fact connected with these distinct forms is, that they are both the offspring of either form. A single brood of larvæ were bred in Java by a Dutch entomologist, and produced males as well as tailed and tailless females, and there is every reason to believe that this is always the case, and that forms intermediate in character never occur.

"To illustrate these phenomena, let us suppose a roaming Englishman in some remote island to have two wives—one a black-haired, red-skinned Indian, the other a woolly-headed sooty-skinned negress; and that, instead of the children being mulattoes of brown or dusky tints, mingling the characteristics of each parent in varying degrees, all the boys should be as fair-skinned and blue-eyed as their father, while the girls should altogether resemble their mothers. This would be thought strange enough, but the case of these Butterflies is yet more extraordinary, for each mother is capable not only of producing male offspring like the father, and female like herself, but also other females like her fellow-wife, and altogether differing from herself."

This is certainly one of the most remarkable points in the history of Butterflies, and why some females should so closely imitate the male form is a problem not easy of solution.

The larva of the Memnon is a large dark-green caterpillar, much humped on the shoulder, and being marked with some pale-brown bands, and a red streak just in front of the hump. It tapers gradually from the hump to the tail, and rapidly from the hump to the head, so that it has very much the aspect of a caterpillar of some Hawk Moth.

The pupa is pale green, patched and streaked with yellow, and is suspended to a twig by a ligature at the tail and a belt surrounding the body.

Like many other insects, the Memnon is subject to considerable variations in colour. There is one very curious example of a tailed female in the British Museum. The upper wings are brown, on which a pattern is traced by the black nervures. The lower wings are black, with white oval patches on the base, and buff spots on the inner margin.

ON this illustration is given the insect to which reference was made in Wallace's description of *Papilio Memnon.*

The resemblance between the two species does not appear in the illustration to be as close as it is in reality, because the size of the illustration is necessarily reduced, the full span of wing being about four inches and a half. The upper wings are pale brown, marked with dark brown as shown in the figure. The lower wings are jet black, with a sort of velvety lustre, and having a very slight bluish gloss in a side light. They are

FIG. 311.—Papilio Coön.
(Black, white, and yellow.)

adorned with a series of large spots, those towards the base of the wing being white, and those at the tip being yellow.

The body is chrome yellow, variegated with black. The colours are nearly alike on the upper and under surface, except that in the latter the markings are not quite so bright as those of the upper surface. There is a variety of this insect which is found in Assam, and in which all the yellow parts, including the body, are changed into scarlet.

Mr. Wallace remarks that it has a habit of fluttering slowly along shady pathways through woods. It is found throughout Java, and in many parts of India.

THE very handsome *Papilio Victorinus* is a native of Mexico, and the specimens in the British Museum were obtained in the well-known voyage of the *Novara*. It is a very large insect, the spread of wings being four inches and a half.

FIG. 312.—Papilio Victorinus.
(Black, with yellow spots.)

There are but few colours in this Butterfly, but they are so boldly contrasted that they produce a very fine effect. The upper surface is velvet-black, diversified with bright yellow spots shaped and disposed as shown in the illustration. Along the inner edge of the upper wings there is a fringe of very long silken hairs of a rich black-brown, which produce a singularly soft and beautiful effect. The body is black.

The under surface is soft brown with a dash of chocolate.

The upper wings are crossed by one complete row of yellow spots, and another row of similar spots extends about half across the wing. On the lower wings are two rows of crimson spots, shaped and arranged very much like the yellow spots of the upper surface. The inner spot of the upper row is rather remarkable, being oblong, and having one half crimson and the other half yellow.

IN *Papilio Leonidas* we have another extremely variable insect. This fine Butterfly is a native of Africa, the specimen which is here figured having been procured from Sierra Leone,

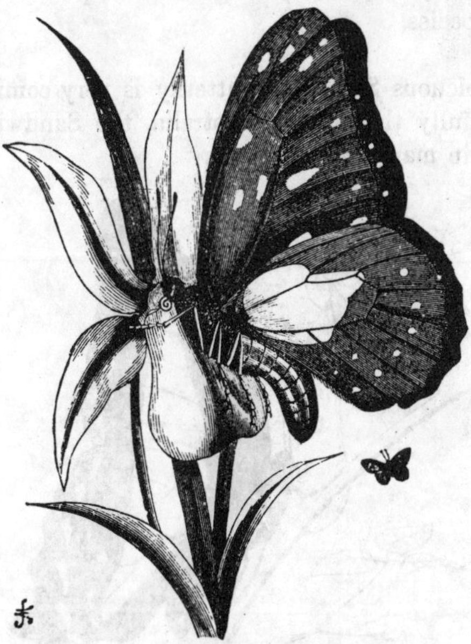

FIG. 313.—Papilio Leonidas.
(Black and pale green.)

and some having been brought from Ashanti and other part of Western Africa. There are six specimens in the British Museum, of which no two are exactly alike. I have therefore selected a specimen from Sierra Leone, which appears to afford the best type of the insect.

Above, the wings are nearly black, and at the base of the lower pair there is a large irregular patch of pale green with a sort of nacreous polish. There are a number of little white spots on both pairs of wings. Below, the wings are rich, deep brown, speckled with white, the patch at the base of the lower pair being of a very much paler green than above. There is one peculiarity about the upper wings which does not at first show itself. This is a streak of very deep scarlet along the under surface of the upper edge. It is widest at the base of the wings, and tapers gradually to the tip. As is often the case with insects, the colour is so deep that it cannot be seen at all except by the aid of a strong and properly directed light. Along the inner edge of the lower wings there is a fringe of very long deep brown hair, much resembling the same portion of the last-mentioned species.

THE conspicuous Sarpedon Butterfly is very common, and is found plentifully throughout Australia, the Sandwich Islands, Borneo, and in many parts of Asia.

FIG. 314.—Papilio Sarpedon.
(Black and green.)

The upper surface of the wings is rich chestnut-brown, and both pairs are crossed by a band of pearly shining green, widest in the middle, and tapering gradually to the ends. Round the margin of the lower wings there is a row of small crimson crescents. The green band assumes a somewhat bluish hue towards the middle. Below, it is similarly, but not so brilliantly coloured, and there is a streak of crimson near the base of the lower wings.

The Butterfly makes it appearance early in May, and remains until the end of the rains in September. It is one of the high-flying insects, frequenting the tops of the oaks, and having a curious jerking or jumping sort of flight, so that it is not easily captured. It has, however, one habit by means of which it can be betrayed into the entomologist's net. It makes regular circuits in its flight, so that if an insect-hunter strikes at a Sarpedon and misses it, he only waits for a time, knowing that the insect will be sure to come back again after completing its round.

The larva of the Sarpedon is a curious dark-green caterpillar, with the segments very strongly marked, and having the singular power of thrusting out a number of stout projections from all parts of its body. In this way it can alter its shape so completely as to be almost unrecognizable. The body diminishes rather suddenly in thickness near the tail. In Ceylon it is known to feed on the cinnamon and sour-sop. The pupa is an oddly-shaped, angular, curved chrysalis, coloured green and yellow, and having a bold ridge down each side. It is bound to the branches by a ligature at the tail and another round the body.

The Indian Butterfly, *Papilio Cloanthus*, bears a remarkable similitude to this species, but may be distinguished by the long tail of the lower wings, and the delicate transparency of the green portions of both pairs of wings.

THE colouring of *Papilio Anticrates* is remarkable for its simplicity and beauty, the boldly contrasting hues being so disposed, that when the wings are opened a sharply defined pattern is formed upon both pairs. The colours are white, with a tinge of creamy yellow, edged and streaked with black in the manner shown in the illustration. Both the colour and markings are liable to slight variations.

The under surface of this Butterfly is much more handsome than the upper. The ground hue is the same, and the markings are very similar, except that the colour is pale brown instead of deep black. The most conspicuous part of the colouring is the second bar from the base of the wing. On the upper surface this forms a nearly continuous bar across both wings, slightly

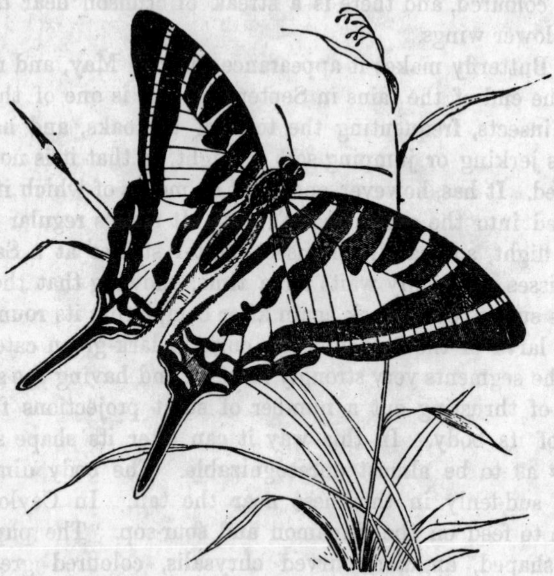

FIG. 315.—Papilio Anticrates.
(Cream-white, and black.)

broken at their junction. But on the under surface the place of this bar is taken by a row of red crescent-shaped spots, each spot being edged with a narrow line of black.

This is one of the Indian insects, and the specimen from which the portrait was taken was brought from Silhet.

HERE is another of the foreign Butterflies which are coloured alike on both surfaces, the only difference being that the under surface is not so bright as the upper. In England we very seldom find this to be the case in the Lepidoptera, our well-known Cinnabar Moth being almost the only example. Abroad, however, there are very many such instances, and in several of them there is scarcely any perceptible difference even in the depth of colour.

In this insect there is but little variety of colouring. The ground hue of the wings is very pale yellow, having almost a washed-out appearance, and they are adorned with a number of dark brown bands, so arranged that when the wings are spread they form a continuous pattern. The eye-like spots at the tips of the lower wings are edged with yellow. This is a native of Australia, and is very rare, only a single specimen being in the British Museum.

FIG. 316.—Papilio parmatus.
(Pale yellow and dark brown.)

The specific name *parmatus* is taken from a Latin word signifying "a shield," but I cannot see where its significance lies, the insect bearing no resemblance whatever to a shield, either in shape or colouring.

CURIOUSLY like the preceding insect are the two species which are shown in the accompanying illustration. Only one of them, *Papilio Alebion,* will be here described, the *Serecinus* coming afterwards with others of its genus. They are, however, placed together in order to show the singular resemblance that sometimes exists between insects of different genera.

The only specimen of this Butterfly in the British Museum was brought from Northern China. Like the last-mentioned insect, it has a sort of faded look about it, and is coloured in almost exactly the same manner on both sides. The ground colour is yellowish white, and the stripes are of a dark brown.

FIG. 317.—Serecinus Telamon. Papilio Alebion.
(White and dark brown.)

Four of them are so arranged that they extend over both wings, while the others are quite short.

Near the tip of the lower wings is a large patch of bright yellow, and beyond this patch is a group of five eye-like spots, the chief portion of which is black, the centre being sprinkled with some tiny azure specks. The long tail of the lower wings is yellow, with a black line running through its centre. In the middle of both pairs of wings the pale yellow is partly translucent.

We now come to another group of Butterflies, called Pierinæ, familiar to us through our "Whites," Orange-tip, Brimstone, &c. Another example of insect mimicry is here given, the insect being a curiously exact copy of another Butterfly named *Thyridia Psidii.* A figure and description of this insect will be found on page 588.

This is a large and handsome genus, a number of species having been brought from tropical America by Mr. Bates. The present species is the largest at present known, and is very scarce, only a single specimen being in the British Museum. It was brought from Tapajos. The colouring is very simple,

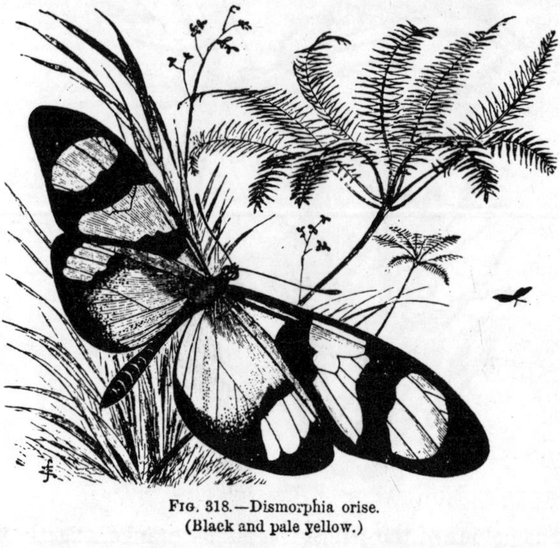

FIG. 318.—Dismorphia orise.
(Black and pale yellow.)

the dark portions of the wing being black, and the rest a very pale yellow, and rather translucent. The body is black, with very narrow white rings on the edges of the segments, and the antennæ are black, except their tips, which are yellow. The wings are similarly coloured on both sides.

Red and yellow are the hues which predominate in Dismorphia, and when a number of them are placed together they have a most gorgeous aspect. The handsomest of them is certainly *Dismorphia Spio*, an inhabitant of St. Domingo. The general colour of this insect is as follows. The upper wings are black, with three large vermilion stripes. The lower pair are also black, marked with one broad band of orange, and another of greenish yellow. It is, however, a singularly variable insect in point of colour, for there are several specimens in the British Museum which have the bands of the upper wings green instead of red.

THE insect which is here shown is a native of the Celebes, and is an example of mimicry, not of another insect, but of vegetable

FIG. 319.—Appias Zarinda.
(Orange red.)

life. The colour of the wings is a ruddy orange, exactly the hue of the Virginian Creeper leaf in the middle of autumn. The long pointed shape of the wings adds to the resemblance, which is so close that, if one of these insects were to settle on a Virginian Creeper, the keenest-sighted entomologist would have very great difficulty in distinguishing it from the leaves among which it had alighted. It is slightly variable in its hue, some specimens having rather more of the yellow and less of the red than the generality. These are probably females.

Like Dismorphia, this is a very large genus, containing species of very different colours, some of them so closely resembling our well-known "Whites" that they can scarcely be distinguished from them without careful observation. One of the most curiously coloured is *Appias placidia*, of Amboyna. Above, this insect is entirely brown, with the exception of a slight edging of white round the wings. Behind, it is also brown, but looks as if it had been thickly dusted with some grey flour.

In colour the *Callidryas Thalestris* much resembles our well-known "Orange-tip" Butterfly, although the colours are distributed differently. The ground colour of the wings is king's

Fig. 320.—Callidryas Thalestris.
(Yellow and orange.

yellow, and near the middle of each of the upper pair is a large oval patch of bright orange. Above this orange patch is a small diamond-shaped mark of jetty black. The abdomen is yellow, the thorax is black, with a fringe of very long bright yellow hairs. It will be seen from this brief description how appropriate is the name Callidryas, *i.e.* "Beautiful Wood-Nymph."

Below, it is dull yellow, like that of a withered leaf, and the surface is covered with a number of large greyish-brown blotches that look exactly like the fungus marks so often seen on decaying leaves. This colouring is evidently intended for the purpose of concealment, as, if the insect were to settle among dying leaves, it would certainly escape the observation which its gaily-coloured upper surface would be sure to attract. These colours are those of the male. The female is coloured in a similar manner below, and above is dull yellow, profusely covered with blotches like those of the under surface. This is probably for the sake of protection, as it certainly causes the female to be much less conspicuous than her mate.

This species is a native of St. Domingo, but the genus is a very large one, and is spread over a considerable portion of the hotter parts of the earth. The general colours are the same throughout the genus, but in some species the orange patch is much larger than that of Thalestris, while in one or two it is spread nearly over the entire wing.

THE gaily-coloured *Ixias Mariamna* is a native of various parts of India.

The colouring of the specimen from which the drawing was taken is as follows:—The upper wings have a brown edge, widest at the tip. Then comes a large scarlet patch occupying the greater part of the wing, with the exception of an irregular black bar which crosses its centre. When the wings are spread, this bar is continued to the lower wings, and runs round their edges so as to form a bold black band, shaped as shown in the illustration. The rest of the wings is white. Below, it is yellow. The upper wings have a patch of yellow immediately under the red of the upper surface, and there is a large black spot near the middle. The lower wings have a row of pale brown spots near their tips.

This is a singularly variable species, the most curious of which is a specimen that was brought from the Punjaub. On the right upper wing of this insect there is a large black spot near the middle, while the corresponding wing of the left side has no spot at all. There is also a similar spot on each of the lower wings.

Many species are yellow, red, and black, distributed in various ways, and in some the male is very gaily coloured, while the female is plain black, white, and grey.

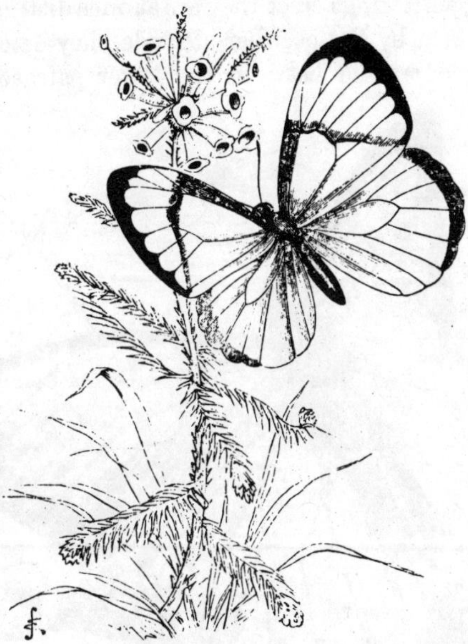

FIG. 321.—Ixias Mariamna.
(Red, white, black, and brown.)

THE insect which is shown on the next page is a native of Boura, one of the islands near Borneo.

The figure which is there given represents the male, there being a marked contrast in colour between the sexes. The upper wings are edged with a band of black, broadest at the tip. The centre of the wing is red, and the rest is bright yellow. The lower wings are entirely yellow, except two angular black spots. The female is quite unlike the male, being simply black and grey, and so dissimilar are the sexes that even an accomplished practical entomologist like Mr. Wallace had some difficulty in determining the identity of the species.

Mr. Wallace has given, in the "Journal of Entomology," a brief but graphic description of the habits of these Butterflies:— "The species of Iphias are all large and handsome Butterflies, frequenting the skirts of forests and the margins of streams in forest districts.

"The males often settle on the ground in damp and muddy places, in company with many Papilionidæ and Pieridæ. When thus resting, with wings erect, they are at once distinguishable from all around them by the peculiar attitude they assume, the upper wings being depressed between the lower pair, so that its basal

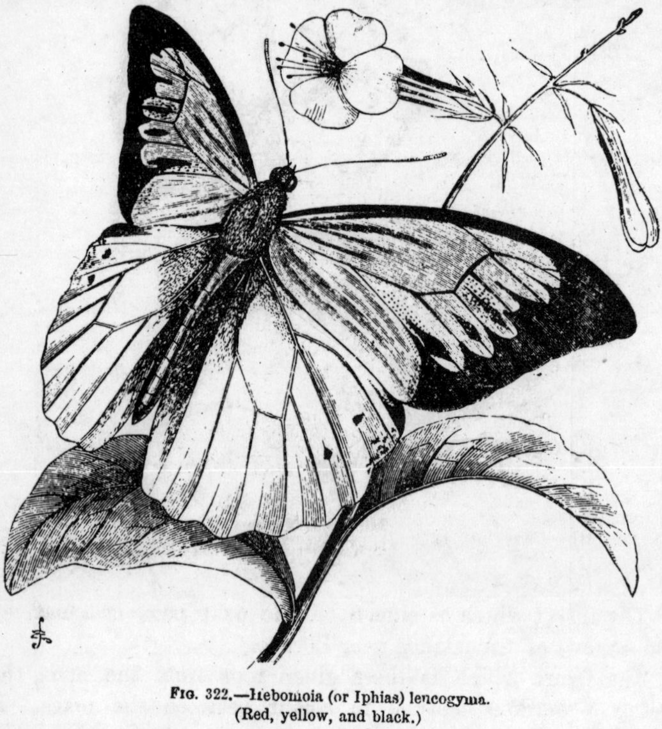

Fig. 322.—Hebomoia (or Iphias) leucogyna.
(Red, yellow, and black.)

half is completely hidden by them. As probably a consequence of this, we find that this basal half of the upper wings is always pale in colour on the under side, and devoid of the characteristic markings of the exposed portions. The females fly rather low, in woods and thickets, and, seldom coming out into the open grounds, are therefore less easily captured.

"I found the female of this interesting species flying among dense thickets in the island of Borneo, and was completely puzzled by its appearance, till I one day caught a glimpse of the underside of its wings, when I knew it must be an Iphias. I afterwards obtained a few males, but it was never abundant."

The specific name, *leucogynia*, is formed from two Greek words signifying "a white female," and is given to the insect on account of the pale colour of the female.

ANOTHER species of this genus is represented in the accompanying illustration. It has a large range of country, specimens

FIG. 323.—Hebomoia Glaucippe.
(Cream-white, red, and black.)

in the British Museum having been found in Java, China, Nepâl Silhet, Ceylon, and the Celebes. The greater part of the upper surface of both wings is a creamy white, and round them runs a deep band of black, with deep, tooth-like projections on the upper pair, and detached, diamond-shaped marks on the lower pair. There is also on the upper pair a rather narrow, waving band of red. The under surface, although not so gaily coloured as the upper, is still very beautiful. The upper wings are white at the base and pale chestnut at the tip, the two colours merging gradually into each other. The lower wings are creamy white, covered with multitudinous wavy pencillings of pale brown, each looking as if executed with the finest possible crowquill pen.

THE genus Teracolas is remarkable for the beauty of colouring displayed by the different species, and the exceeding boldness of

FIG. 324.—Teracolas Ione.
(White and magenta.)

the marking. As for the present species, it is fortunate that in late years the dye called "Magenta" has been invented, for, before that celebrated battle had been fought, and the dye discovered, it would have been a task of no small difficulty to describe this beautiful insect.

The upper surface of the male is white, just like that of our White Butterflies, and the upper wings have on the outer edge a bar of the deepest black, narrowest at the anal angle, and widening at the tip to one-third the breadth of the wing. In the broadest part of the band there are three large spots, which in some specimens are red, and in others magenta. In either case the colour is of the most glowing brilliancy, and flashes like jewels in a setting of jet. The lower wings are white, with a very slight edging of black. Below, it is plain white, and in the female there is neither magenta nor red in the upper wings.

This species is a native of the Natal district. Another species, *Teracolas Phlegyas*, which is found near the White Nile, bears some resemblance to the preceding insect, except that the whole of the band on the edge of the upper wings is magenta; and another, *Teracolas Hewitsonii*, has none of the brillant colours which are usually found in members of this genus, but is dun, crossed with streaks of black.

We now leave the Pierinæ, and take a few examples of the next group, the Papilioninæ.

The first of these is *Parnassius Charltonius*. This genus is tolerably familiar to English entomologists, because the Apollo

FIG. 325.—Parnassius Charltonius.
(White and grey, with blue and red spots.)

Butterfly belongs to it. It is very dubious whether this insect can really be considered as English. Many years ago, however, I found in a drawer in the Ashmolean Museum at Oxford an Apollo Butterfly, which was said to have been caught by a lady and given to the Museum. There was certainly internal evidence that this might have been the case. It had not been captured by an entomologist, for it was pierced all on one side by a darning-needle instead of a pin, and had never been set. I relaxed the wings, replaced the needle with a pin, set the specimen properly, and returned it to the collection.

The larvæ of this genus are odd-looking creatures, very much resembling the caterpillar of a large moth. They have a tentacle in the neck similar to that of Papilio larva. The pupa is enclosed in a large, rude cocoon, made of leaves loosely fastened together.

Most, if not all, the Parnassians are inhabitants of mountainous districts, the present species being a native of the Caucasus. The ground colour of the wings is white. On the upper pair there are three pale grey-black bands, one on the edge and

FIG. 326.—Parnassius Hardwickii.
(Black, white, and red.)

the others crossing the wing. Then come two short black stripes, and towards the base there is a large patch of grey speckles. On the lower wings there is a curved band of black, with blue eye-like spots, and above them are two curved marks of red. The body is black. There is only one specimen in the British Museum.

ANOTHER species of this genus, *Parnassius Hardwickii*, is a native of Nepaul and Chinese Tartary. Its colouring is rather complicated and not easily described, especially as it is an exceedingly variable species, but may be briefly given as follows:—

The upper surface is almost entirely black and white, but on the upper wings there are four patches of red near the upper edge. The insect has a sort of translucent look about it, and is very glossy. Scarcely any two specimens are exactly alike, the chief variation taking place in the red spots on the upper wings. In some specimens they are so much enlarged as to form one patch of considerable size, while in others they are barely half the size of those which are shown in the illustration.

One of these insects, *Parnassius Stubbendorfii*, is entirely white with the exception of the nervures, which are black, so that it bears a very close resemblance to our "Black-veined White" Butterfly.

THE curious genus Serecinus now comes before us. These insects have very long tails to the lower wings, and bear a close resemblance to some of the Papilionidæ. This resemblance is well shown in *Serecinus Telamon*, which may be seen figured on page 572, this being the lower figure of the two. It is a native of Northern China.

The colouring is very simple, the ground colour being white, on which are placed a number of dark brown marks, arranged as shown in the illustration. On the lower wings there is a large black patch occupying the space between the anal angle and the tail, and extending into a black stripe along the lower edge. In this patch there are three round spots, which are powdered with a blue dust. The abdomen is cream-coloured, with some black spots.

The female resembles the male, but the colours are duller, and there is a larger proportion of brown.

ANOTHER fine example of this genus is seen in *Serecinus Montela*, also a native of Northern China. The illustration represents a male, which is coloured as follows. The ground hue is yellowish white, upon which are drawn a number of dark brown stripes and marks. There is a large scarlet patch at the anal angle of the lower wings, and the tail is slightly powdered with blue. Below, the colour is much the same, except that the patch on the lower wings is black, and has only a slight streak of red running through its middle.

In order to show the contrast which often exists between the colour of the two sexes, the female of the same species is given on the opposite page. In this sex the colours are quite

FIG. 327.—Serecinus Montela. Male.
(White, brown, and scarlet.)

as conspicuous as those of the male, though there is about them that almost indefinable dimness which is generally to be found in female Lepidoptera.

The upper wings are brown, and are marked with three distinct rows of yellow spots running in a line with the outer edge, several streaks of the same hue being between the third row and the base of the wing. The lower wings are coloured after the same fashion near the base, but at the anal angle there is an interrupted band of blue, above which is a row of crimson marks. The tails are black, and there is a patch of bright yellow at the base.

PLATE XIII.

1

2

There is but little difference in the colours of the under surface of the wings, except that the yellow, blue, and crimson are not quite so brilliant, and the spots are less sharply defined.

FIG. 328.—Serecinus Montela. Female.
(Brown, yellow, and crimson.)

We now pass to another group of Butterflies, called the Danainæ, several examples of which will be figured, and others will be mentioned or briefly described.

On Plate XIII. Fig. 1 is shown a large Butterfly called *Hestia Idea.* This genus is rather a large one, and as all the species are of very similar colouring, and there is a great tendency to variation, it is not at all easy to distinguish between the species. Mr. Westwood has figured several Hestias in his "Oriental Entomology," and comments upon the difficulty of distinguishing between a species and a variety. Speaking of *Hestia Jasonia,* a Cingalese insect, he makes the following remarks, which are well worthy of notice:—

"How far this may be a good specific character must be left for time (or, more properly speaking, the possession of an extensive series of specimens of these insects from different localities) to determine. It is doubtless in some degree dependent on the form of the apical angle of the wing, and this form of the wing cannot at present, I believe, be fully relied upon. That the form of the wing varies in some Butterflies according to the localities of the individuals, is unquestionable; and if this should be ascertained to be the case here, I think it may possibly be followed by the discovery that all the supposed species of Hestia are only so many local or geographical sub-species of one real species."

This is a very simply coloured Butterfly, the ground colour being white and the markings dark brown. Still, although it has no brilliancy, it is really a handsome insect, owing partly to its size and partly to the bold contrast between the two hues. The abdomen is white, with a narrow black stripe down the middle.

FIG. 329.—Danais insolata.
(White and dark brown.)

ALTHOUGH the colours of this Butterfly are by no means brilliant, it is a very pretty insect, the hues being soft and well contrasted.

In the male the basal half of the upper wings is dark brown, with a rather peculiar silken gloss. The other half is pure white, the outline having a tendency to run into tooth-like projections. The colours of the lower wings are similar, but are arranged in a different manner, the brown and white forming a series of radiating teeth round the edge of the wings. In the female the brown is much lighter than in the male. This species is a native of the Solomon Islands.

There are many species of Danais, their predominating colours being rich brown, orange, white, and black. It is rather remarkable that in all the species there is a tendency for the colours to be arranged in streaks or dashes radiating from the thorax.

THE genus Euplœa is a very interesting one, containing many species which are notable for their beauty, and one, at least, which is remarkable for the use to which it is put.

FIG. 330.—Euplœa imitata.
(Brown and white.)

The species which is here given is a native of the Solomon Islands. Above, the upper wings are brown at the base, becoming white at the tip, the outline being waved as shown in the illustration. The lower wings are smoky grey-brown. Below, the colour is very much paler, and there are three white spots on the upper wings and five on the lower.

ONE Australian species, *Euplœa hamata,* is remarkable for being used as food by the natives, who know the insect by the name of Bugong. In certain seasons the Bugongs arrive in vast swarms, just as do locusts in many parts of the world. They

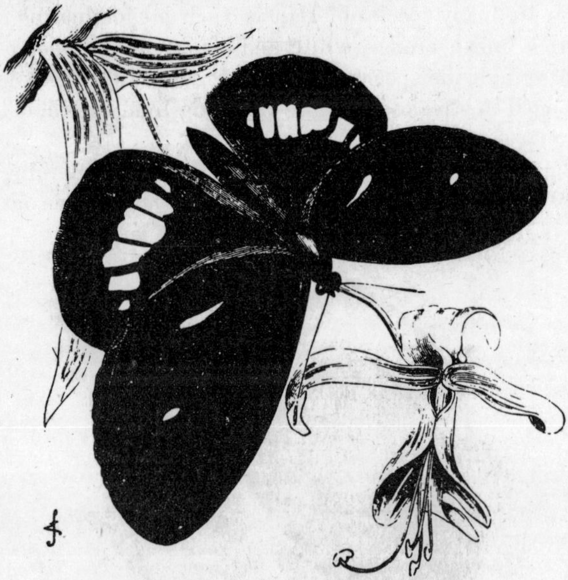

FIG. 331.—Euplœa Lorenzo.
(Brown and white.)

settle upon the rocks, and the natives then light fires so as to smother them with the smoke, when they are swept into baskets. Large fires are then lighted on the rocky ground, and the "moths," as they are called, thrown on the heated ground and stirred about until they are cooked and the wings and legs separated from the bodies. They are then pounded into lumps and are fit to be eaten. Mr. Bennett describes the flavour as resembling that of a sweet nut.

The natives become exceedingly fat upon this curious diet, though at first it always disagrees with them. Birds, as well as men, feed upon the Bugong, and there is a species of crow called

Arabul that is so fond of the Bugong as to dash at it while the natives are cooking it. For this audacity, however, the bird mostly pays with its life, a club being flung at it with the unerring aim of the savage. The popular name of "moth" is probably given to this insect because the body is very stout. The colour of the Bugong is brown, with two round black spots on the upper wings.

THE Lorenzo (given on opposite page) is a native of the Solomon Islands, and appears to be scarce, as there is only one specimen in the British Museum. The colour is brown, with two little white patches on the upper wings, and an interrupted band of white on the lower wings. Both sides are coloured alike.

Although the Euplœas are mostly clad in sober colours, some of them are really handsome insects. There is, for example, *Euplœa Diocletia*, of the Philippines, a really beautiful Butterfly, its wings glowing with changing purple, just like those of our Purple Emperor. Another rather striking insect is *Euplœa Palla*, of Arú, which is quite black except a single row of round white spots upon the edges of the wings.

HERE is the insect to which reference was made in the description of *Dismorphia orise*, page 573. The resemblance between

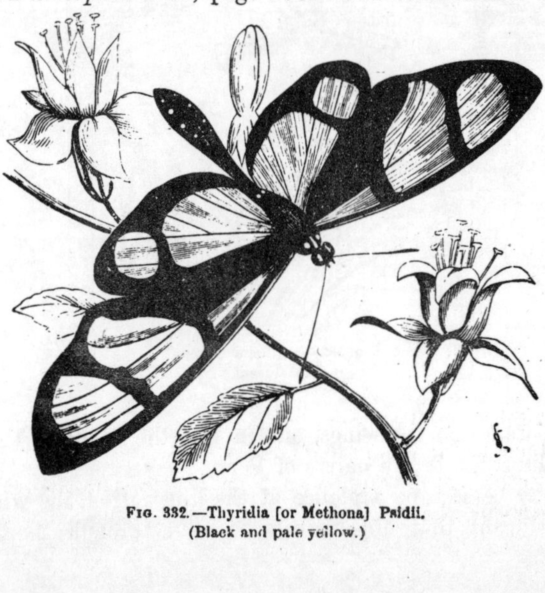

FIG. 332.—Thyridia [or Methona] Psidii.
(Black and pale yellow.)

them can easily be seen by reference to the illustration on that page.

This insect is a native of Guiana. The long, narrow wings are black, and upon each wing are two large patches of pale greyish yellow, these portions being partially translucent. The generic name of *Thyridia,* or "little window," is given to the insect on account of these window-like patches on the black wings. The body is dark brown, with the exception of some round white spots.

There are several species of Thyridia, all coloured very much alike. One of the most remarkable is *Thyridia Ædesia,* in which the translucent parts of the wings are ruddy chestnut instead of pale yellow. The larva of this species is smooth.

OF the group called Satyrinæ a single example will suffice.

The insect which is called *Callitæra Aurora* is a very remarkable one. In the last-mentioned Butterfly there are large trans-

FIG. 333.—Callitæra Aurora.
(Translucent.)

lucent patches on the wings, but in this the whole of the wing is translucent. It is a native of Peru.

As may be seen by a glance at the illustration, the wings are so translucent that objects can be seen through them quite clearly. They have quite a glassy appearance, with the slightest possible haziness about them. The only markings are a couple of eye-like spots, one near the tip of each hind wing. The outer ring of the eye is greyish black, then comes a ring of white. Inside the white is an oval patch of black, and in the centre of the black is a tiny spot of white. The wings are edged with a very narrow band of brown.

There are many species of Callitæra, all much resembling each other, and all natives of tropical America. Some of them have the wings covered with most delicate pencillings and mottlings of light brown, and all of them have the eye-like spot on the lower wings.

ANOTHER group of Butterflies, the Morphinæ, will be represented by one example, *Drusilla mylœcha.* This insect is a native of Louisiade, one of the Solomon group.

FIG. 334.—Drusilla mylæcha.
(White above ; four large eyes below.)

The colouring of the Butterfly is very remarkable. The upper surface is perfectly white, except a narrow black edging to the upper wing. The under surface is also white, but the upper edge of each wing has a black band, which is widest at the base and narrowest at the tip. The remarkable point in this insect is the marking of the lower wings. These are white, but upon them are two large circular eye-like spots. The outer ring of these spots is blackish brown, and within it is a broad ring of yellow. Then comes a large circular patch of black, and in its centre is a little round spot of white. These rings are so exactly circular that they look just like miniature targets. The wings are rather translucent, so that when viewed from the upper surface the eyes can be seen through them.

The specific name of *mylæcha*, or, as it ought to be spelled, *mylæca*, is a very curious one to be given to this Butterfly. It is a name compounded by Pliny from two Greek words signifying anything which inhabits a mill. Pliny used it to indicate some little worm which was found in mills, but its connection with a Butterfly from Louisiade seems rather obscure.

In the British Museum there are many species of Drusilla, and in all of them the eyes of the lower wings are very conspicuous. One of them, *Drusilla bioculata*, of New Guinea, has the spots brought so closely together that they look like a figure of 8. The second ring is blue instead of yellow. The *Drusilla Phorcas*, a native of the New Hebrides, has its wings dark brown, with the exception of a large patch of white on both pairs. The lower wings have each a single circular eye of yellow, with a black middle, and the usual little white dot in the centre of the black.

THE great and important group of the Nymphalinæ commences with the most wondrously magnificent members of the insect race. In mere point of colour perhaps there may be many which rival, even if they do not excel, the Morphos, but then they are so small that their beauties cannot be seen—and, indeed, scarcely suspected—without the aid of the microscope. But the Morpho Butterflies not only are gifted with colours of absolutely dazzling brilliancy, but are among the largest of the insect race. They are all inhabitants of tropical America. Two examples will be here given, the one to illustrate the upper and the other the under surface of the wings.

Our first example of these wonderful Butterflies is *Morpho*

Cypris, an insect which was brought from the emerald mines of Muso, in North Granada, and which seems to partake with the gems the full glory of colour. It is scarcely possible to conceive of a living creature that can surpass this insect in absolute magnificence of colour. The upper surface is radiant azure, as if composed of a sheet of thin mother-of-pearl.

When the light falls in the right direction, the colour is so intense that the eye can scarcely endure its radiance. Yet, with a cross light, the dazzling azure becomes dull blue, and if the

Fig. 335.—Morpho Cypris.
(Azure and yellow.)

light be directed from the tip to the base of the wing, the surface becomes brown. Thus, while holding the insect and turning it in different lights, it often happens that either the entire surface is dull blue, or that one wing is glowing azure, while the other is dark brown. The cause of this change of colour is shown by the microscope. The scales are nearly square, and, as they overlap one another, they are slightly curved in the middle.

It will be seen, therefore, that this curve causes a shadow to be thrown on one side of the scales, while the full light is admitted on the other. It is rather remarkable that if the insect be held up to the light all colour goes out of it, and it becomes of a plain greyish brown colour.

The upper surface is not wholly blue, but is relieved by an interrupted bar of yellow across the centre of both wings, and a number of spots of the same colour, that run nearly parallel to the outer edges. Below, it is pale brown and white, with three large eye-like spots on the upper wings and five on the lower, the two nearest the anal angle being united.

ANOTHER of these splendid insects, called *Morpho Peleides,* is a native of Bogotá. In the illustration the under surface of the

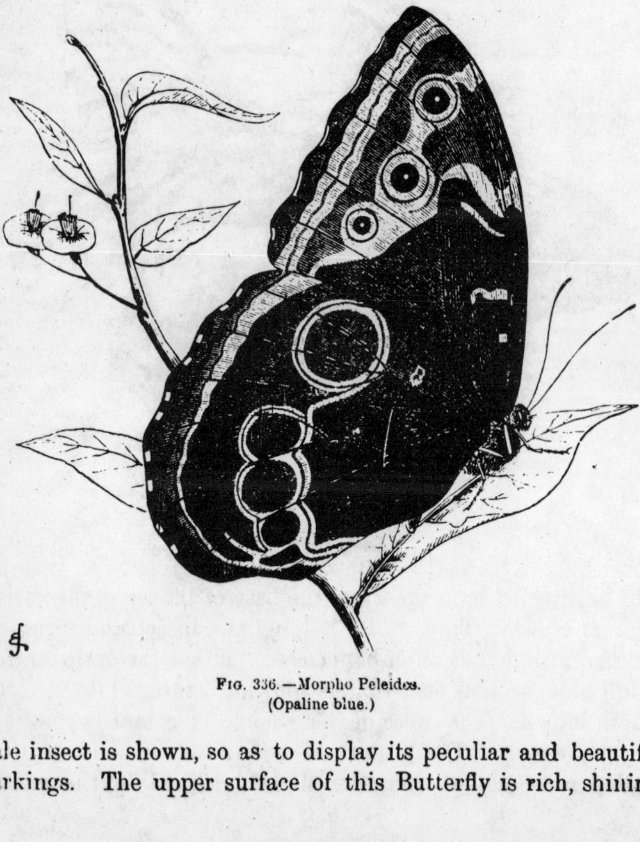

FIG. 336.—Morpho Peleides.
(Opaline blue.)

male insect is shown, so as to display its peculiar and beautiful markings. The upper surface of this Butterfly is rich, shining,

PLATE XIV.

2

1

opaline blue, with a decided dash of green in some lights. The wings are edged with a broad band of black, in which is a row of little white spots. The female is coloured in a somewhat similar fashion, but the blue is less brilliant, and the black belt is replaced by a very broad brown band. In this band are a number of spots, white on the upper wings and red on the lower.

Below, its colouring is equally bold, and so intricate that a minute description would be quite out of place. Described generally, the ground colour is chocolate-brown, and upon the upper wing there are three bold eyes, situated in an irregular belt of grey. The outer ring of these eyes is black, followed by a ring of yellow. Then comes a circular patch of black, and in its centre is a purple spot. A band of pale red runs parallel to the edge of both pairs of wings. The lower wings are likewise chocolate-brown, and have upon them four large circular rings of grey, each ring having a very narrow black line running through it.

THE magnificent insect which is drawn on Plate XIV. is a native of South America. Two views of it are given in order to show the difference between the upper and under surfaces. The former appears at first sight to be plain chocolate-brown, but in certain lights it is seen to be glossed with blue and olive-green. The latter is dun, mottled near the base of the lower wings with white. The lower wings are also dun, covered with profuse mottlings and scribblings of dark brown. In the centre is a single large oval eye-like spot. At the upper end is a semi-lunar line of black, followed by an oval ring of ruddy chestnut. Inside this is another ring of yellow, and the centre is filled with a large oval spot of black, crossed with a few white spots.

When the wings are expanded, the insect bears a startling resemblance to the face of an owl; the oval marks representing the eyes, the body of the butterfly the beak, and the open wings resembling in outline the two great feather-discs that surround the eyes. On account of this peculiarity it is popularly called the OWL BUTTERFLY. I would have had it drawn so as to show the resemblance, but the insect is so large that there would not have been sufficient space on the page.

All the species belonging to the genus Heliconius are of a very peculiar shape. Their wings are long and narrow, so that when they are spread the insect is very much wider than it is long. There is a peculiarity in the colouring as well as in the shape of the wings, the clothing of scales being so slight and thin as to make them partially translucent. There are many species of Heliconius, and they are all inhabitants of tropical America and the West India islands.

Fig. 337.—Heliconius Hermathena.
(Black, yellow, and orange.)

Two species will be given as representatives of the genus; the first of which inhabits Brazil, and is called *Heliconius Hermathena*. The ground colour of the wings is deep black-brown, and near the middle of the upper pair runs a broad belt of bright orange with a dash of brown in it. A long narrow streak of bright yellow runs nearly parallel with the inner edge of the wing, its width being greatest in the middle, and diminishing almost to a point at either end. The lower wings are of the same blackish brown as the upper pair, and upon each of them there is a yellow streak running diagonally from near the base to the tip, together with two rows of spots near the edge, the outer row nearly circular, and the inner rather oblong.

THE second species, *Heliconius Hecalesia,* is a native of Bogotá, and is one of the many rare insects that Mr. Bates brought from South America. There is only one specimen in the British Museum. Its ground colour is velvet black, and near the outer edge of both pairs of wings are some large spots of

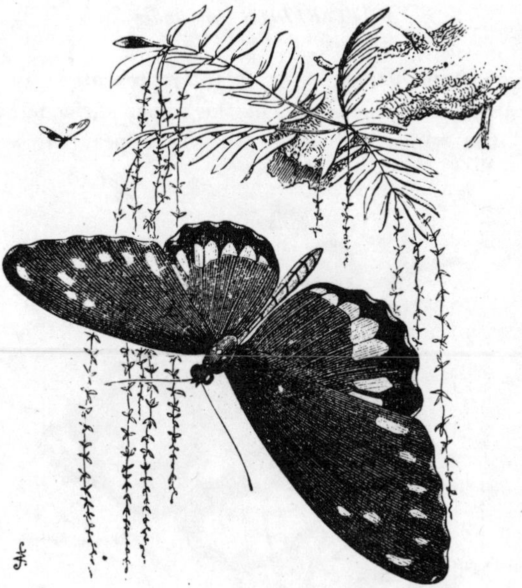

FIG. 338.—Heliconius Hecalesia.
(Velvet black and greenish yellow.)

greenish yellow. At the base of the lower wings is a large patch of bright chestnut. Below, the colours are the same, but rather duller than on the upper surface.

This insect almost exactly imitates another Butterfly of the same district, called *Tithorea Hecalesina.* The two insects fly together in company—perhaps for the purpose of protection. Mimicry is very common among the species of this large genus, and, as is remarked by Dr. Horsfield, the South American genus Heliconius is represented in Asia by the genera Euplœa and Idea. The larvæ of Heliconius feed on the Passifloræ.

CHAPTER II.

BUTTERFLIES (*concluded*).

THE large genus *Junonia* is here represented by *Junonia crebrene,* an African species. On the upper surface the ground colour of the wings is black. On the upper pair is a broad

FIG. 339.—Junonia crebrene.
(Black, chestnut, and yellow.)

waving band of yellow, deepening gradually into chestnut. There is a yellow spot near the tip of the wing, and close to the edge is a narrow line of chestnut. The lower wings are more gaily coloured than the upper. They are black near the base, but have at the tips a patch of yellow deepening into dun. This patch is so large that it occupies almost one-third of the wing. In the British Museum there is a specimen from Plettenberg Bay, which has two dark spots on the yellow patch. Near the base of the wing is an oval patch of blue, which in some specimens takes a purple cast. Beneath, the colour of the insect very closely resembles that of our Meadow Brown Butterfly, and there is a large eye-like spot on the upper wings.

This genus has a very wide range of residence. There is, for example, one species, *Junonia Orithyia*, which is found in Northern Australia, the Celebes, China, Japan, Northern India, West of the Nile, and East Africa. This insect has a greenish tinge, glossed with blue on the lower wings. On the lower pair there are two large eyes, and on the upper, one large and one small eye.

THE two very remarkable insects which are here shown are so well described by Mr. Wallace, in his "Malay Archipelago,"

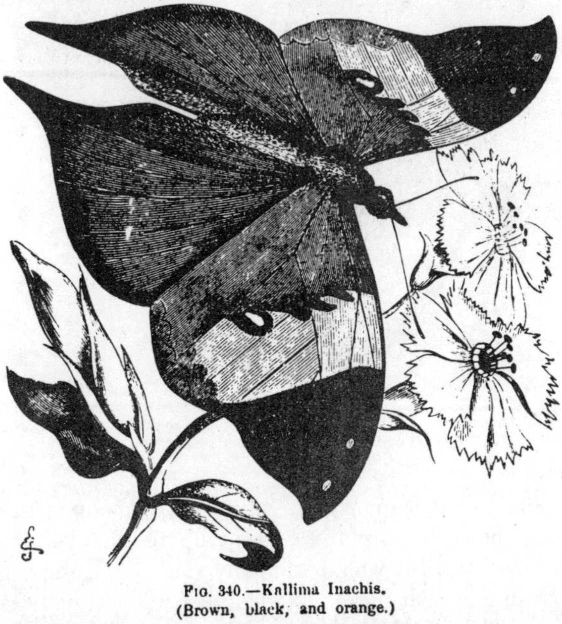

FIG. 340.—Kallima Inachis.
(Brown, black, and orange.)

that I cannot do better than transfer his description to these pages. There are many species of Kallima, most of which are remarkable for the manner in which the colouring, as well as the shape of the closed wings, resembles that of a leaf. The upper surface of the *Kallima Inachis* is mostly brown, the tips of the upper wings being black, and orange-dun bands running diagonally across them.

The following extract is taken from Mr. Wallace's work :—

"This species was not uncommon in dry woods and thickets, and I often endeavoured to capture it without success, for after

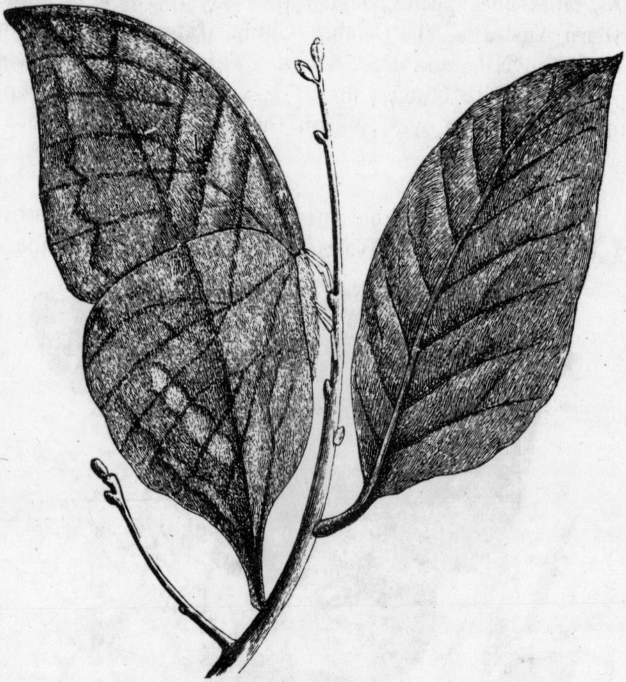

Fig. 341.—Kallima paralekta. The left-hand figure represents the under surface of the butterfly at rest. (Brown, black, and orange.)

flying a short distance it would enter a bush among dry or dead leaves, and however carefully I crept up to the spot, I could never discover it till it would suddenly start out again, and then disappear in a similar place. At length I was fortunate enough to see the exact spot where the butterfly settled, and though I lost sight of it for some time, I at length discovered that it was close before my eyes, but that in its position of repose it so closely resembled a dead leaf attached to a twig, as almost certain to deceive the eye, even when gazing full upon it. I captured several specimens on the wing, and was able fully to understand the way in which this wonderful resemblance is produced.

"The ends of the upper wings terminate in a fine point, just as the leaves of many tropical shrubs and trees are pointed, while the lower wings are somewhat more obtuse, and are lengthened out into a short thick tail. Between these two points there runs a dark curved line, exactly representing the midrib of a leaf, and from this radiate on each side a few oblique marks, which well imitate the lateral veins. These marks are more clearly seen on the outer portion of the base of the wings and on the inner side towards the middle and apex, and they are produced by striæ and markings which are very common in allied species, but which are here modified and strengthened so as to imitate more exactly the venation of a leaf.

"The tint of the under surface varies much, but it is always some brown or ashy colour, which matches with those of dead leaves. The habit of the species is always to rest on a dead twig and among dead or dried leaves, and in this position, with the wings closely pressed together, their outline is exactly that of a moderately sized leaf, slightly curved or shrivelled. The tail of the hind wing forms a perfect stalk, and touches the stick while the insect is supported by the middle pair of legs, which are not noticed among the twigs and fibres that surround it. The head and antennæ are drawn back between the wings, so as to be quite concealed, and there is a little notch hollowed out at the very base of the wings, which allows the head to be retracted sufficiently. All these varied details combine to produce a disguise that is so complete and marvellous as to astonish everyone who observes it; and the habits of the insects are such as to utilize all these peculiarities, and render them available in such a manner as to remove all doubt of the purpose of this singular case of mimicry, which is undoubtedly a protection to the insect. Its strong swift flight is sufficient to save it from its enemies when on the wing, but if it were equally conspicuous when at rest, it could not long escape extinction, owing to the attacks of the insectivorous birds and reptiles that abound in the tropical forests. A very closely allied species, *Kallima Inachis*, inhabits India, where it is very common, and specimens are sent in every collection from the Himalayas. On examining a number of these, it will be seen that no two are alike, but are the variations corresponding to those of dead leaves. Every tint of yellow, ash, brown, and red is found here, and in many specimens there occur patches and spots formed of small black dots, so closely resembling the way in which minute fungi grow on leaves, that it is almost impossible at first not to believe that fungi have grown on the butterflies themselves!

"If such an extraordinary adaptation as this stood alone, it would be very difficult to offer any explanation of it; but although it is perhaps the most perfect case of protective imitation known, there are hundreds of similar resemblances in nature, and from these it is possible to deduce a general theory of the manner in which they have been slowly brought about."

THE genus Eubagis is South American, and contains a great number of species. The present example is a native of St. Paulo, and is one of the many that were taken by Mr. Bates. There is at present only one specimen in the British Museum.

FIG. 342.—Eubagis Sara.
(Black, blue, and white.)

Above, the upper wings are black, with a definite gloss of blue in a side light, and variegated with white spots, disposed as shown in the illustration. The lower wings are glossed with blue, and have three black stripes, one running along the outer edge, and two others nearly parallel to it. On the under surface the upper wings are brown, with some large white spots, and four dashes of blue. The lower wings are much paler, and have two horizontal strips of dark brown.

Of the other species we may notice two, both brought from Ega by Mr. Bates. One is *Eubagis Ines*, the upper surface of which is shining green, edged with black, and the under surface white, mottled with brown. The second is *Eubagis Mœon*, which is white, edged with black on the lower wings, and azure on the upper pair. The azure only belongs to the male, the female being simply black and white.

The genus Catagramma is easily distinguished by the peculiarity from which it derives its name, which is composed of two Greek words, signifying something that is painted or written upon. It is applied to these insects because the under surface of the lower wings is always covered with a boldly delineated pattern of contrasting colours. All these Butterflies are natives of the New World. The painting of the lower wings is very much alike in

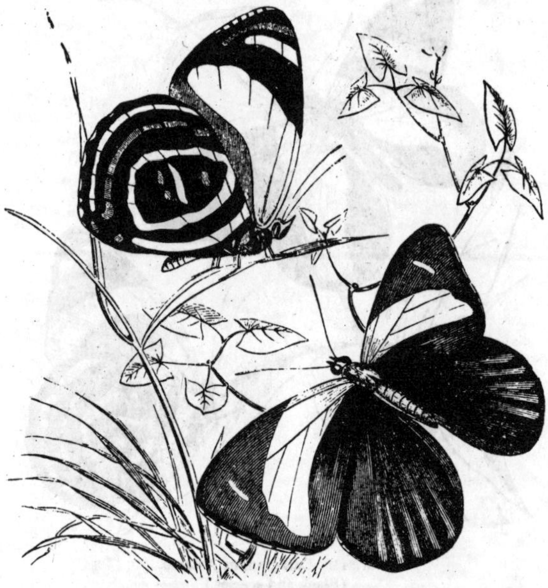

FIG. 343.—Catagramma excelsior.
(Above, black and orange.)

most of the species, but the upper surface varies very considerably, especially in the upper wings. None of the Catagrammas are large insects, those which are here given being of the average size.

There is only one specimen of *Catagramma excelsior* in the British Museum. It is a native of the Amazons district. Above, the upper wings are black, with a broad band of orange reaching from the base nearly as far as the outer edge, and near the tip is a slight dash of the same colour. The lower wings are also black, but not so deep as the hue of the upper pair. Below, the colour of the lower wings is very beautiful. The ground colour is black. Near the outer edge is a long streak of yellow, and then comes a broken line of blue. Next comes a large oval yellow ring, and in the middle is a horizontal blue dash between three spots of yellow.

THE second species comes from Spirito Santo, in Brazil.

Above, the ground colour of both wings is black, with a gloss of purple in a side light. Near the base is a tringualar patch of

FIG. 344.—Catagramma Astarte.
(Black and scarlet.)

scarlet, then a bar of the same colour runs across the middle of the wings, and then comes a slight dash of the same hue near the tip. The lower wings have a single broad and rather wavy bar of the same scarlet, passing from the base almost to the outer edge. Below, the first two-thirds of the upper wings are red, with a bar of black. The rest of the wing is black, with a blue dash close to the tip, and a small yellow bar next to it. The colouring of the lower wings is like that of the previous species.

Generally, the colours of this genus are black and red of some shade. In some, however, a vivid green is substituted for the red. *Catagramma Mionina,* an insect from New Granada, has an orange patch on the upper wings and a shining emerald patch on the lower pair; while one species in the British Museum, as yet without a name, has the patch on the lower wings blue instead of green.

THE extremely rare insect which is here figured is not in the British Museum. It was captured by Mr. Bates, who named

FIG. 245.—Ageronia Alicia. Upper side.
(Slaty green and black.)

it after his daughter. The following is his description of the Butterfly and its habits:—

"Slaty green, silky. Fore wings, above, with many black or dusky variously shaped spots, nearly all of which are margined with a paler hue. Besides these dark spots, there are ten or twelve pale brown spots, one or two between each of the longitudinal nervures. Margins of the wings black.

"Hind wings with a row of black eyes running parallel with the margin and edged with green—some of them have slaty green pupils.

"Beneath, the fore wing ochreous at base, the rest of the wing dark brown, with three belts of white spots. Hind wing, clear saffron yellow; outer margin black, with ochreous spots between.

"This fine and large species was met with only at S. Paulo, Upper Amazons. It has the same habits as its congeners, but it

FIG. 346.—Ageronia Alicia. Under surface.
(Slaty green and black.)

is much swifter in flight. Although I saw several, I was able to capture only one example." The expanse of wing is three inches and three-quarters.

ANOTHER of the Butterflies brought by Mr. Bates from the Amazons is here given. Its name is *Timetes Egina.* The figure represents the male insect. This rare and curiously coloured insect is marked as follows.

Above, both the wings are tawny brown, darkening into black-brown towards the tip, and having several whitish grey spots on the upper pair. Both wings have a number of narrow streaks of dark black brown, looking as if they had been drawn with a pen, the streaks being short on the upper and long on the lower wings. Beneath, both wings are pearly white, with a dash of pinky lilac, very much like the colour of a newly-caught smelt. On the wings are drawn a number of pale brown streaks, one of which is darker than the others and crosses both pairs of wings. The female resembles the male in most respects, but is paler, and has five spots on the upper wings.

It is found in the district of the Upper Amazons. The expanse of the wings is not much more than two inches, so that its length is much greater than its width.

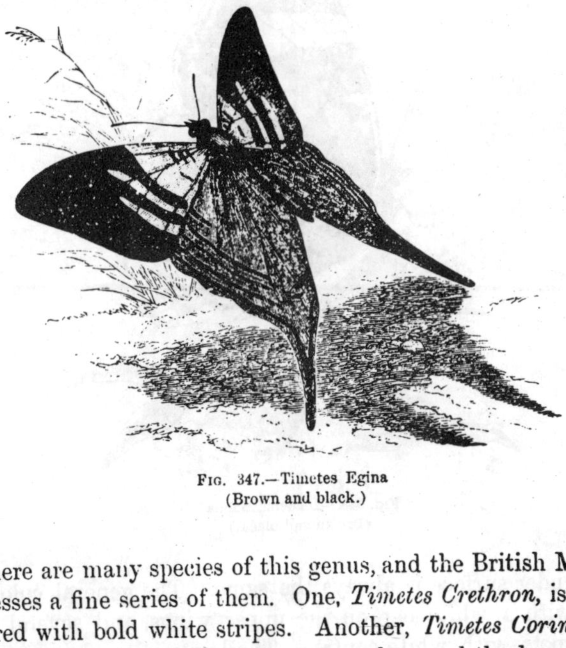

FIG. 347.—Timetes Egina
(Brown and black.)

There are many species of this genus, and the British Museum possesses a fine series of them. One, *Timetes Crethron,* is brown, covered with bold white stripes. Another, *Timetes Corinna,* has the upper wings black, with an orange bar, and the lower wings blue, edged with black and orange. The name *Timetes* is taken from a Greek word signifying "honourable," and is given to the insects on account of their remarkable form.

THE extremely variable insect which is called *Diadema Bolina* has a very large range of residence. The specimen which is figured in the illustration was brought from the South Seas by

Mr. Brenchley, and is remarkable for the exceeding paleness of its colouring.

Generally, the upper wings are velvet brown-black, with a small patch of blue on the upper wings and a large patch on the lower pair. In some specimens, however, the upper patch is white, or has a white centre. It is rather curious that whatever may be the variations in the colouring of the upper surface, that

FIG. 348.—Diadema Bolina.
(Brown and black.)

of the under surface is always the same. The general colour is brown, with a white bar on the upper wings, and several dark brown spots with white centres. The lower wings have a white bar and a row of white spots running parallel to the outer margin.

THE large genus Adolias is represented by two species, and the distinction which exists between the sexes is shown by a figure of the female as well as of the male.

The first species, *Adolias Kesava*, is a native of Northern India, the specimens which are here figured having been taken at Silhet. The male is olive-brown above, with indistinct broad stripes of very dark brown on the upper wings, and a narrow stripe of the same hue on the lower pair. Below, it is dun, with two light brown bars, and the surface is covered with narrow black streaks, looking as if they were scribbled at random with a pen.

The female is considerably larger than the male, and is very different in colour. The upper surface is chocolate-brown, with some dark marks and rings, and a broad, wavy, pale grey-brown

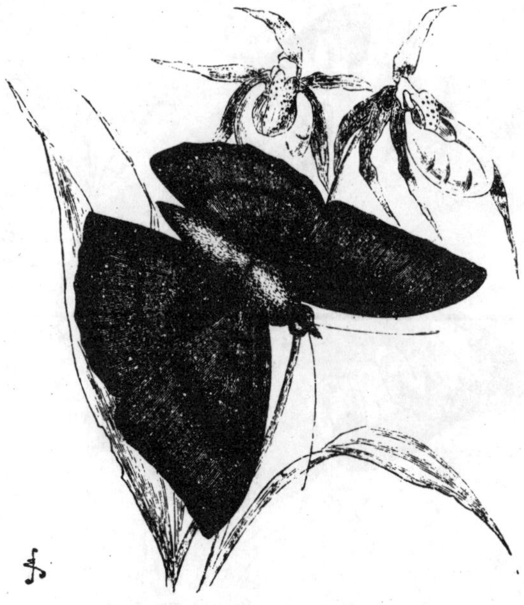

FIG. 349.—Adolias Kesava. Male.
(Olive brown.)

bar across the upper pair. Below, it is pale, mottled with a darker brown.

There is a specimen in the British Museum which at first looks like a variety, on account of a large dark brown patch at the base of the wings. This patch, however, is nothing more than some glue which has been employed for the purpose of fastening the wings to the body, and has been used with too liberal a hand.

Very great changes in the appearance of an insect may thus be made. The reader may remember that in the course of this work the tricks of dealers have several times been mentioned, and it is as well to know that artificial colouring is one of them. The dealers treat the insects very much as foolish ladies treat their hair when they wish to change its colour. They first begin by discharging the original hue, and when the wings are dry, paint them with any coloured dye that they may think suitable. The insect is carefully dried in a strong current of air, so that the delicate hairs of the body may not adhere together so as to betray the deception.

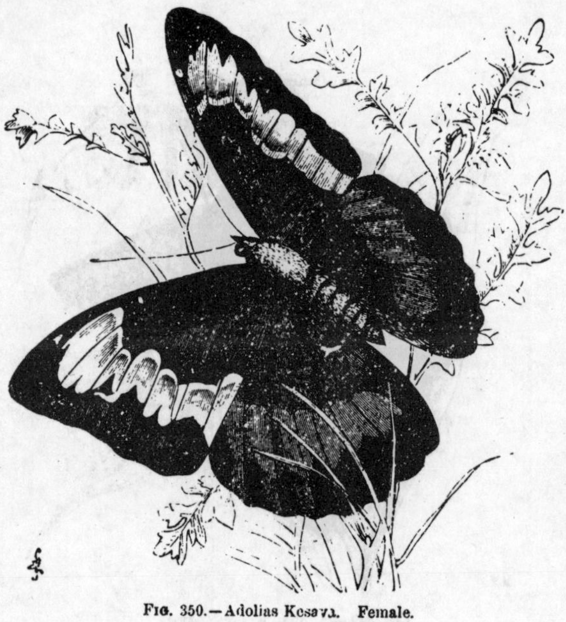

FIG. 350.—Adolias Kesava. Female.
(Chocolate-brown and grey.)

Mr. A. H. Butler, of the British Museum, has quite a collection of such Butterflies. They were dyed by himself, just to show the amount of imposition which can be practised by skilful and unscrupulous dealers. These, it must be understood, are never the owners of the naturalists' shops, who are always thoroughly honourable and trustworthy. But there are itinerant dealers, who are as great in insect forgeries as "Flint Jack" was in antiquities, and who go about with their insect boxes from one collector to another all over the country.

ANOTHER species of this genus, *Adolias Sahadeva*, is here given. As its name imports, it is a native of India, the specimen which is here figured coming from Nepaul. The colour of the upper surface is deep brown, with a distinct wash of olive, and mottled with black. A number of pale dun spots are so arranged as to form a single interrupted bar crossing both wings, and two short bars on the upper pair, near the upper margin. These are edged with black. The under surface is pale green, covered with black scribblings and dun mottlings.

FIG. 351.—Adolias Sahadeva.
(Brown, black, and dun.)

This is a very large genus, and some of them deserve a brief description. *Adolias Anosia* is brown, but is curiously blotched with yellowish grey, so that it has a sort of unwholesome look about it, as if covered with lichen. *Adolias Phemius* is brown, with a pale blue bar at the tip of the lower wings. In *Adolias Ramuda* the male is dark blackish brown, with its lower wings edged with pale blue. The female is very differently coloured, being very pale brown mottled with white. *Adolias Durga* is deep olive-brown, with a bold white bar across the wings, just like that of our "White Admiral." The lower wings are washed with blue. Lastly, *Adolias Epiona* is also olive-brown, but has the bar yellow instead of white.

THE insect which is here given was formerly placed in the preceding genus, but has now been transferred to the genus Tanœcia. It is an Indian insect.

The colouring of this species is very simple. The ground hue of the wings is brown, and both pairs have a broad white band running parallel to the outer edge, and only broken by the dark nervures. On the outer side this band is edged by a jagged line

FIG. 352.—Tanœcia Pulasara.
(Brown, white, and black.)

of black. A small patch of white is on the upper wings, as is a patch of black near the tip, and there are a few black marks and scribblings on both pairs. The insect is similarly coloured both on the upper and under surfaces, except that the latter is rather paler than the former.

The genus Tanœcia has a tolerably wide range, and in the British Museum there are specimens from India, Sumatra, Sarawak, and Singapore. Among them may be noticed *Tanœcia Vikrama*, a Sumatran species. This is pale brown, covered with black arch-like marks and a multitude of black dashes. Then, there is *Tanœcia calliphorus*, of Luzon. This is a very conspicuous insect, being dark brown, with a green stripe crossing the wings diagonally, almost exactly like that of *Papilio Sarpedon*, which has already been described and figured.

THE genus to which belongs the magnificent insect which is here given is familiar to English entomologists on account of the only British species, the well-known "Purple Emperor," *Apatura Iris*. The whole genus is a very splendid one, and is remarkable for the prevalence of rich blue in the males, the females being comparatively plain, and having no hues more brilliant than brown and chestnut.

FIG. 353.—Apatura Lavinia.
(Azure, purple, chestnut, and black.

Of all the Apaturas this is undoubtedly the most gorgeous. In the male insect the upper surface of the wings is dazzling azure, changing to purple in some lights, and having a decided gloss of green in others. A broad band of warm chestnut runs through the centre of both wings, so as to form a continuous band when they are spread, and the wings are edged with a double row of semilunar black marks. The upper wings are edged with black, and have besides three short black bars on the upper margin.

Below, like our own species, it is comparatively plain, being simply buff, with profuse mottlings and blotches of brown and dun. The female is plain, and very much resembles that of our own species.

This is not only the most magnificent, but one of the very rarest of the Apaturas. There are only two specimens in the British Museum, fortunately one of either sex, and for more than twenty years no specimen has been added to the collection. So unrivalled is it in its beauty, that as soon as the drawer is opened its dazzling hues flash on the eye in spite of its splendid congeners around. It is a native of Peru.

THE accompanying illustration represents another of these splendid insects, called *Apatura Laura.* It is a native of Nicaragua.

FIG. 354.—Apatura Laura.
(Purple-brown and dun.)

Although not so fiercely brilliant as the preceding insect, it is a most beautiful creature. At the base of the upper wings it is brown, edged with a streak of black. Then comes a rather broad band of dun, tending to yellow on the lower wings, and the outer edge of both wings is rich blue or purple, according to the light in which the insect is viewed. The base of the lower wings is also blue. Below, it almost exactly resembles *Apatura Lavinia*, except that there is a shining silvery gloss over both wings, and, like that insect, the female is quite plain, without one particle of the brilliant colours that adorn her mate.

There are many species belonging to this genus, all of which are tolerably alike. There are two, however, which are worthy of a brief notice. *Apatura Agathina* is remarkable on account of the bold difference of the sexes as regards colour. The male is very deep purple, while the female is white, speckled with black. Indeed, were it not for the under surface of the wings, no one would think that they could be only the two sexes of the same insect. A curious variation in colour is found in *Apatura Cherubina*, a native of Bogotá. In almost all the Apaturas the wings of the male are either blue or purple, but in this insect they are shining green.

THE beautiful insect which is here figured is a native of Columbia.

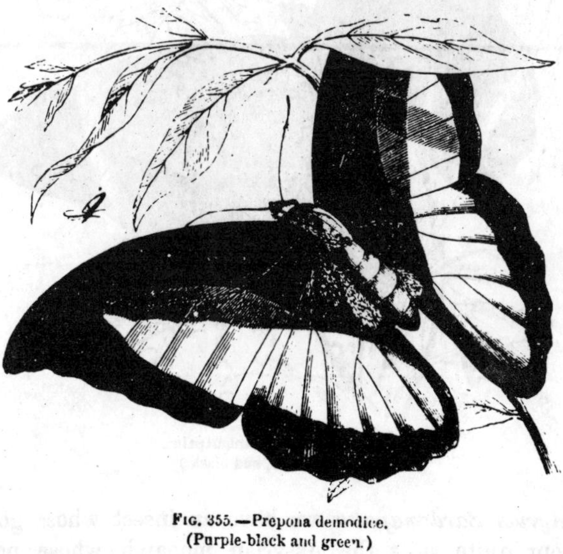

FIG. 355.—Prepona demodice.
(Purple-black and green.)

The greater part of both wings is the very deepest purple, so deep, indeed, that except when viewed with a strong light, it appears to be velvety black. Across both wings runs a bar of green, narrowest on the upper wings, and becoming so wide on the lower pair as to occupy one-half of the surface. In a side light the green takes a blue gloss, and the purple base and edging are much deeper on the lower than on the upper wings. Beneath, it is prettily though not brilliantly coloured. The ground colour is the palest pearly grey, pencilled profusely with black, and on the lower wings are two brown eye-like marks.

The genus is a tolerably large one, and all the species are much alike.

FIG. 356.—Agrias Sardanapalus.
(Crimson, blue, and black.)

In *Agrias Sardanapalus* we have an insect whose gorgeous splendour quite suits the Assyrian monarch whose name it bears. Lacking the dazzling azure and purple of the Apaturas, it is really startling in its bold contrasts of colour. The upper wings are rich crimson from the base to more than half of their surface. Then comes a velvet-black bar extending completely across the wing, and being wider on the upper than on the outer edge. Next is a bar of dark blue, edged with black; and the rest of the wing is brown, except a black edging. The lower wings are brown-black at the base and on the margin, while the centre is occupied with a large patch of bright blue. Beneath, the upper wings are crimson, black, blue, and brown, but not so bright as on the upper surface. The lower wings are mottled very much like the skin of the jaguar, the spots being olive-black with bluish centres.

This species is a native of the Amazons district, and is very rare.

There are several curious insects belonging to this genus, one of which is *Agrias Phalcidon,* which has the base of the wings very deep blue, followed by a broad band of olive and then by black. This insect is remarkable for a pair of brush-like tufts of yellow hair that project from the base of the lower wings Concerning these tufts there is a small story.

It sometimes, though not often, happens that visitors to the insect room at the British Museum are utterly ignorant of entomology, and in consequence are very troublesome to the officers Of course only the most showy insects are selected for exhibition to such persons, who are politely got out of the room as soon as possible. Once, however, two young ladies overpassed the well-tried patience of the officer who was showing the insects, their chief idea of butterflies being the effect which they would produce if worn as ornaments. At last, when the Agrias drawer was opened, their guide gravely pointed out this species, and told them that it was called the Shaving-brush Butterfly, because it used these brushes every morning in shaving itself. Furthermore, he said that it was a swift insect and difficult to catch, but that it could always be taken by putting out over-night a basin of soap-suds, which attracted the butterflies and enabled the collector to catch as many as he wanted. And they believed him.

There is only a single specimen of *Agrias Sardanapalus* in the British Museum.

Mr. Bates has the following remarks on the genus:—" Agrias, I think, is the most magnificent group of the Nymphalidæ in South America. They are very bold, strong, rapid fliers, not at all like the Catagrammas. They fly for a short distance with inconceivable rapidity, and then settle on a leaf high up in a tree; on the trunk of a tree where sugary sap is oozing, or on filth of some kind on the ground, with their wings erect, and are not very easily scared away."

ON Plate XIII. Fig. 2 is shown an insect called *Charaxes Eudamippus*, a native of Silhet and Assam. In this genus each of the hind wings has two projections, and one species, *Charaxes Jasius*, which inhabits the warmer part of Europe, is popularly called the "Pasha of two tails."

Above, the colour of this species is yellow and black, the tails of the hind wings being olive-green. Beneath, it is pale, nearly white, with the exception of a black streak, looking just like a twig with a forked end, and a pale brown band which crosses both pairs of wings. The wings are edged with the same colour.

There are many species of this genus, and in all the colours of yellow, brown, and black predominate. One of the most striking is *Charaxes Nitebis*, of the Celebes, in which the base of the wings is dark yellow-green and the rest black.

The caterpillar of *Charaxes Jasius* is a very curious creature, having its head armed with four yellow horns tipped with red. It is a nocturnal feeder, remaining by day quite motionless among the leaves of its food-plant, which it so closely resembles in colour that it can scarcely be detected. There are two broods in the year, one in June and the other in September.

THE rarest of these insects is *Charaxes Kadenii*, popularly known as the "Calliper Butterfly," because the tails of the lower wings are curved towards each other like the legs of a pair of callipers. A short account of the capture of this insect is given by Mr. Wallace in his "Malay Archipelago":—

"One day, a boy brought me a butterfly between his fingers perfectly unhurt. He had caught it as it was sitting with wings erect, sucking up the liquid from a muddy spot by the roadside. Many of the finest tropical butterflies have this habit, and they are generally so intent upon their meal that they can be easily approached and captured. It proved to be the rare and curious *Charaxes Kadenii*, remarkable for having on each wing two curved tails like a pair of callipers. It was the only specimen I ever saw, and it is still the only representative of its kind in English collections."

The colour of this species is creamy white above, adorned with sundry streaks and spots, arranged as seen in the illustration. The under surface is similarly marked, but the ground-colour is silvery white instead of cream white.

FIG. 357.—Charaxes Kadenii
(Yellow, white, and brown.)

The late General Sir J. Hearsey, who was a good practical entomologist, states that he usually took the Indian species, *Charaxes Fabius*, on wounded apple-trees, the insect feeding eagerly on the sap as it exuded from the tree. They are all strong-winged, and swift of flight.

THE genus Paphia belongs to South America, and the present species was taken by Mr. Bates in the Amazons district. There is only a single specimen in the British Museum.

Above, the colour of this insect is simply Prussian green, glossy, but not vivid. Beneath, it is very prettily marked, being rather pale brown, with multitudinous pencillings of black. On the hind wings there are two whitish spots near the base, and four bright green spots near the tip.

One of the most striking examples of this genus is *Paphia Nessus*, from New Grenada. This insect has the lower wings

FIG. 358.—Paphia Glauce.
(Shining green.)

dark brown, and on the upper pair there are two large patches of red edged with blue. All the rest of the wing is black.

THE splendid insect called *Siderone Thebias* is a native of Bogotá. The upper wings are dark crimson at the base, and a black bar with slightly waved sides runs across the centre of the wing. Then comes a bar of crimson extending nearly across the wing, and the remainder is black. The lower wings are black, tending to brown at the tips, and a bar of crimson passes about half across the wing. Beneath, it is of a dead-leaf brown, much blotched with dark brown, especially at the base of the wings.

Another species, *Siderone Isidora*, of South America, has its wings of a dead-leaf yellow, becoming brown at the tips. *Siderone Archidona*, of Mexico, has its upper wings rather long and boldly hooked at the tip. Above, their colour is pale brown, with some patches that shine as if they were burnished silver.

FIG. 359.—Siderone Thebias.
(Crimson and black.)

WE now come to another group of Butterflies, called the Erycinidæ. In these insects the two front legs of the male are rudimental, while those of the female are fully developed. Some of these species are singularly beautiful in colouring as well as in form, and many of them have the hind wings prolonged into small tails. They are quick of flight, and have a habit of resting on the under surface of leaves with their wings extended. Both the larva and pupa are very short.

THE insect which is given as the first example of the Erycinidæ is a native of Bogotá, and is very rare, only one specimen being in the British Museum.

The upper surface is deep velvet-black, with an interrupted band of shining blue across the middle, followed by another of rich crimson near the base. Both bands are narrow at the top and widen by degrees, and they are so formed that when the wings are extended they form two continuous bands across both pairs of wings. Beneath, it is quite as handsome as above. The upper wings have an azure glossy surface, traversed by

FIG. 360.—Necyra manco.
(Black, blue, and crimson.)

black nervures, and having a single crimson patch at the inner edge. The lower wings have a single broad crimson stripe.

The specimen which is shown in the illustration was captured in 1871.

THREE examples of the typical genus Erycina will now be given.

The first is called *Erycina ocollo,* and is a native of New Grenada. It is very nearly two inches in expanse of wing.

It is a very beautiful species, and, though distinct from any other, given to variation. The specimen from which the illustration was drawn is coloured as follows. The head, antennæ, and body are black, and the upper wings are black, with a single broad bar of bright orange passing diagonally across them. The hind wings are very much lengthened at the tips, so as to form two tails, which diverge boldly from each other. Like the upper pair they are black, but are more variegated as regards colour. On the centre of the wing is a yellow band, and a broad patch of bright blue crossed with black nervures occupies the surface of the wing between the white spots on the outer margin and the yellow band.

FIG. 361.—Erycina ocollo.
(Black, yellow, and blue.)

THE insect on the left of the illustration, on page 624, is a very rare species, called *Erycina Atahualpa.* It was brought from New Grenada, and the specimen is now in Mr. Hewitson's collection. The upper wings are much pointed. Their colour is black, and across them runs diagonally a single narrow streak of crimson. Parallel with the outer edge is a row of blue spots. The lower wings are lengthened at the tips into a short and rather rounded tail, the two diverging from each other. Their ground colour is black, and across them runs a band of crimson which joins that of the upper pair when the wings are spread. Parallel with and close to the outer edge is a band of dark blue, and just within it is a similar band of paler blue. There is a row of little white spots on the edge of the wing.

THE second species is a native of the Amazons district, and is called *Erycina Calphurnia.* The illustration represents the male. The upper wings are brown, with a white band drawn across the centre, and a blue band on the lower half of the outer edge. The lower wings are elongated so as to form two diverging tails, and are beautifully and elaborately coloured. A white band passes over the middle like that of the upper wings, but as it descends it changes gradually to blue, and maintains that colour to the end of the tail. The outer edge of the wing is

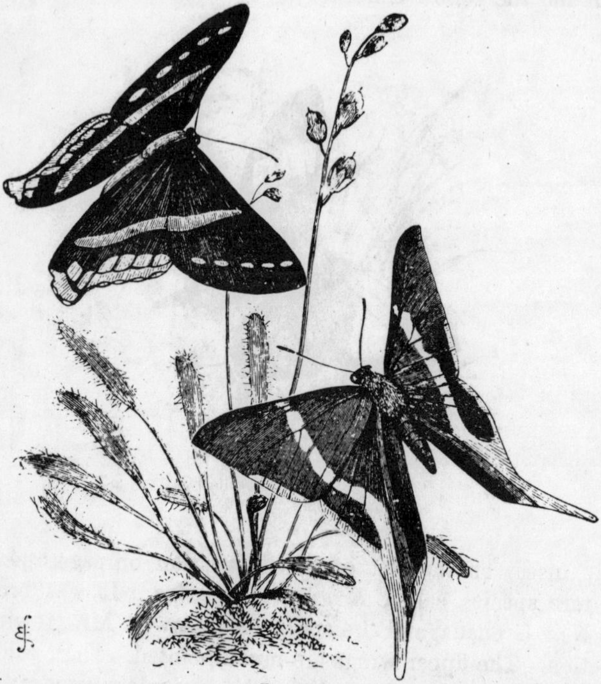

FIG. 362.

Erycina Atahualpa. (Black, crimson, and blue.)

Erycina Calphurnia. (Brown, blue, crimson, and white.)

also blue. From the base of the wing a broad crimson band runs parallel to the white band, and the inner edge is brown. The head, thorax, and abdomen are brown.

FOR our knowledge of the beautiful genus Zeonia we are almost wholly indebted to the researches of Mr. Bates. The following remarks on the genus are from a letter from Mr. Bates to Adam White, dated Ega, May 2, 1857, published in *Trans. Ent. Soc.* vol. v.:—

"The beautiful Zeonia, of which I sent you a large series last July, I met with in a part of the forest near Ega, which I had traversed and examined before, many times, in all seasons. The first specimen I found was a straggler in a different part of the forest. On July the 21st, after a month of unusually dry and hot weather, in ascending a slope in the forest by a broad pathway mounting from a moist hollow, choked up with monstrous arums and other marsh plants, I was delighted to see another of what had always been so exceedingly rare a group of butterflies; it crossed the path in a series of rapid jerks, and settled on a leaf close before me. Before I had secured it I saw another, and then shortly after a third. I mounted to the summit of the slope, followed a branch pathway which led along the brow of the ridge, without seeing any more, but returned again to examine well the exact spot where I had captured the three, for it very often happens that a species is confined to a few square yards of space in the vast forest, which to our perceptions offers no difference throughout its millions of acres to account for the preference. I entered the thicket from the pathway, and a few yards therein found a small sunny opening, where many of the Zeonia were flitting about from one leaf to another, meeting one another, gambolling, and fighting; their blue transparent tinge, brilliant crimson patch, and long tails, all very visible in the momentary intervals between the jerks in their flight. I was very busy, you may imagine, at first in securing a supply of specimens; I caught perhaps 150, two-thirds of which fell to pieces in the bottom of the net, so fragile is their texture. I then paused to look around the locality, and endeavoured to find the larvæ and pupæ.

"I walked through the thicket in all directions, and found the space peopled by the species was not more than from twenty to thirty square yards in extent: so far as the eye could reach, the leaves were peopled with them; it is possible the brood belonged to some one tree. The only two pupæ I could find, it is true, were on two distinct kinds of trees, but this is no proof that the larvæ may not have fed on one tree only. I was disappointed at not finding the larvæ, although I searched well during this and the three following days. On the second day the butterflies were still coming out; on the third they were much fewer, and nearly all worn; and on the fourth day I did not see a single perfect specimen, and not a dozen altogether. During all the time I worked in the neighbourhood of the city of Pará I found but one specimen of a Zeonia. This was in 1848. The next time I saw the genus was at Altar do Chao, where I took a few of a very small long-tailed species at flowers. At Ega, a few miles up the Teffi, I took one of another very handsome species at flowers, very distinct from all the others."

The colours of this large genus are very similar throughout, and are generally black, scarlet, and white, the scarlet in some species giving way to yellow.

Our first example, *Zeonia Faunus,* has the greater part of both wings nearly transparent. The upper wings are entirely

FIG. 363.—Zeonia Faunus
(Black, scarlet, and white.)

surrounded with a band of black, powdered with tiny grey specks, and a rather jagged bar of the same hue runs through the middle. The upper part of the lower wings is edged with jetty black, and the lower part with black, powdered like the upper wings. In the midst of the black are two spots of scarlet, with a slight tint of orange—something like that lovely but too fugitive "pure scarlet" of the colour-makers—one of the spots being large and oval, and the other small and circular. The colours are nearly identical on the upper and under surface of the wing.

There is only one specimen in the British Museum.

ON the accompanying illustration are given the two sexes of *Zeonia Batesii,* in order to show the curious difference of shape as well as colour between the males and females. The colours are arranged in much the same manner as those of the preceding species, the edges of the wings being black, the centre transparent, and a scarlet patch on the lower wings, which in this species is followed by two little white spots. At the extremity of the tails of the lower wings there is a short streak of yellowish white. The reader will probably have noticed that,

FIG. 364.—Zeonia Batesii.
(Black, white, and scarlet.)

whereas in the males the projections of the lower wings are tolerably straight, in the females they diverge considerably, and turn a bold curve. Both these insects are natives of the Amazons district.

Now we come to the Lycænidæ, a group of Butterflies which is familiar to English entomologists on account of the well-known "Copper," "Blue," and "Hair-streak" Butterflies. They are small and slightly made, have the fore-legs fully developed in both sexes, and very tiny claws. The larvæ bear a singular resemblance to woodlice.

Only a few examples can here be given, the first of which is *Chalybs coronata,* a native of Bogotá. The whole genus is a singularly splendid one, the upper surface being metallic blue, green, or gold, and often two or all of these colours. This metallic aspect has earned for the insect the generic name of *Chalybs*, a Greek word signifying "steel."

The species which is here represented is very rare, and there is only a single specimen in the British Museum. The upper surface is metallic blue or green, according to the direction of the light; the green predominating near the base, and the blue towards the tip. Both pairs of wings are surrounded with a

FIG. 365.—Chalybs coronata.
(Blue-green, black, and orange.)

black edge, which merges almost imperceptibly into the blue of the centre. The double tail of the hind wings are jetty black, and above each of them is a large spot of orange.

Beneath, it is even handsomer than above. In both pairs of wings the base is dark green, edged with glittering emerald. Then comes a band of ruddy mahogany. In the upper pair is a stripe of pale brown, while in the lower the colour is pink, speckled with green, and then followed by rich green. On both surfaces the tails are black.

All the species of this genus are remarkable for their exceeding beauty, and the singular fact that, although their upper surface is magnificently coloured, their under surface is even more beautiful. For example, there is *Chalybs Actæon*, the upper surface of which is metallic blue and black, while below the upper wings are emerald powdered with tiny black specks, and the lower are green pencilled with black. Then there is *Chalybs Pholcus*, the upper surface of the male being very dark metallic blue, bordered and edged with black, while the under surface is black, barred with green. The female is very different in colour, being brown on both surfaces, with yellowish green and white spots on the under wings.

All the species are natives of tropical America.

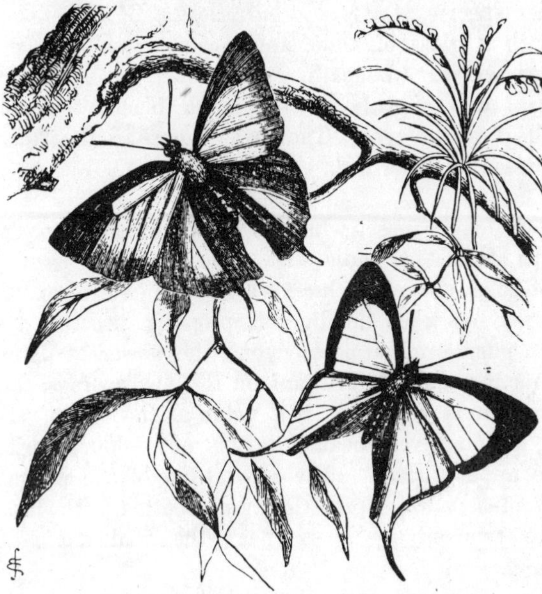

FIG. 366.

Amblypodum quercetorum. (Blue and brown.) — Loxura Surya. (Pale red and black.)

THE genus Amblypoda derives its name from the structure of the feet, the word signifying blunt or rounded feet.

THE insect which is here represented is a native of Northern India, being taken at Silhet and Darjeeling. In expanse of wing it measures very nearly two inches and a half.

The upper surface is violet-blue, fading to white in the centre. Near the tip of the upper wing, and at the end of the discoidal cell (*i.e.* the space enclosed by nervures in the centre of the wing), is a large dark spot divided by nervures so as to look like several distinct spots. The wings are edged with dark brown, and at the anal angle of the lower wings there is a short tuft of the same colour.

Beneath, it is buff-brown, the upper wings having a series of seven oval and semilunar spots across the wing and parallel with the outer margin. The lower wings have five black spots near the base. The illustration represents the male insect, the colours of which are more intense than in the female.

Another species, *Amblypoda quercetorum*, of Silhet, is brown above, with a gloss of blue, and a white spot on the tip of the upper wings. Beneath, it is brown, washed with dark olive-green, and slightly mottled with black, the mottlings taking the form of eyes. The lower figure in the illustration will be presently described.

THE very lovely insect which is shown on the opposite page is a native of Eastern India.

Except when viewed with a very strong light, it appears to be dark brown, but when the light is properly directed, it is seen to be of a purple rich almost beyond the power of description. This colour is peculiarly brilliant on the lower wings, the inner edge of which is yellow, as is a patch at the end of the tails. Beneath, although very beautiful, it is not coloured so brightly as on the upper surface. The general hue of the wings is pale brown, profusely barred, mottled, and spotted with black, and there are two silvery spots near the anal angle of each lower wing.

The insect is a native of Eastern India.

THE lower figure of the illustration on page 629 represents our last example of the Lycænidæ.

As its specific name imports, the *Loxura Surya* is a native of India.

Above, the colour of the upper wings is rich, warm dun, edged with dark, blackish brown, which extends quite to the base of the wing. The lower wings have a patch of dark brown near the base, and the interior edge is lighter brown. Beneath, it is entirely dark ochreous yellow. The lower wings are developed at their tips into two long curved tails, which diverge widely from each other in a diagonal line with the upper wings.

FIG. 367.—Myrina Phocides.
(Purple, brown, and yellow.)

This peculiarity is noted in the generic name, the term *Loxura* being formed from two Greek words, one signifying diagonal, or slanting, and the other "a tail."

There are many species of *Loxura,* varying much in colour, but yet adhering mostly to brown, red, and black. Some of them, however, are deep blue, edged with black or brown; and one species, *Loxura Atymnus,* is red and black above, and yellow-brown beneath.

CHAPTER III.

MOTHS.

THE Lepidoptera fall naturally into two great divisions, namely, the Butterflies and the Moths. As a general rule, these may easily be distinguished from each other by two points. First is the shape of the antennæ, which in the Butterflies are straight, inflexible, and terminated by a knob; and in the Moths are often curved, flexible, and end in a point. Many of the Moths have the end of the antennæ swollen into a sort of club, but even in this case the club ends in a point, and is much longer than the rounded club of the butterfly's antenna. There are, however, exceptions to nearly every rule, and this is the case in the present instance. A Georgian Moth, called *Castnia Yucca*, has the antennæ quite straight, and terminated by a knob as bold as that of any butterfly. It has, however, the flexible abdomen, and in this way we are able to decide which it is.

As a rule, the Moths are nocturnal in their habits, but there are many that prefer the dusk or twilight for coming abroad, while there are some, such as the Uranias, which fly in the brightest noon-day, and have the habits as well as the appearance of butterflies.

WE begin with the swift-winged Hawk Moth, of which a singularly beautiful example is here given. This rare and splendid insect is a native of India, the specimen in the British Museum having been brought from Silhet. It imitates the humming birds in the brilliancy of its plumage, and, as Mr. Westwood remarks, possesses even the tufted legs which distinguish many species of these birds. The wings are gold-green, and in the middle of the upper pair is a long patch of gold and crimson, the two colours alternating most beautifully as the insect is moved about. The lower wings do not possess the crimson patch, but are shining green and gold, slightly glossed with blue. The whole of the thorax and abdomen are green, except the front of the thorax, which is fiery copper. Even in the abdomen, however, a coppery gloss is visible in certain lights. The hind legs are remarkable for the long tufts with which they are adorned, and which are composed of much elongated scales. The colour of these tufts is brown.

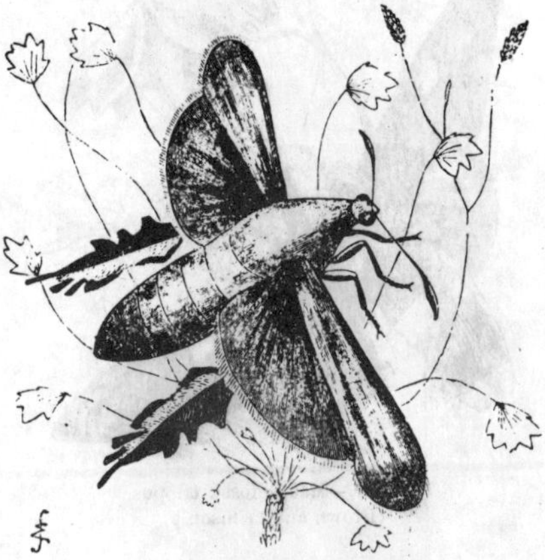

FIG. 368.—Lenyra Ashtaroth.
(Green, gold, and crimson.)

Of this genus only one species is at present known, but there is an allied genus, called Melitta, which very much resembles it, and of which there are many species. Like Lenyra, the hind legs are heavily tufted. The members of this genus are spread over a large portion of the world, specimens having been brought from many parts of Africa, Asia, and Southern America. One of the prettiest is *Melitta pulchipes*, of Venezuela, in which the upper wings are edged with crimson, and the lower are transparent. Generally, bright colours prevail throughout this genus, but there is a curious exception in *Melitta Eurytion*, of Northern India, in which the colours are simply black and white.

THE genus Macroglossa is familiar to English entomologists on account of the well-known Humming-bird Hawk Moth, whose habits make it so attractive to all who are fond of studying the ways of insects.

Of this genus there are very many foreign species, and as a rule they are all of the same sober brown, grey, and black, in which our species is clad. But the present species, which comes from Northern India, presents a bold contrast to its kinsfolk, being adorned with bright and conspicuous colouring.

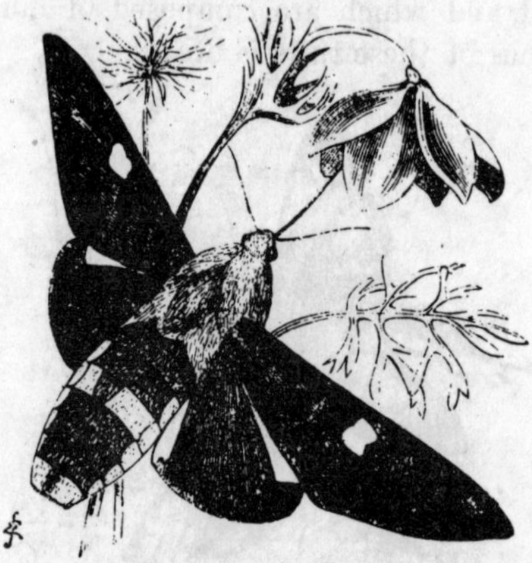

FIG. 369.—Macroglossa triopus.
(Brown and crimson.)

The upper wings are brown, mottled with black, and upon each of them is a square white spot, looking just as if a piece of talc had been let into the wing. The lower wings are black, with a large patch of white on the upper edge, and a rose-red border on the inner margin. The abdomen is splendid rose-red, banded with black, and the under surface of the lower wings is rose-red, like that of the abdomen, but not quite so brilliant. The head and thorax are brown, and upon the latter are some obscure whitish streaks.

ALTHOUGH not possessing the bright colours of the preceding species, *Thyreus Abbati* is a pretty, and even a conspicuous insect when its wings are spread. It is a native of the United States, and the specimen from which the drawing was taken was captured near New York.

Both pairs of wings are olive-brown, changing to olive-green in some lights, and the upper pair are traversed by numerous wavy bands of black. The lower wings are nearly plain, but along their upper margin runs a broad stripe of bright yellow, which is very visible when the wings are spread. There are many species of this genus; one of the most remarkable is *Thyreus Nessus*, also of New York. This insect is smaller in size, has the abdomen banded with white, and the yellow streak

FIG. 370.—Thyreus Abbati.
(Olive-brown, with a yellow streak.)

is replaced by one of blood-red, to which the insect owes its specific name. The classical reader will scarcely need to be reminded that the centaur Nessus was pierced to the heart by the arrow of Hercules, and that his flowing blood is fancifully supposed to be represented by the crimson streak of the lower wings. The generic name *Thyreus* is Greek, signifying "a shield," and is probably given to the insects in allusion to their shape when their wings are closed.

THE genus Deilephila is well known to English entomologists on account of the rare and valuable Spurge Hawk Moth, which is so seldom taken in its perfect state. The generic name is formed from two Greek words, signifying "something that loves the afternoon," this name being given in consequence of the habits of the Moths.

There are very many species of this genus, of which the present is certainly one of the handsomest. The colours of this insect are so complicated that a description is not an easy task. Beginning with the upper wings, the ground colour is a

FIG. 371.—Deilephila daucus.
(Brown, red, yellow, and white.)

very dark, rich, chocolate-brown. From the base of the wing to the tip runs a bold streak of pale dun, and a border of yellow runs round the entire wing. On the middle of the upper edge there is a small but conspicuous patch of white, and a number of very narrow white lines run diagonally across the wing. These lines, together with a mark on the caterpillar, have earned for it the specific name of *lineata*, or "streaked," which has been bestowed on it by some authors.

As to the lower wings, their ground colour is red. Two broad black bands cross the wings, and they are edged with yellow. The thorax is pale brown, with a grey-white streak running down it; and the antennæ are brown, except the tips, which are white. The abdomen is rose-red, barred with black and diversified with white marks.

This is a West Indian species, the examples in the British Museum having been brought from New York, Canada, Mexico, and Jamaica.

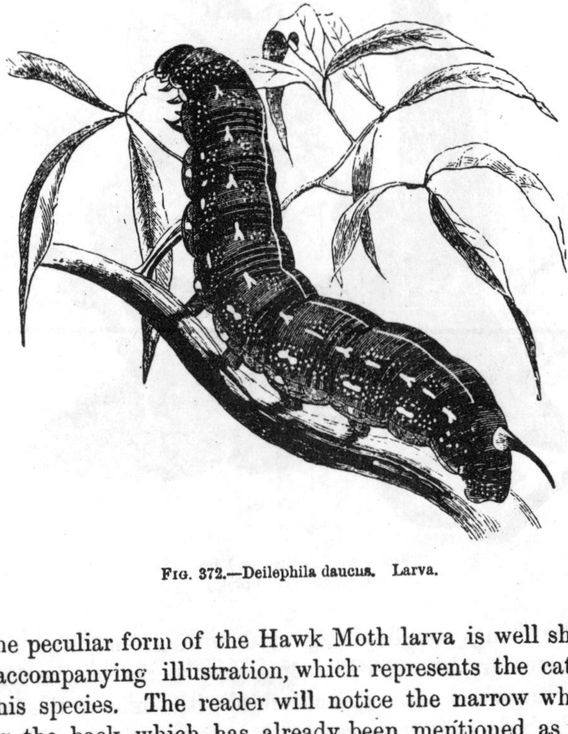

FIG. 372.—Deilephila daucus. Larva.

The peculiar form of the Hawk Moth larva is well shown by the accompanying illustration, which represents the caterpillar of this species. The reader will notice the narrow white line along the back, which has already been mentioned as earning for the insect the specific name of *lineata*.

THE Elephant Hawk Moths are so called because the larva has the power of elongating or contracting the head and first three segments of the body in a way that bears some resemblance to the mobility of an elephant's "proboscis." The generic name *Chærocampa* signifies "swine-caterpillar," and is given to the insect on account of the resemblance in form to the snout of a pig.

The present species has a very wide range of locality, specimens having been brought from Natal, Sierra Leone, Italy, Greece, and Ceylon. It is a handsome insect, the ground colour of the upper wings being pink, on which are a number of black mottlings and grey-white specks. Just at the base of the wings there is a large square mark of very dark olive green.

Fig. 373.—Chærocampa Nerei.
(Brown, green, and pink.)

The lower wings are brown, glossed with green. The thorax and abdomen are brown, with some grey marks on the former, and the margins of the segments edged with white in the latter; the whole body having a pretty silken appearance. Altogether it bears no small resemblance to our Oleander Moth.

It is a very variable insect, both in size and colour, and in some specimens there is little except brown. In all, the colours merge so gradually with each other that it is not easy to define any line at which one colour ends and the other begins.

In the Museum there is an empty pupa-case with the cast larval skin still adhering to it. The original label is preserved, written by the person who reared the insect. It runs as follows: "Oleander Moth: Caterpillar and skin and moth-bread." When I first read the label I was puzzled, knowing bee-bread well enough, but never having heard of "moth-bread." However, it was soon apparent that the writer meant to express that the Moth had been bred from the skins in question.

This specimen came from Sierra Leone, and it is much to be wished that other travellers would take the trouble to rear insects, and to preserve the larvæ and perfect skins as well as the insect "bread" from them.

THE insect which is here given is a native of various portions

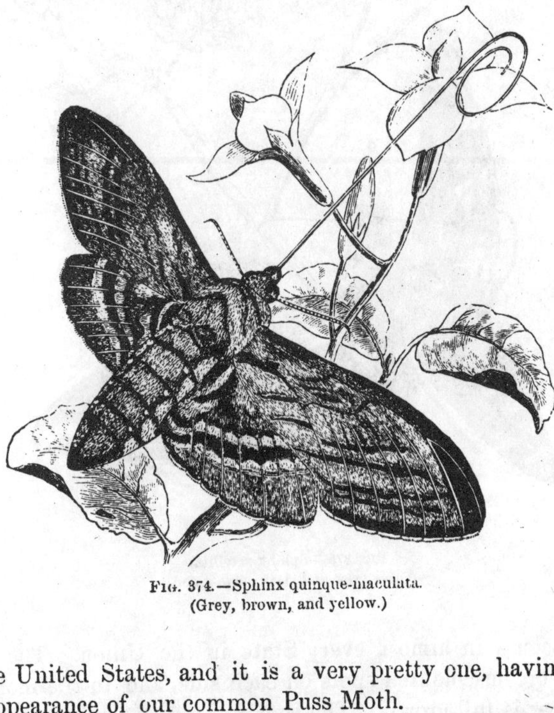

FIG. 374.—Sphinx quinque-maculata.
(Grey, brown, and yellow.)

of the United States, and it is a very pretty one, having much the appearance of our common Puss Moth.

The ground colour is a pale silver-grey, beautifully mottled with chocolate-brown and black; and if the light be favourable, a slight pinkish tinge is seen to be spread over the surface of the lower wings. The abdomen is also pale grey, but a black line runs down the centre; each segment is edged with a thin line of black, and along each side are five large oval patches of yellow, edged with black, and each having a little white spot immediately above it.

The *Sphinx satellita* is here given because it is an insect very plentiful in North America, and is apt to do harm to the grapevine, on which it feeds, unless its numbers are kept down by hand-picking. The following extract is a digest of an article in the "American Entomologist":—

FIG. 375.—Sphinx satellita.
(Olive-grey and dark olive-green.)

"It occurs in almost every State in the Union. The larva has five cream-coloured spots on each side, and in the month of September is full-grown. The eggs are glued firmly and singly to the leaves of the plant. When just hatched, and for some time afterwards, the larva is green, with a tinge of pink along the sides, and with an immensely long pink horn at the tail. This horn soon begins to shorten, and finally curls round like a dog's tail. As the larva grows older, it changes to a reddish brown, and by the third month it entirely loses the caudal horn.

When about to enter the chrysalis state, it enters a short distance into the ground, and soon works off the larval skin, becoming a pupa of a dark brown colour. The moth generally makes its appearance in the June of the following year, though it has been known to issue in the same year, and in these instances it doubtless becomes barren, as is the case with other insects under similar circumstances. The colour of the perfect insect is olive-grey, variegated with dark olive-green, as seen in the illustration.

The reader will note that very curious point in the history of this larva, namely, the gradual change in shape, and lastly, the disappearance of the horn at the end of its tail. The object of these horns, which are common to the Hawk Moth larvæ, is very problematical. The creature never uses them in self-defence, they are not venomous, not very sharp, and in some insects, such as our Death's-head Moth, are blunt and rounded at the tips. Nor is it likely that birds would be afraid of them, for the instinct of birds tells them whether or not an insect be fit for their food. And here we have an instance where, when the larva is very small and inconspicuous, the horn is very long. When it becomes larger and more easily seen, the horn curls up so as to lose all offensive aspect, and when it becomes a large and conspicuous larva, the horn disappears altogether, and leaves the creature defenceless. That the horn must serve some needful purpose is evident by the fact of its existence, but what that purpose may be is at present a complete mystery.

OWING to the exigencies of space, I am reluctantly compelled to have the figure of *Macrosila cruentus* much reduced.

It is a very giant among Hawk Moths, being so large that the specimen in the British Museum can only just be got into a drawer, its tail touching the head of the drawer, and the tip of its enormous proboscis reaching to the foot. The measurement of its expanded wings is rather more than seven inches, the proboscis alone measures nine inches and a quarter, and the total length of the insect is rather more than a foot, thus evidently exceeding the length of our page. The insect is a native of Brazil.

The general colour of the wings is very much like that of our Death's-head Moth, with the exception of a bold yellow patch at the base of the lower pair. The whole of the body is pale grey, powdered with tiny black specks, and each segment is edged with black, while along the sides are five bold patches of orange. The enormous proboscis is very wide and flat at the base, and tapers with a most beautiful gradation to the tip, where it is comparatively small.

I have not been able to obtain any information as to the habits of this rare and splendid insect, but I think, judging by the length of the proboscis, that it must feed on the wing, and obtain its nourishment by thrusting the proboscis into the nectars of some long-belled flower, which could not be reached by the proboscis of any ordinary insect.

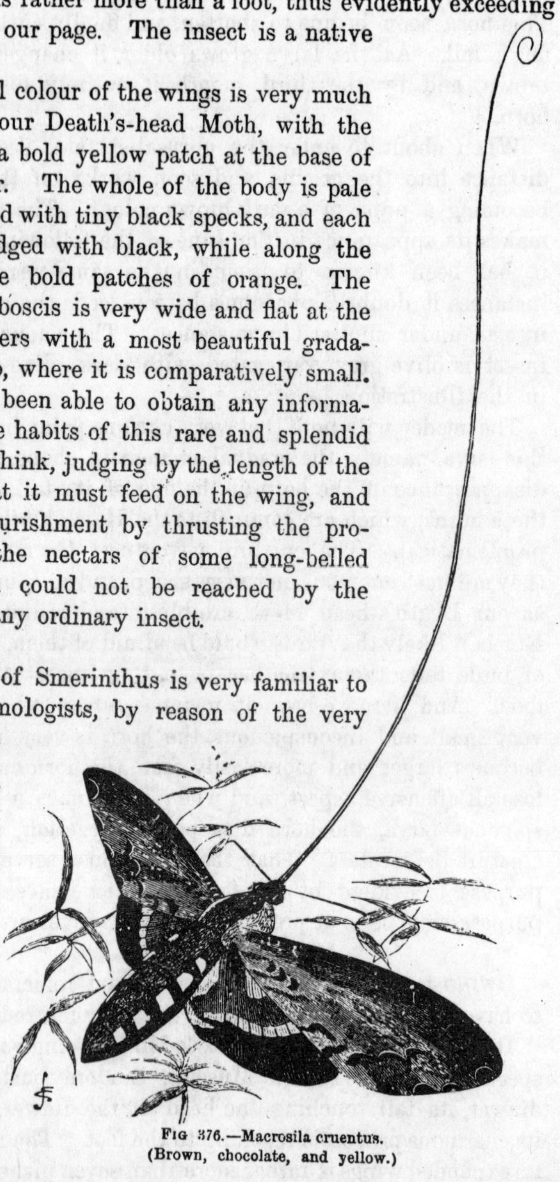

FIG 376.—Macrosila cruentus.
(Brown, chocolate, and yellow.)

THE name of Smerinthus is very familiar to English entomologists, by reason of the very pretty Lime Hawk Moth, which belongs to this genus, and which is so difficult to see as it hangs among the leaves with its wings drooping just like the foliage on which it rests.

The word is Greek, and literally signifies a fishing-line, or a cable.

The insect which is given as the representative of the genus is an inhabitant of Natal, and is a very handsome species, looking, indeed, very much like our own insect greatly magnified. The colours are so mixed with each other that they are not easily described, but they may be briefly taken as follows. In the upper wings there is a large patch of grey-brown, slightly

FIG. 377.—Smerinthus Dumolinii.
(Chocolate, grey, and black.)

mottled and having a narrow bar of darker brown upon it. Then comes a large patch of dark chocolate-brown, in which are two marks of pure white, one nearly round, and the other having a sort of anchor shape. This chocolate patch is interrupted by a jagged bar of the lighter colour, which runs completely through it as far as the upper edge of the wing, where it spreads so as nearly to reach the tip.

The lower wings are grey, and towards the tip of each there is a faintly-marked crescent of pale brown. The body is pale, the edges of the segments being marked with white, and the head and thorax having some large tufts of very long and jetty black hairs.

On Plate XV. Fig. 1 is shown that rather striking insect called *Cœquosa Australasiæ*, which, as its specific name implies, is a native of Australia.

Its colouring is very simple, and yet exceedingly bold and beautiful. The shape of the upper wings is rather remarkable, on account of the peculiarly bold curved edge where they overlap the under wings. Their colour is pinkish near the base, and the rest is brown, with the exception of a large, nearly triangular patch across the middle of the wing, one side of the triangle resting on the upper edge. The under wings are brown, but have at the lower edge a large patch of red extending along the whole edge of the wing, and widening gradually from the tip. This patch is edged with black, and has a most singular effect, strongly reminding the observer of the redstart as it appears with extended wings.

The body is smooth, shining, silken grey, the segments being edged with pink, and a dark chocolate stripe passing along the centre of the thorax.

We now come to those beautiful Moths the Uranias. They look very much more like butterflies than moths, and, indeed, were until quite lately classed among the former insects. Not only do they look like butterflies, but they possess all the habits of butterflies, being diurnal, and flying quite high in the full rays of the sun. There are very many species of Urania, spread over a considerable portion of the globe. The generic name of *Urania* signifies "heavenly," and is given to these insects partly on account of their high-flying habits, and partly by reason of their splendid colouring, which places them among the most magnificent of all the Moth tribes.

I will briefly describe the colours of the two species which have been selected as examples.

The insect which is here shown really looks too gorgeous for a Moth, the brilliant colours which adorn its wings being of

PLATE XV.

metallic brilliance, and shifting about with every change of light. The ground colour of the wings is velvet-black, variegated with glittering emerald-green marks disposed as seen in the illustration. The lower wings are also velvet-black, but they are crossed in the centre by a broad bar of singularly bright

FIG. 378.—Urania orientalis.
(Black, emerald, and crimson.)

colouring. First it is bright blue, which changes to green in the middle of the wing, and that again to crimson. At the anal angle of the wing there is in recent specimens a large eye-like patch of fiery crimson, but unfortunately the colour is as evanescent as it is splendid, and a specimen with this crimson patch in good condition is very rarely seen.

Below, it is quite as handsome as on the upper surface, the colour being metallic blue-green, crossed with transverse black bars. The under wings are copper-red in the centre, the rest being emerald variegated with velvet-black spots.

The insect is a native of Madagascar.

THE next species, *Urania Sloanus,* is an inhabitant of the West Indies, and is quite as beautiful as the preceding insect.

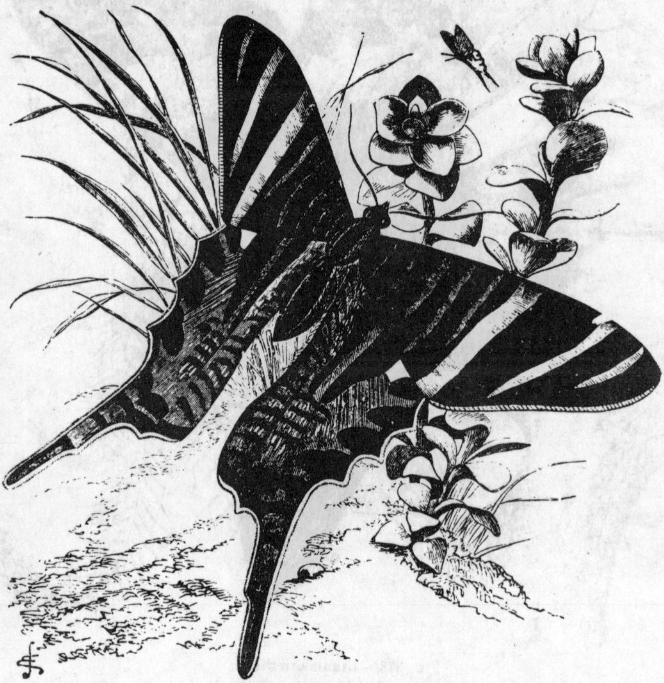

FIG. 379.—Urania Sloanus.
(Black, emerald, gold, and crimson.)

The upper wings are velvet-black, and next the base come five narrow emerald bars. Then comes a broad bar of ruddy gold extending across the centre of the wing, then a narrow bar of the same colour, and lastly, a short stripe of emerald near the tip. The lower wings are crimson glossed with gold and spotted with black, while the tips are emerald-green.

A long and admirable description of this Moth and its habits is given by Mr. Gosse in his work on Jamaica, but want of space prohibits it from being inserted here.

In describing this beautiful insect, the want of adequate means to express colour becomes more and more apparent. Even as it appears in the sober black and white of the printer's ink, it is evidently a striking insect, but in its natural colours it is simply superb. There is but little colouring in the wings, which

FIG. 330.—Cocytia Durvilii.
Wings transparent. Body blue-green.)

are quite transparent and edged with a bold black line, the only exception to which is an orange patch at the base.

It is in the body that the chief beauty lies. The thorax is deep black, and so is the tip of the tail, with the exception of a little patch of gold-coloured hair. The rest of the abdomen is the most brilliant blue, glossed with green, and having a satin-like sheen about it. This beautiful insect is a native of New Guinea.

We now come to the typical genus of the large group called Castniidæ. I may here remark that the best systematic entomologists have long entertained doubts as to the right arrangement, not only of the Moths, but of Butterflies, and that, as I have already mentioned withr egard to the Hymenoptera, an entirely new arrangement seems to be imminent. Even as it is, a month scarcely passes over without some alteration in the relative positions of insects. I have not therefore in this work insisted strongly on any one system, because in a few years it may be superseded by another.

The specimen of *Castnia diva* which is here given is a portrait of the male insect, and is given of its natural size.

Fig. 381.—Castnia diva.
(Brov.n, black, and red.)

The female is twice as large as her mate, and not quite so deeply coloured. The upper wings are of the peculiar brown of a withered leaf, and have a few greyish white spots scattered over them, as shown in the illustration. The lower wings are black, with the exception of a rust-red edging. Behind, the colour is ruddy chestnut.

The specimen which is here figured was taken at Chortales, in Nicaragua.

The figure of the second species is necessarily reduced to half its size, the insect being among the largest of the Castnias, some of which are so large that they look like bats rather than moths.

As is the case with most of these insects, the colouring of *Castnia Zerinthia* is very simple. The ground colour of the upper wings is pale brown mingled with a little white, and a bold black stripe about the middle. The lower wings have a little more colour, the basal half being white, and the rest black mingled

FIG. 382.—Castnia Zerinthia.
(Pale brown, yellow, and white.)

with yellow spots. The thorax is dark brown, and the abdomen white with a number of tiny brown specks. The insect is a native of Brazil.

A SMALL group called the Agaristidæ is illustrated by two species.

The first is an Australian insect called *Agarista contorta*, and is rather a conspicuous one on account of the boldly contrasted hues of its colouring.

The ground colour of the wings is deep black, and upon them are several bold spots and lines of bright yellow, as seen in the illustration, one deeply curved line running through both wings, and gaining for the insect the specific name of *contorta.* The base of the abdomen is black, and the tip red. It is rather pretty below, the colour being black, and the legs clothed with long crimson down.

This is a native of Australia, and all the insects of the genus, which is a very large one, are Australian. Most of them are brightly coloured, and all have a light tip to their tails. As a

FIG. 383.—Agarista contorta.
(Black and yellow.)

rule, the Agaristas are black and yellow, but there are exceptions, such as *Agarista agricola,* which is black, with spots of emerald-green, yellow, blue, and scarlet.

OF the genus Alypia only two species are known, both of them belonging to North America.

The generic name is Greek, signifying "harmlessness;" but its application to the insect is not very easy to see unless it refers to the larva. The colour of this insect, like that of the preceding, is very simple, being entirely yellow and black. The former colour is deeper on the upper than on the lower wings, and is arranged in symmetrical spots, two on each wing, which have given to the insect the specific name of *octomaculata*, or

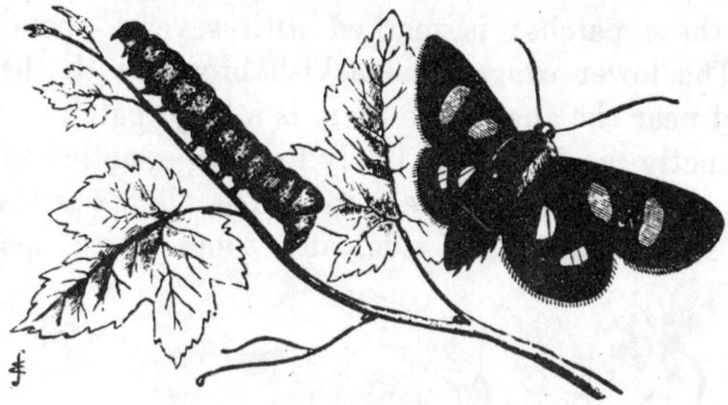

FIG. 384.—Alypia octomaculata. (Black and yellow.)

"eight-spotted." There is a stripe of similar yellow on each side of the thorax.

THE group of Moths called the Zygænidæ is familiar to English entomologists on account of the well-known Burnet Moths, which, although not large, are among the most beautiful of British insects. Why such a name should be given to these Moths, or indeed to any insect at all, is more than I can understand, for the word, which is Greek, signifies a kind of shark, and is used by Aristotle in that sense.

FIG. 385.—Eunomia hæmorrhoidalis. (Scarlet and black.)

The accompanying insect is a beautiful example of the Zygænidæ, and loses none of the prestige of its family. The wings are transparent, but are edged with black. The head, part of the thorax, and the middle of the abdomen are black, and the rest of the abdomen is rich scarlet, this colour gaining for the insect the specific name of *hæmorrhoidalis*, or "blood-stained." The end of the abdomen has a peculiarly soft, velvet-like appearance. The insect is a native of Brazil.

ALTHOUGH not so brilliantly splendid as the preceding species, the insect which is here given is a very handsome one. The ground colour of the upper wings is glossy olive-green, crossed by the nervures, which are black. On each wing there are two patches of black, one near the base and the other near the tip. Each of these patches is marked with several spots of clear white. The lower wings are blackish brown, with three white spots, and near the anal angle there is a large patch of blue, not very distinctly marked, and likely to escape notice unless the insect be held in a favourable light. The thorax is black, with a white streak on either side, and some white spots. The

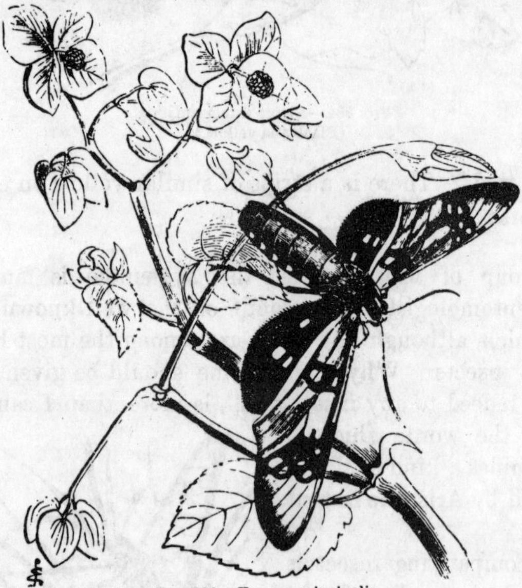

FIG. 386.—Eupyra principalis.
(Olive-green, black, and white.)

abdomen is very beautifully marked, being black, with a gold-coloured ring on the edge of each segment, and a row of snowy white spots along each side.

The insect is a native of Mexico.

THE beautiful though simply coloured insect which now comes before us is a native of Venezuela.

It has a very peculiar aspect, owing, as far as I can make out, to the shape of the wing-scales. At first sight the wings look as if they were transparent, but a closer examination shows that, although they are not so opaque as the wings of Moths usually are, they are yet not sufficiently transparent to allow anything to be seen through them.

The colour is a rather dull but pure and very soft white, with a kind of downy look about it. The wings are edged with

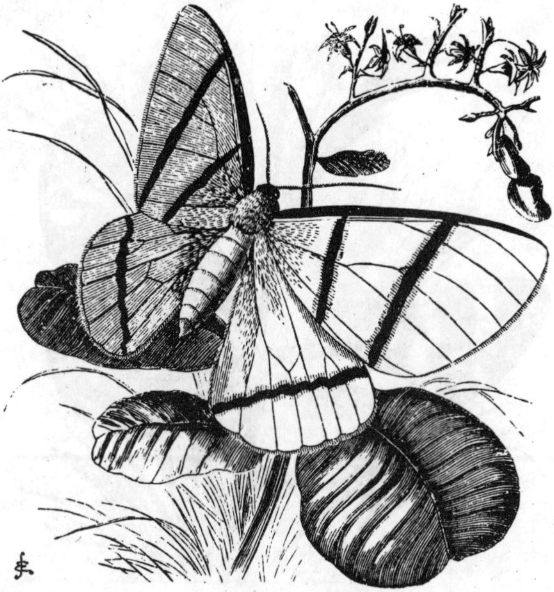

FIG. 387.—Carpella districta.
(White and brown.)

pale brown, and are covered with rather indistinctly marked bars of the same colour, as shown in the figure. It is rather remarkable that a Moth called *Genussa celerenaria*, a native of Pará, is exactly like the Carpella except that it is very small—not being larger than our common "Orange-tip."

THE reader will probably have noticed how widely the phenomena of imitation prevails among insects, and how close is the resemblance, not only in form but in colour, and generally in manners. Take for example a recent instance, *Eunomia hæmorrhoidalis*, and see how closely it resembles the Clear-wing Hawk Moths, and how closely they in their turn imitate bees hornets, wasps, gnats, and other insects; the resemblance extending to their habits and even their movements, as well as to shape and colour. The family of Pericopidæ, which belongs to the great group of Bombycidæ, is remarkable for the closeness with which its members imitate the Heliconias, just as the Uranias imitate the tailed Papilios. They are all West Indian insects.

FIG. 388.—Pericopis angulosa.
(Deep brown and yellow.)

The species which is here figured is a native of Venezuela, and, as will be seen, resembles the Heliconias in colour as well as in form. The ground colour of the wings is very dark blackish brown, with a dash of chocolate in it. The lighter portions of the wings are warm chestnut, with the exception of the spots at the tip of the upper wings, the bar and spot which immediately follow, and the upper part of the bar that crosses the middle of the wing. All these are bright yellow.

THE insect which comes next on our list was taken at Waigiou, an island of the Eastern Archipelago, and is one of the species that was brought to England by Mr. Wallace.

On the upper surface it is a handsome and boldly-coloured insect, but on the lower surface its beauty is an absolute surprise. The ground colour of the upper wings is deep velvety black, with a tapering bar of crimson across the centre, and a large triangular patch of the same colour at the base, shading off into yellow. The lower wings are black and orange, the colours being arranged as shown in the illustration. If, however, it be turned over and held in a strong light, its beauty is marvellous.

FIG. 389.—Bizarda optima.
(Black, crimson, and yellow.)

At first sight it seems to be coloured as above, but when a side light falls upon it, both pairs of wings are seen to be of the most brilliant metallic blue as far as their centre, the colour being quite as splendid as that of any of the Morpho Butterflies. Even the legs are of the same splendid blue. An allied species, *Bizarda clarissima*, of Ara, is black and white except the base of the wings and the whole of the head and body, which are rich blue-green.

A BEAUTIFUL Brazilian insect is here given, both of its names being more appropriate than is generally the case. Its colour, though very simple, is very bold, and makes it quite a conspicuous insect. The only colours are yellow and black, and, as may be seen by reference to the illustration, are so equally divided that it is not easy to decide which is the ground colour.

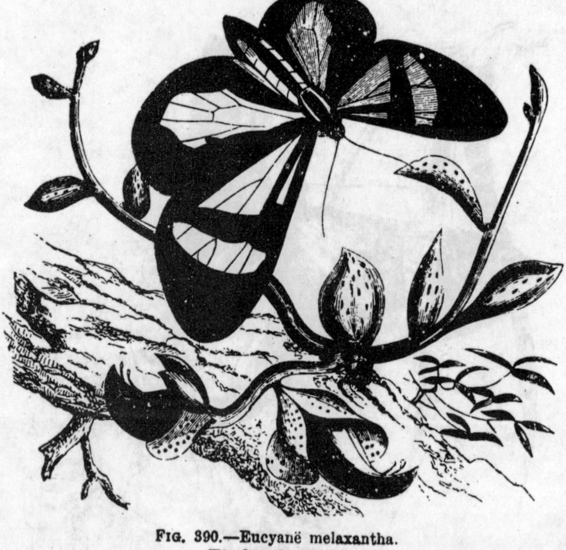

FIG. 390.—Eucyanë melaxantha. (Black and yellow.)

The generic name *Eucyanë* is formed from two Greek words, one signifying "beauty," and the other any dark colour, especially one which has a dash of blue in it. The specific name *melaxantha* is also formed from two words signifying "black and yellow." For my part I should like to see all generic names formed from the Greek, and all specific names from the Latin; and in this case the name would have been *Eucyanë nigroflava*, or *flavopicta*, which would have been a prettier title than *melaxantha*, and quite as descriptive.

THE insect which is known as *Eucyanë glauca* is a very remarkable one, on account of the striking variation to which it is subject. Of the series of specimens in the British Museum, all but one are coloured as follows:—

The ground colour of the wings is black, the basal portions of both wings being gold-green glossed with blue, the colours changing their relative positions in a strong light. In the centre of each wing is a slightly-curved bar of rich crimson. The body is of the same splendid colour as the base of the wings, except that the abdomen is banded with black.

FIG. 391.—Eucyanë glauca.
(Black, green, and crimson.)

But there is one specimen which has the band across the wings white instead of crimson. When I first saw this, I naturally took it for a variety, but was informed by Mr. A. H. Butler—who, like most of the officers of the Museum, is most liberal of information to those who wish for it—that the specimen in question was really the typical insect, and that either the others must be varieties, or that they must be separated into two distinct species. The difference of appearance is singularly striking, the white-banded specimen having quite a plebeian look among its companions, the blue and green of the base of the wings not being set off by their complementary colour, which enhances the brilliancy of both.

The specific name *glauca* refers to the green colour which has been mentioned. There are seven species of this genus in the British Museum, and all are natives of South America.

In the Moth which now comes before us, we have an example of the kind of nomenclature to which I have just referred. The generic name *Euschema* is formed from two Greek words signifying a beautiful form or outline, and is given to the insect on account of the bold and graceful outline of its wings. The specific name *flavata* is Latin, and signifies something that is coloured with yellow but is not wholly yellow.

FIG. 392.—Euschema flavata.
(Black, white, and yellow.)

The ground colour of both pairs of wings is black, which in a strong light is seen to be glossed with purple. The large light patches at the base and near the tip of the upper wings, and in the middle of the lower wings, are nearly white and partly translucent. The remainder of the spots are yellow. The body is black, banded with the same colour, and the front of the thorax is also yellow, so that the name of *flavata* is a very appropriate one. There are many species belonging to this genus, and the present one is a native of Timor.

In nearly all the members of this genus, purple, more or less vivid, asserts itself as the ground colour.

In most of these it is of so deep a hue that it appears to be black, except in a favourable light; and also, as a general rule, the lighter portions of the wing are yellow. There are, however, some, as in the present case, where the purple is sufficiently vivid to show itself with a moderate light. The rest of the wing is nearly white, except in the middle, where it is yellow.

FIG. 393.—Euschema Bellona.
(Purple, white, and yellow.)

Still, even in this species, the characteristic purple and yellow are the leading colours.

This is a very widely spread species, being found distributed over the greater part of India and the neighbouring parts.

THERE is a great variety of colouring displayed in the Moth called *Præsos Mariana.*

Its name, by the way, is as bad as that of *Euschema flavata* is good, simply because it conveys no idea to the mind of the reader. Anyone who was absolutely unacquainted with the latter insect, and who had a slight acquaintance with Greek and Latin, would gather at once from the two names that it was gracefully formed, and that there was a good deal of yellow about it. But no idea whatever is conveyed in the present insect. In the first place, the generic name *Præsos* is—at least to me—a sound without meaning. *Præsos* signifies "a presi dent," and the word might perhaps have some occult meaning; while the name *Mariana* might as well be any other name.

The ground colour of the wings is black. In the upper wings there is a narrow waved line of pale green near the base, another of similar form just beyond the large central patch, and all the other markings are white. The black has a slight gloss of green

FIG. 394.—Præsos Mariana.
(Black, white, yellow, and pale green.)

in a favourable light. The lower wings are deep yellow, marked with black, similar to that of the upper wings. The thorax and base of the abdomen are black, and the rest of the abdomen is yellow, banded with a narrow band of light brown at each segment. It is an Australian insect, and at present is the only species known of its genus.

THE handsome insect which is here shown fully deserves its title of *pulchella*, or "beautiful." It is a native of Northern India, and the specimen which is here figured was taken at Silhet.

It is one of the insects which are difficult to describe, because its colouring is not only gorgeous but intricate, and the effect when the insect is at rest is so different from its aspect with outspread wings, that when two specimens are placed alongside of each other, one "set" as if flying, and the other with closed wings, they would scarcely be recognized as belonging to the same species.

We will begin with the upper wings. The ground colour is velvet-black, crossed with a number of narrow streaks of shining, glittering, emerald green. On the wing are a number of white stripes and patches, and there is one point which requires

FIG. 395.—Erasmia pulchella.
(Black, green, orange, and yellow.)

special notice. I have already mentioned the conspicuous difference between the appearance of the insect in two different attitudes. This is partly due to the general outline of the insect, which is heart-shaped when the wings are closed, but chiefly to the shape and colour of one of the markings on the upper pair of wings. If the reader will refer to the figure, he will see that at the base of the wing there is a white patch, followed by a grey stripe, and then by a curved bar of a light colour. Now this bar is bright orange, and when the wings are closed, these bars form a continuous collar-like mark, and have a singularly conspicuous effect.

The lower wings are brightly coloured. At the base they are

green, which presently gives place to yellow, and then to black on the edge; the nervures retaining their green colour and giving a series of green lines to the very edge of the wing.

On Plate XV. Fig. 2 is pictured an insect which, even under the exigencies of printer's ink, shows itself to be a conspicuous one. Its very appropriate name is *Cyclosia sanguifera*, and it is a native of Northern India.

The ground colour of the wings is glossy black, and upon the upper pair near the base are a number of circular spots of yellow and blue. On the rest of the wing is drawn a complicated pattern of stripes, looking just as if they had been painted with blood. The lower wings are black from the base to two-thirds of their length, and are adorned with circular spots of vivid blue. A broad band of the same blue occupies the edge of the wing, and on it is a row of white spots.

The generic name *Cyclosia* is formed from a Greek word signifying "a circle," and is given to the insect on account of the many circular spots upon its wings. The specific name *sanguifera* is a Latin word signifying "blood-bearing," and refers to the red stripes on the upper wing. When the insect is at rest its outline assumes a beautiful shape. The under wings are completely covered by the upper, the spots and streaks forming a most singular and striking pattern.

In the British Museum are two empty cocoons of an allied species, *Cyclosia subcyaneus.* They are of slight material, rust-red, and from their angular shape have evidently been attached to a branch.

There are many species of the genus Hypsa, and in most of them the chief colours are yellow and grey.

The present species is remarkable for the difference in appearance between the sexes. The figure represents the female, which is coloured as follows. Both pairs of wings are from the base to two-thirds of their length pale yellow, edged with white and sprinkled with black spots. On the edge of the wings is a band of pale brown, very broad at the tips of the upper pair, and narrowing gradually to the angle of the lower pair. This band is traversed by narrow grey streaks, showing the course of the nervures. The male has the yellow part of the wing much smaller than the female, and on the lower wings is a large and

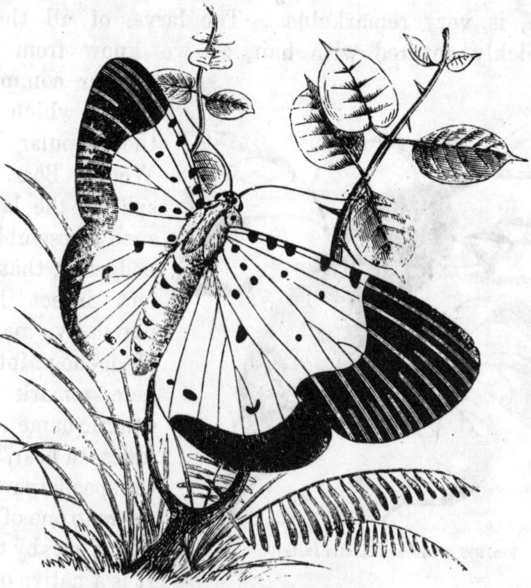

FIG. 396.—Hypsa orbicularis. Female.
(Pale brown, yellow, and black.)

nearly circular patch of greyish brown. This mark has earned for the insect the specific name *orbicularis*, or "circular." The insect is a native of the East Indies.

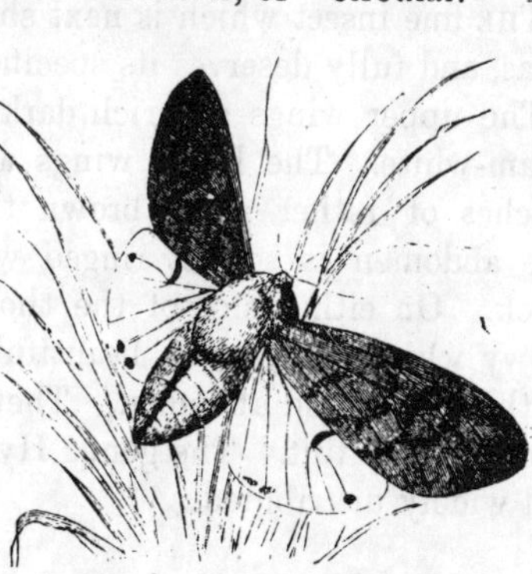

FIG. 397.—Arctia Isabella.
(Pale brown.)

THERE is nothing very remarkable in the Moth which is called *Arctia Isabella,* the insect being small, and soberly coloured. The upper wings are pale brown, with a few indistinct dark spots, and the lower wings are greyish yellow, with some dark spots, and nearly transparent. The legs are red, and the abdomen yellow, spotted with black. The larva, however, which is here shown, is very remarkable. The larvæ of all the Arctias are thickly covered with hair, as we know from the larva of our common Tiger Moth, which goes by the popular name of Woolly Bear. In this species the larva bears such a resemblance to a hedgehog, that the perfect insect has been popularly named the Hedgehog Moth. I may here remark that the generic name *Arctia* signifies "a bear," and that the specific name *Isabella* refers to one of the bears which goes by that name. It is a native of Georgia.

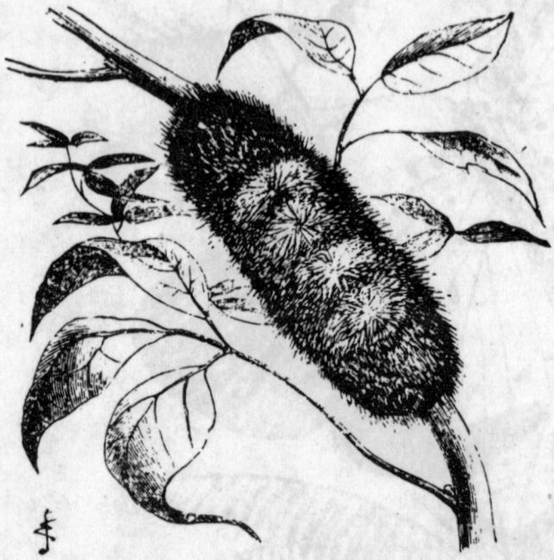

FIG. 398.—Larva of Arctia Isabella.

In the British Museum there is a specimen of the larva of *Arctia hyperborea,* the hairs of which are so long that the insect might well be called the Porcupine Moth.

THE fine insect which is next shown is a native of the Himalayas, and fully deserves its specific title of *imperial.*

The upper wings are rich dark brown, boldly streaked with cream-white. The lower wings are deep yellow, marked with patches of rather paler brown than that of the upper pair. The abdomen is scarlet ringed with black, and the thorax is black. On either side of the thorax is a large pointed tuft of snowy white, contrasting beautifully with the black and scarlet of the thorax and abdomen. There is a little black spot in the centre of the tuft. The genus Hypercampa is a very large one, and widely distributed.

NOT very long before writing this account I was in the British Museum, when a great sensation was caused by the arrival of a new and beautiful insect allied to the Tiger Moths. It was so remarkable that an alteration was at once made in my list, and the new insect inserted. It was found to belong to the genus *Anaxita*, and Mr. A. H. Butler conferred upon it the appropriate specific name of *Sannionis*, i.e. "harlequin," the colours of the insect being exactly those of a harlequin's dress. The insect is a native of Mexico.

So complicated a pattern and such varied colours are not easy of description, except in technical language which would not be understood by the general reader. I will try, however, to make them intelligible. The ground colour of the upper wings is

FIG. 399.—Hypercampa imperialis.
(Brown, white, and yellow. Body scarlet.)

scarlet, changing gradually through orange in the centre to yellow at the base. At the upper edge of the wing there is a large and well-defined patch of bright yellow. The curious pattern at the base and the stripes which run to the edge of the wing are green edged with blue, so that we have here the red, green, gold, and blue of the harlequin's dress.

The lower wings are scarlet and black, very much like the colours of our well-known Cinnabar Moth. On either side of the thorax there is a very long tuft of hair, yellow at the top;

and the abdomen is scarlet above and black beneath, with a line of black running along the centre of the upper surface.

FIG. 400.—Anaxita Sannionis.
(Red, yellow, green, and blue.)

The only other known is called *Anaxita decorata*, of somewhat similar colours, but much paler, and there is more yellow about it.

As may be conjectured from the specific name of the insect

FIG. 401.—Egybolia Vaillantina.
(Olive-green and orange.)

here represented, it is a native of Southern Africa, being named in honour of the traveller Le Vaillant.

There are but few colours in the insect, but they are boldly contrasted; and it is a very handsome though small Moth. The colour of the upper wings is glossy olive-green, darkening into black towards the base. Just beyond the base of each wing there is a broad curved bar of bright orange. The head and antennæ are of the same colour. The lower wings are also dark olive-green, but with a favourable light a decided gloss of blue is perceptible.

BOTH names of the insect called *Asthenia machaonaria* are very appropriate. The generic name is formed from a Greek word signifying "weakness," and is given to the insect on account

FIG. 402.—Asthenia machaonaria.
(Satiny-white and pale brown.)

of the pale and feeble hue of its colouring. The name *machaonaria* is given to it in consequence of its resemblance to our familiar Swallow-tail Butterfly, *Papilio machaon.* Perhaps the title would have been still more appropriate if it had referred to the Podalirius, in which the markings are paler than in the Machaon, and arranged much like those of the present insect.

The ground colour of the wings is very pale, soft, greyish white, with a satin-like gloss on the surface, and over them are drawn several bars of very pale brown, arranged as shown in the illustration. The edges of the wings are marked with a very narrow band of darker brown, and the spots at the tips of the lower wings are dark brown, approaching to black. The insect is a native of Pará.

THE two figures here given represent the male and female of the Processionary Moth, an insect which, happily for us, has not taken up its residence in England. The smaller figure represents the male and the larger the female. The colour is pale brown, with markings of a darker brown, and the female is altogether darker as well as larger than her mate.

The insect derives its name from the singular habits of the caterpillars, which, when full-fed, set off in company to seek a

FIG. 403.—Bombyx processionen.
(Pale brown, marked with dark brown.)

place of repose in which they can pass their pupal state. This journey they accomplish in single file, one taking the lead, the next burying his head in the hairy tail of his predecessor, and so on until a long and continuous line is formed. A sympathetic feeling exists between them, for, if the leader should halt even for a moment, the whole line also halts; while, if one of them be pushed aside, the one next in order moves up in double-quick time, followed by its successors, so as to leave the line unbroken.

These caterpillars are doubly disliked by the people. In the first place they are terribly destructive to vegetation, and in the next, their hairs, like those of several British caterpillars, have a horribly irritating quality, and are said to penetrate through the clothes and so to enter the skin. Some persons aver that they make their way even through thick boots, but this I take

PLATE XVI.

to be an exaggeration. This irritating power remains even in those hairs which adhere to the pupa after it has buried itself in the earth and shed its larval skin.

In its larval state it spins large webs for its protection, just as our Little Ermine Moth does, and even fir-trees are so cut to pieces by these larvæ, that they seem to be nothing but bundles of sticks and webs.

THE larvæ of the group of Moths called Saturniidæ also spin webs, but, instead of doing harm, the webs are utilized—some of the best silks being made from them. I need hardly mention the familiar names of Eria, Arrindy, and Tussore silks, all of which are made by insects of this group.

On Plate XVI. Fig. 1 is given a figure of one of these Moths, called *Attacus Jorulla,* a native of Orizaba, in Mexico. As is the case with most of its kind, it possesses soft and rich, though not brilliant hues, and the general impression caused by it is that of a soft, downy, pinkish brown. Taking this as the ground colour, we find at the base of the upper wings a well-defined patch of which the centre is dun, surrounded first by a line of white and then by a narrow boundary line of black. Through the middle of the wing runs a waved white bar edged with black. Then comes a faintly-defined and very irregular line, the space between which and the edge of the wing is decidedly pink, and towards the tip of the wing is a bold patch of dark brown. The lower wings are coloured in much the same manner, except that a row of dark brown marks takes the place of the narrow waved line. The abdomen is pale brown, and the thorax nearly white.

One point has yet to be noticed, namely, the transparent patch in the middle of each wing, the object of which no one knows. The two young ladies who have been mentioned on page 617 asked that question, which was really a sensible one, and perhaps deserved a better answer than they got, *i.e.* that they were windows through which the insect could see the approach of a foe. But much allowance must be made for the feelings of a scientific man interrupted in his work.

A NORTH AMERICAN species of this group is given. Its colours are much the same as those of the preceding insect, but seem to be more compressed, if I may use that term. The ground colour is rather pale warm brown, slightly speckled with yellow. In the middle of each wing is a kidney-shaped mark of dun with a white centre, followed by a whitish grey band running across the wing. Near the tip of the upper wings is a

FIG. 404.—Samia Cecropia.
(Pink-brown, yellow, and white.)

bold oval mark of dark brown, followed by a pink bar which extends irregularly to the angle of the wing. The thorax is rich warm chestnut, with a pointed brush of hairs diverging boldly on either side, and the abdomen is of the same hue, but the edge of each segment is marked with white.

IN consequence of the exigencies of space, the figure of *Samia Calleta* is only half the size of the insect itself. However, the reader can form a good idea of the appearance of the insect by doubling in his eye the distance between the tips of the wings, and then tracing an imaginary outline of the Moth. The insect is a native of Mexico.

In colour this has darker and deeper hues than the preceding insect. Taking dark brown as the ground colour, we

FIG. 405.—Samia Calleta.
(Dark-brown, grey, dun, and white.)

find near the base of the upper wings an angular stripe of greyish dun, followed by a triangular spot of grey. A narrow and slightly waving bar of pale dun traverses the whole wing, and then becomes of a much lighter brown, warming to chestnut towards the edge. Both pairs of wings are coloured in much the same way, except that the waving bar which in the upper wings is pale dun, becomes nearly white in the lower wings.

IT is to be supposed that the specific name of *Polyphemus* was given to the accompanying insect on account of the eye-shaped marks on its wings. The Polyphemus of mythology, however, had but one eye, whereas the Moth has four, so that the only mode of accounting for the nomenclature is to consider that one eye is reckoned with each wing. The insect has rather a large range of locality, being found both in North and South America.

The figure represents the male insect, in which the colours are more distinctly shown than in the female, and the marks more closely resemble eyes. I take the description from a specimen in my collection. The upper wings are reddish brown, becoming rather pinkish on the outer edge, and having a narrow pink line running parallel with the edge. A waved mark of a similar hue is near the base of the wing, and near the centre is

FIG. 406.—Telea Polyphemus.
(Pale brown, pink, and yellow.)

a transparent eye-like spot. The lower wings are of a darker colour, and the pink stripe is accompanied by one of a blackish hue. The transparent eye-like spot is about the size of that of the upper wings, but is so surrounded with yellow and black as to bear a singular resemblance to a human eye with dark eyebrows.

The body is of the same colour as the upper wings, and the thorax is clothed with long hairs, which in the male project in two long tufts over the base of the wings. The insect being a very large one, the figure is little more than half its real size.

THE two following illustrations represent an insect very beautiful both in form and colour, the *Attacus* [or *Telea*] *luna* of North

America. This Moth has been bred in England, and might perhaps take its place among the insects which supply silk for commerce. The description is taken from a specimen in my collection. In consequence of the size of the insect, my specimen measuring seven inches across the wings, the figure is necessarily reduced.

The general colour is pale green, with two narrow bars of a darker hue in the upper pair, one being much lighter than the

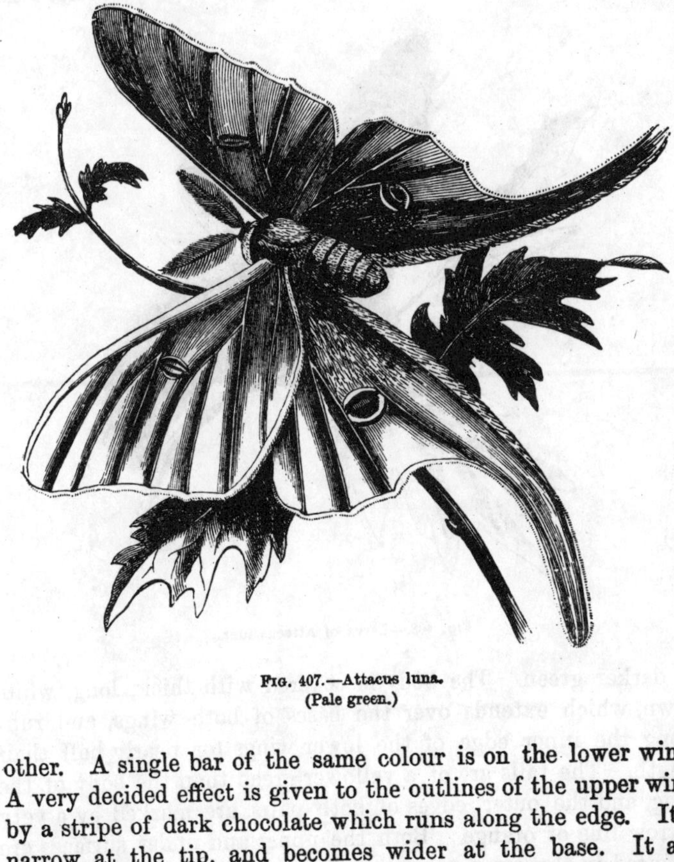

FIG. 407.—Attacus luna.
(Pale green.)

other. A single bar of the same colour is on the lower wings. A very decided effect is given to the outlines of the upper wings by a stripe of dark chocolate which runs along the edge. It is narrow at the tip, and becomes wider at the base. It also crosses the front of the white thorax, so as to produce a very bold effect. The legs are of the same dark chocolate, and so is the narrow line which represents the eyebrow, if it may so be called, of the eye-like spots. These are the only dark parts of the insect.

In this species the transparent part of the eyes is reduced to a scarcely perceptible stripe, and the ground colouring of the eyes may be briefly described as follows. First comes the dark chocolate eyebrow, through which runs a line of pure white, then comes the little transparent streak, and then a patch of dun, separated from the pale green of the wing by a narrow line

FIG. 408.—Larva of Attacus luna.

of darker green. The body is covered with thick, long, white down, which extends over the bases of both wings, and runs along the inner edge of the lower wings for nearly half their length. The tails are of a yellower green than the body of the wing, and the outer edges of both pairs are marked by a very narrow line of orange. Both the upper and under surfaces are coloured in the same manner. The cocoon is about as large as a pigeon's egg, and of a very dark brown.

A SLIGHTLY reduced figure is given on page 675 of another of these silk-producing Moths called *Antherea Pernyi.* The figure represents the female, as may be seen by the shape of the antennæ, which in the male are doubly feathered, and are singularly beautiful.

The general colour of this insect is dun-brown, with a few light and dark streaks arranged as shown in the illustration. As is the case with many of these insects, the outer edge of the wings takes a pinkish hue, and is separated from the rest of the wing by a dark bar. The upper edge is marked by a blackish streak, as shown in the illustration.

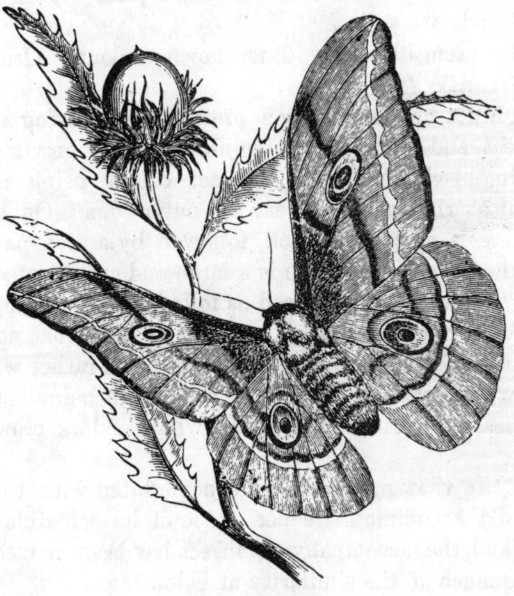

FIG. 409.—Antheræa Pernyi.
(Brown.)

The eyes of both pairs are very similar, except that in the upper pair the transparent portion is larger and more decidedly circular than in the lower pair. The colouring of the under surface is rather lighter than that of the upper, and the place of the dark streaks is taken by a row of dark spots.

The cocoon differs little in colour from the body, and the silk which it furnishes is smooth and strong. I possess specimens of the Moth, the cocoon, and the silk, and the descriptions have been taken from my specimens, which are Chinese.

We have seen many examples of tailed insects, but few in which the tails run to such an extraordinary length as in the *Tropæa Leto,* figured at No. 1, Plate XVII. The insect is a native of the East Indies. This is not the largest species, as it is much exceeded by *Tropæa Mænas* of Northern India.

The colour is very simple, the light parts being greenish yellow, and the dark parts pinkish brown. On the lower wings there is a rather large spot of orange, and near the middle of the upper pair is a large eye-like spot, the upper part of which is dark brown, followed by a black curved stripe, and then by a partly translucent spot. The tails are pink brown, and their widened ends are yellow.

On the same Plate, Fig. 2, is shown a South African Moth called *Ginanisa Isis.*

Though not brilliant, it is a pretty insect, having a soft owl-like aspect, and its colours being almost every possible mixture of brown, black, and grey, the last colour being most predominant at the base and near the outer edge. On the upper wing there is a spot of black, followed by a transparent spot, and on the lower wings there is a large and complicated eye, the colours of which are arranged as follows. In the middle is a transparent spot surrounded with black, and that again by a larger circle of the same hue. Then comes a rather wide circle of yellow, followed by another of pink, both being bounded by black lines. The outer edge of the wings is dark brown.

I presume that my readers are acquainted with that pretty little bird the common Creeper. One of its scientific names is *Certhia,* and the accompanying insect has been named after it in consequence of the similarity of colouring.

In the Moth as well as the bird, brown is the leading colour, but it is so varied and broken up with grey, black, and yellow, that it is impossible to state what is really the ground colour. The outer edge of the wing is yellowish, and the two light patches near the tip are yellow. The series of angular marks are white, and look just as if they had been painted with Chinese white. The base of the upper wings is very dark brown. The insect is a native of Northern India.

The genus Hyperchirea is a very large one, and is spread

PLATE XVII.

over the whole of the West Indies. The species which is represented on page 678 is a native of Guatemala.

As may be inferred from the specific name *rubescens*, or "ruddy," a reddish tint is spread over the wings, and is more conspicuous on the upper than on the lower pairs. The general hue is pale yellow, washed with red, and two pinkish brown lines traverse the upper wings, one nearly straight running from

FIG. 410.—Brahmæa certhia.
(Brown, black, and grey.)

the tip to the inner edge, and the other, a curved line, being near the base.

The lower wings are marked more definitely than the upper pair. The most conspicuous mark is a large circular eye. The spot in the middle is white upon an olive ground; then comes a rather wide circle of black and another of yellow, divided from the brown of the wing by a narrow black line. Of the three curved lines which run parallel to the top of the wing, the outer is pinkish yellow, the next yellow, and the last and innermost dark olive-green. One species, *Hyperchirea lineosa*, is very

FIG. 411.—Hyperchirea rubescens.
(Pink-brown and yellow.)

curiously and prettily coloured, the wings being brown, and marked with lines by the yellow nervures, a peculiarity which has gained for it the specific name of *lineosa*.

AMONG the Moths, examples of imitations seem to be endless. Already we have seen some imitations of the Heliconia butterflies, and here we have one which actually outdoes them in the transparency of its wings. It is a native of Spirito Santo.

It is a most ethereal looking creature, for, as may be seen by reference to the illustration, objects are almost as visible through its wings as if they were made of glass or talc. The colour of the wings is the palest imaginable yellow, becoming rather darker towards the base. Towards the edges some tiny black specks are seen, and similar specks are scattered very sparingly over the whole surface of the wing. They have rather a curious look about them, which, on examination with a magnifier, is shown to be owing to the fact that each speck is a single black scale, very long in proportion to its width. There is a slight yellow line marking the edges of both pairs of wings. I need

FIG. 412.—Heliconisa impar.
(Transparent, black-speckled.)

scarcely say that the colour is exactly the same on both sides. Even the body has a very butterfly-like aspect, as if to increase the resemblance. The thorax has a tuft of long, pale brown down, and the abdomen is brown above and yellow at the sides.

THE genus Clisiocampa is familiar to English entomologists on account of the pretty and variable little Ground Lackey Moth (*Clisiocampa castrensis*).

The present species is spread over a considerable portion of Europe. Like our own insect, it is so variable that to describe it is not an easy task, the description which would apply to one specimen being quite unsuitable when applied to another. The male is smaller than the female, and of rather brighter colours, the upper surface of the first pair of wings having a beautifully gilded appearance, which extends even to the long silken hairs which clothe the thorax and abdomen. This lovely golden hair also runs along the edge of the lower wings, but it cannot be seen without a favourable light, which brings it out in all its radiance

FIG. 413.—Clisiocampa sylvatica and Larva.
(Brown and dun.)

The general colour of the larva is dark black-grey with light grey and yellowish streaks. In the background is seen the web constructed by this larva, which much resembles that which is spun by the larvæ of the common English Lackey Moth.

OWING to the size of the insect, which measures six inches across the wings, the figure of *Ceratocampa regalis* is much reduced in dimensions. It is a native of North America, and is more common than welcome.

The colour of the upper wings is olive, streaked with light red, and the lower wings are rust-red, paling into yellow towards the upper edge. The thorax is rust-red, edged and streaked with yellow, and the abdomen is coloured in the same manner, the edges of the segments being marked with yellow.

As may be seen by the illustration on page 682, the larva is a formidable looking creature, with its panoply of horrent spines. In most places where it lives it is dreaded almost as much as if it were a rattlesnake, and very few can be found who are bold enough to put a hand upon it. The popular name for it is the "Hickory Horned Devil." It feeds upon the walnut and allied trees.

Its colour is greenish yellow, and upon it are patches of black, blue, and orange. The spikes are black and orange. The

FIG. 414.—Ceratocampa regalis.
(Olive, red, and yellow.)

length of the full-grown larva is almost five inches, and its formidable aspect is increased by an odd habit of wriggling its body sharply from side to side, as if to use the spikes as offensive weapons.

THE simply-coloured but beautiful Moth which is figured on page 683 is an Australian insect, and is not very easy of description, in consequence of its strong tendency to variation, both in colour, markings, and dimensions.

Brown is the prevailing character. Upon the upper wings the brown is dark, and near the base are some silvery markings, thrown up by a nearly black irregular streak just above them. A row of similar silvery spots runs from the tip parallel to the outer edge of the wing. The insect derives its specific name from a most intricate and labyrinthine pattern of different browns, which covers the wing, but in so subdued a way that some trouble is needed in order to trace it fully. As this can

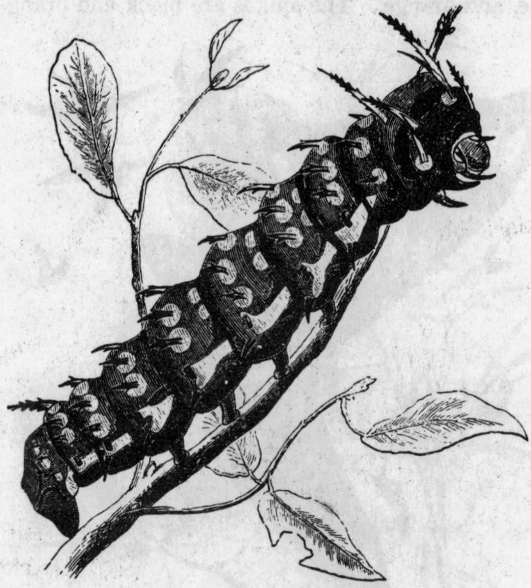

FIG. 415.—Larva of Ceratocampa regalis.

only be done by shifting the insect about so as to change the direction of the light, the artist has indicated rather than copied the marks as they appear in one particular light.

The lower wings are pale brown without any markings, and the sides of the body are fringed with very long brown hairs.

THE genus Xyleutes is closely allied to our Cossus, or Goat Moth, and both insects appear to have somewhat similar habits.

The present species is a native of North America, and as the caterpillar chiefly attacks the black locust tree, it is popularly known as the "Locust Carpenter." In some parts of the country it is so numerous that it has killed whole groves of the trees on which it feeds. It has been found that a tree may be tolerably protected against the insect by smearing the trunk well with soft soap, as high as the brush can reach. This application prevents the female from gaining a foothold, and so debars her from depositing her eggs. The oak, as well as the locust, needs this protection.

The colour of this insect depends much upon the sex. The female, which is larger than the male, is entirely grey, white, black, and brown, while the male is generally darker than the female, and has the hind wings of an ochreous yellow, of which

FIG. 416.—Pielus labyrinthicus.
(Brown and silver.)

colour the female has none. When the caterpillar is full-fed, it spins a cocoon within the body of the tree, and changes to its perfect state about June or July. As soon as it has issued from the tree, its first care is to find a mate, and its second to deposit its eggs. If, therefore, by the application of soft soap or any such substance, the Moths can be prevented from settling on the trunks during June and July, they may be considered as tolerably safe.

I HAVE already mentioned that, owing to the impending changes among the arrangements of the Lepidoptera, the smaller divisions of these insects will not be noticed, and only the larger groups be mentioned. One of these is the Noctuites, of which we shall have several examples.

The first is the beautiful insect called *Euglyphia hieroglyphica,* both names being derived from the pattern which is traced on

FIG. 417.—Xyleutes Robinea. Female.
(Brown, grey, and yellow.)

its surface. The ground colour of the upper wings is pale golden brown, and upon it are bold lines and a dull row of spots. The colour of the lines is shining metallic green, shifting to blue in certain lights, and the spots are dark brown with a gloss of copper. The lower wings are simply pale brown.

The generic name is formed from two Greek words signifying "beautifully written," and the meaning of the word *hieroglyphica* is self-evident. Mr. A. H. Butler tells me that one specimen has been taken in England, but that as this is a West Indian insect, it has probably been brought from Jamaica in the pupal state and developed after its voyage.

ANOTHER beautiful insect is called *Eudryas grata.*

The colouring of this Moth is rather complicated. The ground colour of the upper wings is yellow, changing to creamy white

FIG. 418.—Xyleutes Robinea. Male.
(Brown, grey, and yellow.)

in the centre. The dark border which surrounds the wings is deep purple-brown with a very glossy surface. The lower wings are shining yellow, with a stripe of purple-brown near the lower

FIG. 419.—Euglyphia hieroglyphica.
(Golden brown and green.)

edge; and the body and thorax are also glossy yellow, with purple marks along the centre.

One of the most remarkable points in this insect is the structure of the fore-legs, which are so thickly covered in front with long white down, that they look as if the insect had put its feet into a couple of white muffs, and as it has a way of holding them side by side in front of the head, the effect is very remarkable. The insect is a native of North America, and the larva feeds upon the grape-vine. The generic name is formed from two Greek words, one signifying "beautiful," and the other "a wood-nymph."

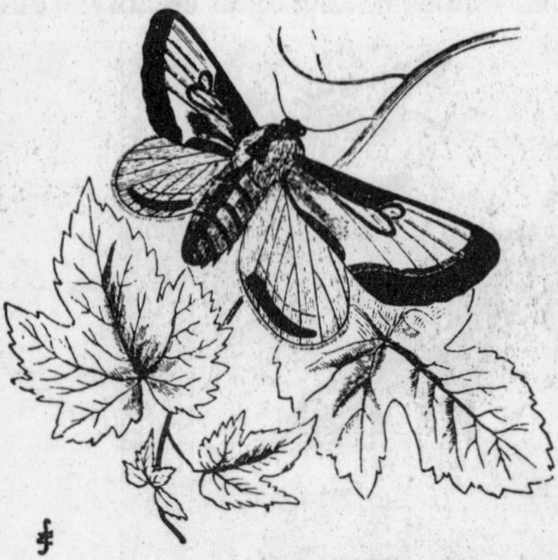

FIG. 420.—Eudryas grata.
(Cream-white, yellow, and purple.)

FIG. 421.—Nyctalea superciliosa.
(Brown.)

THE reader would scarcely think, on looking at the illustration of *Nyctalea superciliosa,* and seeing the simple word "brown" given as applicable to its colouring, that it could possess any beauty. Its specific name expresses the same idea, inasmuch as it is a word which is sometimes used to signify anything that is sad or dull. The generic name, *Nyctalea,* which signifies "nocturnal," also refers to the dull, dark colouring. Yet, that it does possess beauty we shall presently see.

The surface of the upper wings is rather warm brown, covered with a profusion of marks of different qualities of brown. These run transversely across the wing, and look as if incursive waves of colour had washed over the wing and left their marks, just as do the sea-waves upon a sandy shore. The only way to see these marks properly is to hold the insect so as to look along the wing from base to tip. The artist has therefore represented the creature as it appears to an ordinary glance, and indicated a few of the marks only. The insect is a native of San Domingo. The under surface is shining grey.

THE name of the next insect, which literally signifies "sun-fringed," refers to the colouring of its wings, though in this case the word signifies beauty, and not dulness. The genus is a large and very pretty one, shining pink, white, and gold being the leading hues of the wings. None of the species are large, and some are much smaller than the present one.

FIG. 422.—Heliothys armigera. (Pink-brown and gold.)

The ground colour of the upper wings is pink-brown with dark markings, and the light-coloured specks that run parallel to the outer edge are dun. The lower wings are grey-brown, broadly edged with dark brown on the lower and outer edges; while along the upper edge runs a streak of brilliant shining gold. This gold streak exists more or less throughout the genus, and has gained for it the name of "Sun-fringe." The thorax is boldly mottled with brown and white.

There are very few insects which have so large a range of locality as this. There are many specimens in the British Museum, and they were taken in the following localities, which I give in the same order as they occur in the Museum, without any attempt at grouping them :—Europe, Gibraltar, Navigator's Island, Rio de Janeiro, Natal, Congo, Venezuela, Georgia, Australia, Jamaica, Mexico, Northern India, Ceylon.

THE insect called *Praxis corvus* is a native of Tasmania. Its general colour is black, but with a side-light there is a gloss of

FIG. 423.—Praxis corvus.
(Sooty black.)

blue, like that of iron. The specific name *corvus* signifies "a crow," and is given to the insect on account of this blue-black colour, which is just that of the crow's plumage.

The upper wings are boldly scolloped at the edges, and are crossed by three irregular bands of jet black. The lower wings are similarly coloured, but have only two black bands, and along their inner edges is a greyish down. As the nervures are somewhat thick, they become shining in an old and worn specimen, and consequently make it look very different from a young and fresh one. The abdomen is sooty black, with the edges of the segments grey, and the sides rather greyish.

THERE is a group of large Moths called from their sombre colours, Erebidæ. The reader will remember that Erebus was the name given by the ancient Greeks to the lower regions,

FIG. 424.—Thysanira Agrippina.
(Grey, brown, and black.)

which were represented by them to be dark, dull, and sombre. In consequence of the exigencies of space, the insect is drawn of barely half its proper size, the extended wings of the Moth itself measuring about seven inches across. The Erebidæ are South American insects, and the present species is a native of Brazil.

The colour is pale grey mottled and banded with brown and black, and the wings have a curious aspect which cannot be better expressed than by the word "peppered."

The habits of these Moths are very much like those of our large Underwings (*Catacola*). They will sit motionless on the trunk of a tree or any similar surface, the mottled grey, the brown and black of their wings so exactly coinciding with the object on which they rest, that they can scarcely be detected even by a practised eye. Sometimes, when disturbed, it will fly deliberately to some trees, suddenly whirl, and settle so quickly that it is practically undiscoverable. Mr. Gosse mentions that the under side of felled trees is a favourite resting-place for the Erebidæ. Sometimes one specimen takes a fancy to a particular spot, "to which it resorts with such uniformity during its hours of repose, that it may almost with certainty be dislodged on any afternoon by giving a smart rap on the outside of its shelter. Out it rushes with such a startling suddenness, and with so irregular and zigzag a motion, as often to defy capture, even though we are all on the watch for it."

THE handsome and variable Moth called *Brana calopasa* is a native of Ceylon. There is but one species of the genus at present known to entomologists.

Although there is some variety both in the colour and the markings, the insect may be briefly described as follows. The ground colour of the upper wings is pale brown glossed with gold, and the marks which stud its surface are black, edged with white. At the tips of the wings there is a large patch of dark blackish brown, traversed by a narrow white bar. The lower wings are sooty brown edged with white.

FIG. 425.—Brana calopasa.
(Pale gold, brown, and black.)

The thorax is grey with a brown tuft, and the abdomen is black, with a patch of bright grey at its base, and the last few segments are of the same colour. The name *calopasa* is formed from two Greek words signifying "entirely beautiful."

THERE is a small group of Noctuites called Ophiderides, or Snake-backed Moths, of which we shall take two examples. The first is *Ophideres apta*, a native of Santarem. The ground colour of the upper wings is light brown with a pinky gloss, and upon it are multitudinous markings, dispersed as seen in

FIG. 426.—Ophideres apta.
(Pinky brown, orange, and black.)

the illustration. There are also some dark brown spots and mottlings. One of the most conspicuous points in the upper surface is the bold streak of pure white that is drawn across the centre of the wings. The lower wings are more handsome than the upper, their ground colour being orange, with a broad edge and large spot of black washed with purple. A number of white spots run round the outer edge of the wing.

In the Museum is a cocoon of this Moth. It is so wrapped in leaves that it is not easily seen, but in forçing its way out the insect has brought with it a piece of the cocoon, so that its texture is visible. It is very slight in texture, like the finest muslin, and when examined with the aid of a magnifier, is seen to be a delicate lace-like structure, with a sort of indefinite pattern about it.

THE second species, *Ophideres dividens*, is a native of Java. At the base the upper wings are brown, with a wash of olive-green, and a broad band of the same colour occupies the outer edge of the wing. The intermediate space is paler brown,

FIG. 427.—Ophideres dividens.
(Brown, yellow, and black.)

washed with pink. The lower wings are coloured much like those of the last-mentioned insect, except that there is not so much red about it, the ground colour being yellow instead of orange, darkening towards the base. The thorax is soft brown, and the abdomen yellow.

There are many species of Ophideres, and the similarity of colour is so close that it is not easy to distinguish between several of them. There are two, however, which stand out rather conspicuously from the rest. One is *Ophideres Salminia*, a native of India and Java, in which the upper wings are beautifully glossed with shining green. The other is *Ophideres smaragdi-picta,* in which the wings are purple-brown, on which is laid a pattern defined as sharply as if painted with emerald-green. The specific name is Greek, and signifies "emerald painted."

ON Plate XVI. Fig. 2 is seen a Moth called *Phyllodes consobrina,* a native of Silhet.

The generic name is formed from a Greek word signifying "a leaf," and is given to the insect on account of the singularly leaf-life appearance of the upper wings. They are dark brown in colour, and have a line along the centre which looks just like the central rib of a leaf. Towards the tip the brown takes a purple gloss, and there is a doubly curved mark of chocolate in the middle.

The lower wings are dark brown, changing to rich purple, just like that of our Purple Emperor. Towards the anal angle of the wing there is a large spot of bright scarlet, with a white centre. The body is brown, glossed with purple. The reader will see that the distribution of the colours is intended for the protection of the insect. The brilliant scarlet, white, and purple of the lower wings would make it exceedingly conspicuous, but when their glories are veiled under the leaf-like upper wings, the insect becomes scarcely distinguishable from dead foliage.

THE insect which is shown on page 694 is found in India, China, Borneo, the Philippines, and Java.

It is one of the most variable insects, scarcely any two specimens being alike. That which is the subject of the illustration is coloured as follows. The upper wings are dun brown from the base to half their length, and then change to yellowish brown speckled with black. The spots are black, edged with white. A similar division of colour occurs in the lower wings, except that the basal portion is chocolate. In the middle there is a large oval mark of pale blue. The specimen which has been described was taken in Silhet.

ANOTHER inhabitant of Silhet now comes before us called *Nyctipao albicincta,* both names being very appropriate.

The ground colour of both pairs of wings is dark brown,

taking a chocolate hue towards the edges. A bold white belt runs nearly parallel to the outer edge of the wing, and from it diverge a number of streaks of the same colour. The specific name *albicincta*, "or white-girdled," refers to this belt. In the centre of the upper wings there is a large eye-like spot, almost too complicated for description. It looks like a combination of

FIG. 428.—Potamophora manlia.
(Brown, black, and blue.)

the eye-spots on our well-known Peacock Butterfly, some streaks of bright blue occupying the centre, and surrounded with black, chocolate, olive, and dun, all blending together in the most exquisite manner.

There are many species of Nyctipao, but none in which the eye-spot so much resembles that of the Peacock Butterfly. The generic name signifies "Night Peacock," and is given to the insect on account of this peculiarity.

THE insect which next comes before us is Australian.

It is a very beautiful species, and curiously variable. The ground colour of the upper wings is a light chocolate, taking a pinkish hue towards the tips, and being covered with a multi-

FIG. 429.—Nyctipao albicincta.
(Dark brown, white, and olive.)

tude of little brown marks. From the base of each wing a bold streak of white runs towards the tip, and is edged on either side with black. Five stripes run from the tip of the wings to the inner edge, one being straight and the others wavy. The colour of these stripes is very variable, ranging from white to yellow.

FIG. 430.—Calliodes orbigera.
(Chocolate and crimson, or yellow.)

On the middle of the wing is an eye-like mark, coloured as follows. In the centre is a crescent-shaped spot of dark brown, edged with black, and being surrounded with a circle of chocolate. Then comes a black circle, then a white one, and lastly a very narrow white line separating it from the chocolate of the wing. The under wings are either crimson or yellow, crossed by continuations of the stripes of the upper wings, and the end of the abdomen is either yellow or crimson, according to the hue of the wings.

THERE is scarcely a more curious Moth in existence than that which is here figured. It belongs to a group called Sphingomorphas, or Sphinx-shaped Moths, and affords another example

FIG. 431.—Sphingomorpha fulgurifera.
(Reddish brown and grey.)

of the imitative forms so often seen among insects. The resemblance which is borne by these insects to the Hawk Moths is so remarkably close that anyone who saw a Sphingomorpha for the first time would be nearly certain to rank it among the Hawk Moths rather than to place it in its proper position.

The upper wings of the insect are divided into two totally distinct portions by two shades of brown. The upper half of the wing is light chestnut, and the lower dark brown, the line of demarcation running from tip to base. Upon the wing are drawn a number of beautiful silver-white lines, as shown in the illustration. The lower wings are dark brown, and in the middle there is a triangular patch of a lighter hue. The abdomen is light brown, barred with a darker hue.

The strangest part of the insect is to be found in the tail, which is furnished with a large brush of brown and grey hairs, the former occupying the upper and the latter the lower portion. The appearance of the tuft is curiously like that of the Brush-tailed Porcupine. The hairs, which are, in fact, nothing but developed scales, are exceedingly long and flat, and are widened at the ends so as to resemble very much elongated battledores.

There are many species of this group, mostly Brazilian, but none so large as this. Mr. A. H. Butler describes a very fine species which he has named *Tarsolepis remicauda*, a native of Java, and has given an admirable figure of the insect as it appears in life, clinging to a twig, so that the double tail-tuft displays its peculiar construction. The specific name *remicauda* is Latin, signifying "oar-tail," and is given to the insect because the long tail-hairs with their widened and flattened ends look very much like oars.

FIG. 432.—Achæa Chameleon. (Brown, olive-grey, and white.)

THE CHAMELEON MOTH well deserves its name, for it is so exceedingly variable in colour that two specimens can scarcely be found which are exactly alike. It has a tolerably wide range of country, the specimens in the British Museum having been brought from almost all parts of Southern and Western Africa.

The specimen which is here figured has the upper wings chocolate brown from the base to nearly half their length, the remainder being browns of various shades. The lower wings are brown, with a spot of grey in the middle, and some white marks on the outer edge. This, however, is only one out of the twenty-five specimens in the British Museum, in which the colours of brown, grey, olive-green, chocolate, and white are so indifferently spread over the surface that it is hardly possible to decide upon any particular specimen as the type of colouring.

THE Moth which is here figured inhabits India, Ceylon, Sumatra, and Java, and is a pretty though not conspicuous insect.

The upper wings are olive-brown and pink, arranged as follows. First comes olive-brown, extending from the base to nearly the middle of the wing. Then comes a pink bar, extending completely across the wing; and the rest is olive-brown, with the exception of a curved pink stripe stretching from the lower edge nearly, but not quite, to the tip. The lower wings are brown, edged with a paler hue, and having a yellow patch in the middle.

FIG. 433.—Ophiusa fulvotænia.
(Brown, pink, and yellow.)

There are many species of this genus, one of which—perhaps the most remarkable in colour—has not yet been described. The upper wings are rich deep brown, with a slight blue gloss. Across the middle of each wing is drawn a broad diagonal bar of chalky white, so arranged that when the wings are closed the bars unite and form a saddle-shaped mark over the back. The wings are edged with a row of little chalk-white marks like the cogs of a wheel. As the thorax is red, the appearance of the insect when at rest is sufficiently remarkable.

The specific name *fulvotænia*, or "tawny-band," refers to the reddish bar across the upper wings.

THE generic name of *Trigonodes* is Greek, signifying a triangle, and is well applied to all the members of the genus. The triangle is the chief character of the insects, no matter where they may live. They are found in India, China, Africa, Australia, and Jamaica. None of them reach any great size, the present species being, as may be inferred from its name, the largest of the genus. There is but little diversity in colour among them, brown, chocolate, yellow, and grey being the prevailing hues.

FIG. 434.—Trigonodes maxima.
(Brown and yellow.)

In the present species the ground colour of the upper wing is pale yellowish brown, on which are placed three bold marks of dark chocolate-brown. The lower wings are yellow-grey, and the two pointed stripes upon them are rather dark brown. This species comes from Hindostan.

FIG. 435.—Cardamyla carinentalis.
(Orange, grey, and purple.)

OF the great and important group of the Pyralidæ we can take but two examples, the first of which is called *Cardamyla carinentalis*, and is a native of Australia.

It is one of the many insects which require a favourable light before their beauties are appreciated. At first it looks as if it were simply coloured with black and orange, but with a good light it is seen to be really a splendid example of colouring.

The ground colour of the upper wings is sooty brown, with a glossy silky surface, and upon it are a number of lines of shining grey glossed with gold. The lower wings are orange, with a spot and broad edging of a colour which at first sight appears to be black, but is really of the deepest purple, with a velvet-like texture. Only two species of this genus are as yet known, and both of them are Australian.

THERE is a small and most splendid group of Pyralidæ called Margarodidæ, or Pearl Moths, because the ground colour of their wings is exactly like mother-of-pearl both in colour and in iridescence. It is scarcely possible to imagine anything more magnificently dazzling than a collection of these Moths, one of the largest of which is the present species, a native of Domingo.

FIG. 436.—Lypotigris reginalis. (Pearl and purple.)

The ground colour of the upper pair of wings is rich deep metallic purple, washed with green, and, as is often the case with insects, there are some lights in which it looks simple dark brown. Upon this wing are drawn three bars of lustrous, opalescent pearl. This latter colour forms the ground hue of the lower wings, whose only other adornment is an edging of the same deep metallic purple as that of the upper wings. The thorax is mottled black and white, and the abdomen is barred with the same colour, thus accounting for the generic name, which signifies "Wolf-Tiger."

One of the most curious of the group is *Phakellura hyalinotatis*, of South America. With outspread wings it is very triangular in shape, and the wings are glossy in the middle, with an edging of gold-brown. The tail is ornamented with a tuft of diverging oar-shaped hairs, almost exactly resembling those of the Sphingomorpha. The generic name, which literally signifies "bundle-tail," refers to this peculiarity.

As all entomologists know, the group of the Geometridæ is so enormous that only a few characteristic species can be selected as representatives. The name signifies "land-measurer," and is given to the insects because the caterpillars do not crawl when walking, but double themselves up in an arched form, and proceed as if they were engaged in measuring the ground. From

FIG. 437.—Erebomorpha fulguraria
(Brown, yellow, and grey.)

the shape which they then assume they are popularly called Loopers. A full description of them will be found in "Insects at Home," p. 446.

In the present genus the resemblance to the Erebus Moths is so close as to earn for the insect the name of *Erebomorpha.* The ground colour of the wings is brown, covered with minute pencillings of paler brown, grey, and yellow. Over both wings is a curious, irregular jagged pattern of greyish white lines, which has given to the insect the name of *fulguraria.* or Lightning Moth. There is a tuft of yellow at the base of the thorax, which, with the abdomen, is brown.

THIS is really a difficult insect to describe. As long as there is any definite pattern, that pattern can be traced. As long as there is any definite colour, that colour can be indicated. But there are cases, as with the present insect, where exists neither definite pattern nor colour, and where the powers of description are utterly baffled. Without a figure no description could be of the least service, and, even with it, I can only offer the following approximation to a description.

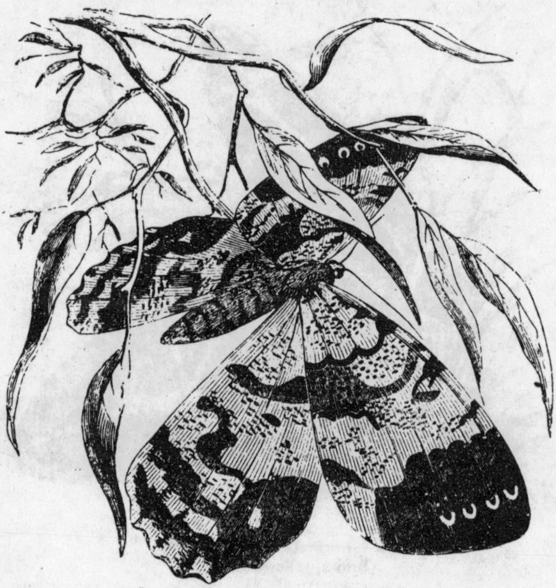

FIG. 438.—Elphos hymenaria.
(Yellow, brown, grey, and black.)

Take your Moth and wet it. Take some pepper-boxes, and fill them respectively with raw and burnt umber, gamboge, Indian ink, Chinese white, and sepia. Shake them indiscriminately over the Moth, let the colours all run together on the wet surface, and these will be a good representation of the ordinary colouring of this insect. Perhaps the yellow may be the predominant colour, or perhaps the white, or the black. It does not in the least matter, for the actual insects exhibit just such eccentricity of colouring, and it is absolutely impossible to say definitely what the ground colour really is. Some specimens are almost entirely sooty brown, others are mostly grey, like lichens; in others the yellow predominates, while in some the prevailing characteristic is a series of black blotches and spots.

It is equally variable in size, and in this insect sex has nothing to do with the variation, some of the smallest specimens in the British Museum being females. This specimen is a native of Northern India.

THE delicate-looking insect which is here represented is a native of Sarawak, and belongs to the small family called Micronidæ.

The colour is a peculiarly soft, creamy white, with a kind of sparkle upon it here and there as if powdered glass had been thinly sprinkled over the wings. On the upper wings are six transverse stripes of the palest brown, four being long stripes and the other two short. On the lower wings are two stripes and a few pencillings of the same hue. The only positive colouring in the insect

FIG. 439.—Micronia astheniata. (White and pale brown.)

is found in the little black spots along the edge of the upper wings, and the short streaks on the edge of the lower wings.

The specific name *astheniata* signifies "enfeebled," and refers to the paleness of the colours. Another species, *Micronia justasia*, of New Guinea, is almost exactly like this insect, except that it has three brown bands on each wing. There are twenty-nine species in the British Museum.

THE genus Panagra is a very large one, and is mostly African or Australian, from which latter country the present species was brought. Generally they are dull coloured and small, and this is the only one which takes the eye at a first glance.

FIG. 440. Panagra tricolor.
(Brown, yellow, and orange.)

From the base to the centre the colour of the upper wings is dark brown. Then comes a stripe of greenish yellow, and the rest of the wing is chocolate-brown. The lower wings are dark brown, and in the centre there is a large patch of warm orange.

THE genus Abraxas is familiar to all English entomologists on

FIG. 441.—Abraxas tigrata.
(Orange and black.)

account of the Magpie Moths. On taking out the drawer containing this genus, it is rather startling to come upon our Currant Magpie and Clouded Magpie, looking like old friends in a strange land.

The present species is a native of Northern China. In common with most insects of this genus, it is much liable to variation, as may be seen by inspecting the four specimens in the British Museum. In one of them the ground colour is entirely orange. In another, both pairs of wings are edged with orange, the centre fading into greyish white; and in the two others the upper wings are entirely orange and the lower are grey, edged with orange. In all the spots are black.

The body is orange banded with black. The insect is called *tigrata* because it bears some resemblance to the Tiger Moths.

WE now come to the beautiful group of the Erateinas, which look so much like butterflies that a casual observer would be nearly certain to mistake them for those insects. They are mostly Brazilian, and in some respects remind the observer of the Catagramma butterflies, some of which have already been described. Some species are tailed, while others have the hind wings simply rounded.

FIG. 442.—Erateina leptocircata.
(Brown, green, and orange.)

The present is an example of the tailed Erateinas. The upper wings are olive green at the base, changing gradually to dark brown at the tips. Across the centre runs a band of pale, shining yellow-green. The greater part of the lower wings is orange, paling to yellow at the end of the tails, and having a dark brown stripe on the outer edge.

This species inhabits New Granada. Another species, *Erateina Julia*, somewhat resembles it, except that each of the lower wings is traversed throughout its whole length by a bold, wavy, black stripe.

As several of the Erateinas are remarkable for the beauty of the under surface, two species will be given, so as to show both surfaces of each.

FIG. 443.—Erateina lineata. Upper surface. (Dark brown, green, red, and yellow.)

The first is *Erateina lineata,* a native of Bogotá. The upper surface of the upper wings is dark brown with a peculiarly glossy surface, and across the middle is drawn a streak of pale green, very much like that of the preceding species, but a trifle brighter and with more green in it. From the base of the lower wings to the centre or beyond it, the colour is dark brown, traversed by a number of yellow lines, which have earned for the insect the specific name of *lineata.* The remainder of the wing is red, but the width of the red edging is exceedingly variable.

FIG. 444.—Erateina lineata. Under surface.

The under surface of the upper wings is rich warm chestnut, with a narrow gold-brown streak running parallel with the outer edge. A bar of pale green coincides with the mark on the upper wing. The lower wings are chestnut, warming into bright red near the tips, and upon them are drawn a number of golden lines disposed as shown in the illustration. Round the edge of the wing are alternate spots of very dark brown and bright yellow, so that the under surface of the insect is very much handsomer than the upper.

FIG. 445.—Erateina regina. Upper surface. (Copper-red, silver and gold, and white.)

THE last of these beautiful insects is *Erateina regina*, one of the rarest and, as far as is at present known, the handsomest of the group. There is only a single specimen in the British Museum. It is a native of Bógotá.

Although the upper surface of this insect is handsome, it has not much to distinguish it from the other species of the same genus. The upper wings are rich copper red, becoming darker towards the edge, and there is no green mark across them as is usually the case with the Erateinas. The lower wings are olive brown for half their length, when they are crossed by a narrow wavy line of bluish white, followed by a very wide bar of black-brown, edged with snowy white.

FIG. 446.—Erateina regina. Under surface.

On the under surface the upper wings are silvery grey at the base, followed by chocolate. Near the outer edge of the wing is an indistinct bar as of powdered silver, and across the middle stretches a bold and well-defined bar of burnished silver. The lower wings are olive-brown at the base, traversed by gold lines. Through the middle runs a broad silver bar edged on either side by a line of ruddy chestnut. The next portion of the wing is powdered with gold, and the rest is rich chocolate brown, edged with snowy white.

THE last of the Moths which can be described in this work is *Nelcynda rectificata*, a native of Darjeeling, in Hindostan. This is the only species at present known.

FIG. 447.—Nelcynda rectificata.
(Brown, white, and grey.)

The ground colour of the upper wings is soft grey-brown towards the base, becoming darker near the tip. A little roundish spot of white is near the middle of the wing, which is crossed by several narrow bands of the same hue. A row of small dark chocolate-brown spots runs parallel with the outer edge of both pairs of wings.

The lower wings are very pale grey-brown, nearly translucent towards the base, and they are transversely pencilled with a brown very slightly darker than the hue of the wings.

HEMIPTERA;

OR,

HETEROPTERA.

HEMIPTERA;

OR,

HETEROPTERA.

BOTH these titles are used as names of the next order of insects, and both are appropriate. The former word signifies "half-wings," because the upper pair, which are analogous to the elytra of the Beetles, are partly hard and opaque, and partly membranous and diaphonous. The word Heteroptera signifies "different wing," and is given to the insects because the upper wings are partly opaque and partly transparent.

The mouth of these insects is modified into a piercing and sucking apparatus which may be called its beak; and there are some species in which the beak is so sharp and strong that it can inflict a wound on the human skin which, for a time, is nearly as painful as the sting of a wasp. Details of this organ may be found in "Insects at Home."

We will now pass to the foreign species of Hemiptera, taken in the order which they occupy in the British Museum, which arrangement can but be considered as a provisional one.

OF all the variable creatures in the world, commend me to the insect called *Cimex* (or *Tectocorix*) *Banksii*. It has a very wide range of locality, having been taken in Java, New Caledonia, Australia, Timor, the Celebes, and Tonga.

The specimen which is here figured is coloured as follows. The ground colour of the insect is yellowish brown, and the marks upon the elytra are either blue or green, according to the light, and are glossed with gold. The marks on the thorax are purple. As for the other specimens, here are a few examples of variation: scarlet, barred with black; blue, edged with green; orange, with a few brown pencillings; yellow, spotted and edged with green; all scarlet; all brown. And, as if to carry variation to its furthest extent, some specimens are not half as large as others.

FIG. 448.—Cimex [or Tectocorix] Banksii. (Almost any colour except black or white)

HERE is another insect called *Scutellaria nobilis*, a native of India and Siam.

Above, the insect exhibits every imaginable shade of blue and green, varying from deep violet to emerald. In many cases the colour, whether it be blue or green, is so deep that no spots are visible upon it. When, however, the spots are visible, they are always black.

No matter what may be the colour of the upper part of the body, the under surface is invariably scarlet barred with black, and the legs are scarlet as far as the tibia, which, with the tarsus, is black.

FIG. 449.—Scutellaria nobilis. (Violet, green, and black.)

IN the insect called *Phlœa corticata*, there is little room for variation, the colour being pale brown.

It is an odd-looking being—the sides of the head, thorax, and abdomen being flattened until they are thinner than the paper on which this book is printed. Each segment of the abdomen is cut into a toothed form at the tip, and the combined outlines are exceedingly graceful. They are so thin as to be partly translucent, and the only opaque portions of the insect are those which are occupied by the vital organs and covered by the wings.

Fig. 450.—*Phlœa corticata.* (Pale brown.)

The general appearance of the insect so closely resembles that of a piece of dead bark or withered leaf, that it really seems wonderful how such an insect could have been detected at all. Only a few species of this genus are known, and they are all Brazilian.

Fig. 451.—*Catacanthus incarnatus.* (Brown, black, and scarlet.)

The insect which now comes before us is rather widely spread, the specimens in the British Museum having been taken in India, Ceylon, Malacca, the Celebes, Java, Siam, and Borneo.

Like many of its kin it is exceedingly variable, not only in the colour, but in the number and shape of its markings. The specimen which is figured is red, with a kidney-shaped black mark in the middle of each elytron. The ends of the wings are dark blue-brown.

Some specimens have a large black oval spot on the two upper angles of the scutellum, while others have the ground colour brown or dun. But, no matter what may be the colour of the upper surface of the elytra, the under surface is always red.

FIG. 452.—Edessa cornuta.
(Grey, brown, and yellow.)

THE insect which is here given is a native of Pará, and the specimen from which the figure was drawn was brought to England by Mr. Bates.

It derives its specific name *cornuta*, or "horned," from the shape of the thorax, which is prolonged on either side so as to look like a pair of horns. The colour of the thorax is rather variable, being in some specimens pale brown and in others greyish olive. The scutellum is yellow, and the upper part of the body azure. The upper wings are brown with a purple gloss, edged with golden yellow on the upper margin. Below it is yellow pencilled with black.

The genus is West Indian, and is a very large one, more than one hundred and thirty species being known.

BOTH names of the accompanying insect are descriptive, one of its form and the other of its colour. The name *Brachystethus* is Greek, signifying "short-breasted," and is given to the insect on account of the shortness of the thorax. The Latin name *rubromaculatus* signifies "red-spotted," and refers to the large red spots upon the black surface.

These indeed are the only colours. The ground hue is shining black with a green gloss, and the other portions are bright scarlet. The scutellum is very deeply punctured, and the rest of the surface slightly so. The colour below is exactly the same as it is above. The insect is a native of Brazil.

On Plate XIX. Fig. 3 is seen an insect with some external resemblance to *Edessa cornuta*. It is a native of Sarawak, and its name is *Pygoplatys lancifer*.

The oddly-shaped thorax is blackish brown, changing to yellow in front. The scutellum is also brown, and is lengthened behind into a curious double spike like two fingers laid side by side. The ends of the wings are very dark brown, and the flattened abdomen, which projects on either side of the wings, is barred black and brown.

Fig. 453.—Brachystethus rubromaculatus. (Black and red.)

The peculiar beauty of the accompanying insect cannot be seen until the wings are spread. Above, its colour is soft brown tending to chestnut, and very finely punctured. When the wings are spread, the upper surface of the abdomen is seen to be deep velvet-black, on which is a tesselated pattern of rich panelled brown, the two colours looking much like those on the sides of our common cockchafer.

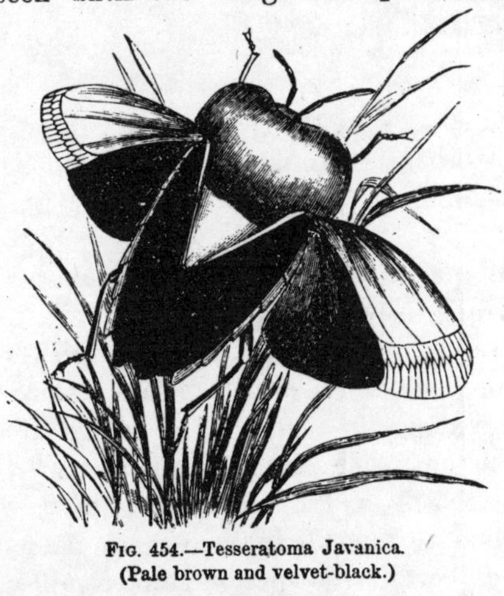

Fig. 454.—Tesseratoma Javanica. (Pale brown and velvet-black.)

As its name implies, it is a native of Java, but is also found in India. The genus is also spread through the Philippines, Celebes, Timor, Malacca, and Burmah. There are between twenty and thirty species.

THE name of Atlas is given to the next insect because its enormous thorax bears some resemblance to that of the Atlas Beetle.

It is a curious looking creature, being very much flattened, and the thorax developed into the singular form which is here given. This part of the insect is very shining, and has a few punctures sparingly scattered over it. The scutellum is brown, and so is the end of the wings, while the body of the wings is

FIG. 455.—Amissus Atlas.
(Yellow-brown.)

yellow. There are only two species of the genus, and both are natives of Singapore. The other is *Amissus nitidus,* and is entirely shining yellow-brown.

ON Plate XIX. Fig. 4 is depicted an insect called *Oncomeris flavicornis,* a native of Australia, New Guinea, and Ava.

It is a very handsome creature. The thorax is black, thickly punctured, and the very long scutellum is of the same colour, with a yellow mark running along its centre. The wings are blue, with a yellow pattern upon them, changing to fiery copper at their tips. The legs are black, and the hind pair are very widened—a peculiarity which is denoted in the generic name, which signifies "swollen legs," while the specific name signifies "yellow-horned," and is given to the insect because the antennæ are bright yellow

PLATE XIX.

THE pretty insect called *Sephina formosa* is a native of Venezuela.

The general colour is black with a violet gloss, and upon it are sundry markings of red disposed as seen in the figure. The thorax is fringed with black hair. Below, it is mottled with black and scarlet, and along the sides run a row of scarlet wedge-like spots, with a black spot in the middle of each.

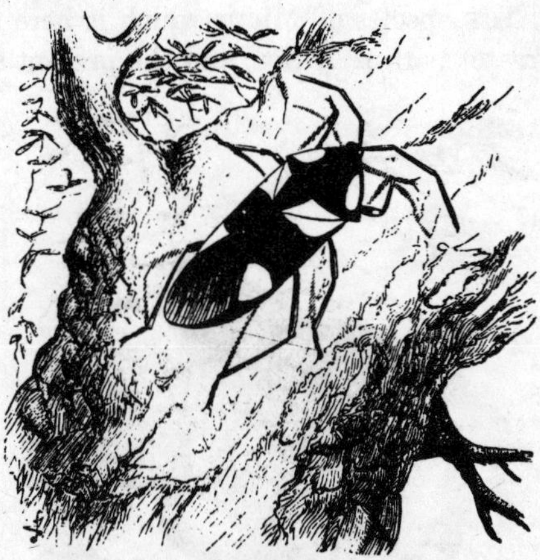

FIG. 456.—Sephina formosa.
(Black and scarlet.)

Two figures are given of *Dalader acuticosta*. One is seen on Plate XIX. Fig. 2, in order to show its appearance with closed wings; while in the accompanying illustration a figure is given with the wings spread as if in flight.

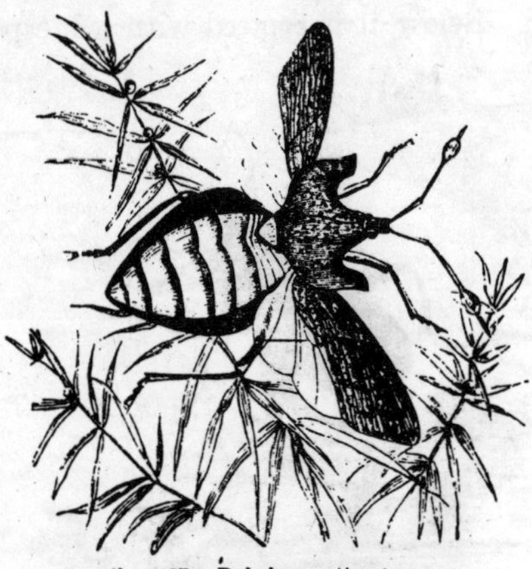

FIG. 457.—Dalader acuticosta.
(Brown and yellow.)

Although its colours are simple, being only various shades of brown and yellow, it is a really pretty insect. It is flat, with the abdomen very much dished, and the whole of the surface is marked with the two colours already mentioned. The thorax is covered with tiny spikes, just like that of a very small spider-crab, and these spines make the sharp ends of the thorax rather formidable. The specific name *acuticosta*, or "sharp-ribbed," refers to this structure. Towards the end of the antennæ is a round flattened plate. The insect inhabits India, Burmah, Borneo, and Siam.

THE species of Mictis which is here shown is spread over the greater part of Africa, and the present species has been selected on account of the singular shape of the hind legs, which has earned for the insect the specific name of *curvipes*, or "curve-footed."

FIG. 458.—Mictis curvipes.
(Grey-brown above, red-spotted below.)

The general colour of the upper surface is dark grey-brown, profusely punctured. The thorax comes into a spike at each angle, and the antennæ are black, changing to red at the tips. When the wings are spread, two spots of yellow are seen on the upper part of the abdomen. Below, it is spotted with red, especially on the sides of the thorax. The thigh of the hind legs is thick, massive, boldly curved, and furnished with several sharp spikes.

FIG. 459.—Mictis symbolica.
(Brown, with yellow cross on back.)

ANOTHER and rather striking example of the same genus is here given. It has a very wide range of country, specimens in the British Museum having been taken in Australia, New Caledonia, New Hebrides, Celebes, and Ceram.

Above, its colour is brown, dark towards the head, and light towards the extremity of the body. Bold yellow lines are distributed in such a way on the back, that when the wings are closed they assume the form of St. Andrew's cross, and thus give rise to the specific name *symbolica.* When the wings are opened, the abdomen is seen to be reddish above, and below it is pale brown.

BOTH names of the following insect refer to the shape of its hind legs. The generic name is formed from two Greek words, one signifying "a flat plate" and the other "a leg." The specific

FIG. 460.—Petascelis remipes.
(Brown, yellow, and chocolate.)

name is Latin, and signifies "oar-footed." It is a native of Southern Africa.

The thorax is brown edged with yellow, and having a stripe of the same colour down the centre. The wings are chocolate-brown, deepening at the tips. Below, it is brown slightly mottled with yellow. The most conspicuous point in the insect is the structure of the hind legs, which are very large, flattened like an oar-blade, and are edged on the inside with a coating of thick red down.

In many of the Hemiptera the two sexes can easily be distinguished by the hind legs, the thighs of which are large in the male and small in the female. This is the case with *Molchina compressicornis*, which is a native of Pará.

The general colour of this insect is velvet-black, with a number of metallic emerald-green scales. If examined by the

Fig. 461.—Molchina compressicornis
(Black, with emerald spots.)

aid of a magnifying glass, these scales are seen to be gathered thickly round certain centres. This is most conspicuous on the wings. Their ground colour is brown, powdered with golden scales, and upon each is a velvet-black spot surrounded with several rows of the most brilliant emerald scales.

The ends of the wings are bronze, and below it is purple-brown, changing to pinkish on the sides. The antennæ are black, except the first half of the flattened portion, which is yellow.

Flattening in unexpected places is one of the principal characteristics of the Hemiptera, in which the legs, the antennæ.

the thorax, the abdomen, and sometimes the whole body, are as flat as if they had passed between rollers.

In the genus Metapodius, of which the present insect—a native of Brazil—is a good example, the hind legs are the portions affected. The colour of the insect is a dull red-brown, much like that of a cockroach, the former hue predominating in a line along the middle of the hind legs. In those limbs the thigh is round, while the tibia is quite flat, except a narrow red ridge which traverses the centre. All the legs are armed with

Fig. 462.—Metapodius latipes. (Reddish brown.)

many spikes on the inner edge. It is a very odd-looking insect, and when the large hind legs are stretched at right angles with the body, its aspect is absolutely ludicrous. Below, it is brown flecked with white.

In the two following illustrations the same insect is represented in the perfect and larval stages. This is a Mexican insect, and in either stage of existence is very handsome. The principal colours are scarlet and black. This bold contrast of colours is well shown on the flattened portions of the antennæ, one half of which is scarlet and the other half black. The wings are velvet-green, traversed with shining yellow stripes.

and at the tips they change to copper-green. The lower wings

FIG. 463.—Pachylis gigas.
(Green, scarlet, and black.)

are shining purple, and the upper surface of the abdomen is

FIG. 464.—Larva of Pachylis gigas.
(Black and scarlet.)

scarlet. Beneath, it is dull white. These colours are exceedingly brilliant even in the dried specimen, but in the living insect must even be more vivid.

The larva is coloured very much like a harlequin, the whole of the creature being alternately red and scarlet, with the exception of the undeveloped elytra and the spots along the back, which are bright yellow.

ANOTHER species of the same genus is here given. This is a native of Orizaba.

Without being so gorgeously coloured as its relative, it is a very handsome insect, and is remarkable for some peculiarity

FIG. 465.—Pachylis acutangulus.
(Black, orange, and purple.)

of form. The flat plate on the antennæ is half yellow and half black. The thorax is dark brown, and the wings are black, traversed with orange lines. Towards the tips they become olive green with lines of metallic coppery red. The males have the thighs of the hind legs very much thickened and armed with sharp spikes. The most characteristic point in this insect is, however, the structure of the abdomen, which is much flattened, and has each segment developed into a sharp point, as is indicated by the specific name, which signifies something which has sharp angles.

On Plate XIX. Fig. 1 may be seen a representation of *Diactor bilineatus.* The former of these words signifies a conductor, or steersman, and is given to the genus because the hind legs are flattened so as to resemble the peculiar oar or paddle with which the ancients, who had no real rudders, were accustomed to steer their vessels.

It is very variable in size and colour, but as a rule it is dark red-brown, with two yellow stripes on the thorax and passing over the head. The upper surface of the abdomen is green. The flattened blades of the hind legs are reddish, tipped with yellow, and having several yellow spots upon them, mostly, but not always, four in number. It is a remarkable fact that even the larva has the flattened hind legs.

The genus Chariesterus appears to be exclusively a South American one, and, as far as is known, all the existing species came from that part of the world. None of them attain any great dimensions, the present species being the largest. The figure is slightly magnified in order to show the peculiarities of colouring and form.

Fig. 466.—Chariesterus mæstus. (Reddish brown.)

The general hue of the upper part of the body is red-brown, and that of the extremity of the wings is dark brown; the antennæ, with their flattened joints, being of the same hue. The lower wings are translucent. The upper surface of the abdomen is velvet-black, and its edges are white.

When its wings are closed, the accompanying insect bears a singular resemblance to our common Wasp Beetle (*Clytus arietis*).

The colour of the upper wings is brown, with two yellow patches, and crossed with a bar of translucent material. The body is dark brown, barred with yellow, and so shaped that when the insect is seen in profile with spread wings, it looks almost exactly like one of our common sand wasps. It is a native of New Guinea, and one of the many insects that were captured there by Mr. Wallace. The figure is slightly enlarged.

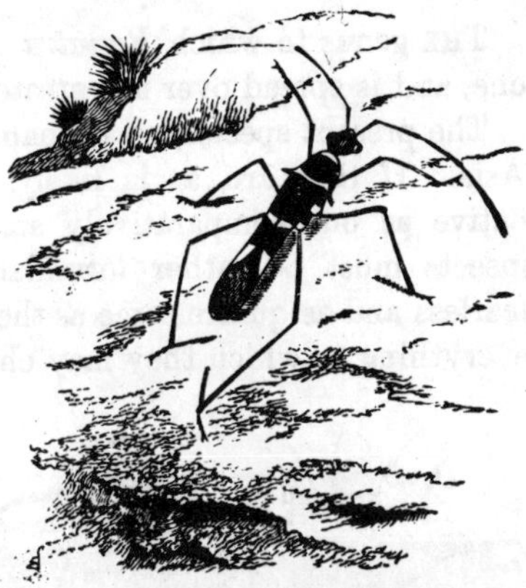

Fig. 467.—Marcius generosus. (Dark brown and yellow.)

It has been already mentioned that many of the Hemiptera are flattened in various places. In the next insect, the body is very much flattened, and the limbs are greatly elongated. It is a native of India, Siam, Java, and the Philippines.

The general colour of this insect is reddish brown. The upper wings are red at their base, and have a large black spot on the upper edge. At the tip they become dark brown with a blue gloss, and, when crossed

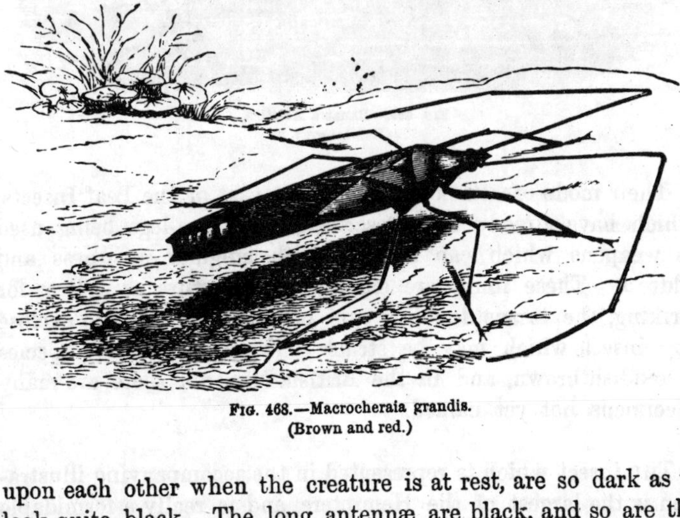

Fig. 468.—Macrocheraia grandis. (Brown and red.)

upon each other when the creature is at rest, are so dark as to look quite black. The long antennæ are black, and so are the legs except the thighs, which are red. The abdomen is very flat and scooped, and is red above. Below, the insect is red spotted with black.

THE genus to which *Ranatra Asiatica* belongs is a very large one, and is spread over the greater part of the world.

The present species, as its name imports, is an inhabitant of Asia. If they are, as is likely, as fierce, voracious, and combative as our comparatively small species, some of the exotic insects must be rather formidable. Our own species are as fearless and as quarrelsome as the great Rove Beetles, and attack everything to which they may choose to take an objection.

FIG. 469.—Ranatra Asiatica.
(Red-brown.)

Their mode of attack is exactly like that of the Leaf Insects, which have already been described, their fore-legs being used as weapons which can be used with singular swiftness and address. These limbs are employed for capture as well as for striking, the tarsus doubling over on the tibia so as to enclose any insect which may be struck. The colour of this species is reddish brown, and in the British Museum there are many specimens not yet named.

THE insect which is represented in the accompanying illustration is the largest of the Hemiptera, and is really a formidable creature. It is here only represented about half its real dimensions, the length of a full-grown specimen being little short of five inches, and the spread wings measuring more than seven inches from tip to tip. It can strike sharply with its fore-legs, capture prey, and draw it to its large, sharp, and powerful beak, which is then driven into the body and the juices sucked. Seeing that several of our little Naucoridæ, to which family this insect belongs, can inflict a painful wound with their beaks, I should think that the Belostoma could not be handled without

FIG. 470.—Belostoma grandis.
(Brown.

extreme care, its beak alone being nearly as long as the entire Naucoris.

The colour of this insect is brown, the thorax having a yellowish edge. Beneath, it is paler than above. This species is a native of Pará.

THE last of the Hemiptera which can be mentioned in this work is the little insect which is popularly known as the Chinch-bug (*Micropus leucopterus.*)

It is a North American insect, and is one of the pests of the country, feeding in its larval state upon the roots of wheat, and sometimes destroying half the crops of a district. On pulling up a wheat-plant, hundreds of the minute eggs may sometimes be seen adhering to the roots, where the mother insect has placed them, having made her way underground for that pur-

FIG. 471.—Micropus leucopterus.
(Blackish ; white wings.)

pose. Fortunately the larva is killed by wet, so that a rainy season will be of the greatest service by destroying the young larva before they are able to produce young in their turn. In droughts, however, the Chinch-bug increases with fearful rapidity, and though the insect feeds chiefly on wheat, it does not disdain other vegetables. In fact, as an aggrieved farmer said of the insect, "nothing comes amiss to it."

The figure is necessarily magnified.

HOMOPTERA.

HOMOPTERA.

THE HOMOPTERA, or Equal-winged Insects, are so called because both pairs of wings are of the same character. The mouth is modified into a proboscis, and the feet never have more than three joints. In our own country the species are but small, and not at all conspicuous, but in other countries they often attain

FIG. 472.—Cicada septemdecem.
(Green; wings edged with brown.)

a great size, and play a conspicuous part in the economy of Nature, mostly as destructive agents.

One of the most celebrated examples of the kind is the insect so familiar in North America under the name of Seventeen-years Locust. It has gained this name from its almost regular recurrence in the same spot once in every seventeen years. It does not appear and disappear simultaneously over the whole country, but takes one district at a time, appearing in vast swarms, doing great damage for a season, and then vanishing until the time for its next periodical visit. In some places its term of re-appearance is thirteen years.

Its colour is green, and the wings are edged with brown.

ANOTHER example of the Cicadas is given on Plate XVIII. Fig. 1, where *Cicada adusta* is mentioned. I very much regret that want of space debars me from inserting a long and very interesting account of the habits of certain species of Cicada, which I had preserved for this work. Suffice it to say that they are tree-feeders, and that the males are remarkable for the loud shrilling noise which they produce by means of an apparatus called the "drum," which is placed in the under side of the thorax, and is covered with a horny plate that can mostly be seen from the upper surface of the insect.

The present species is a native of Siam and Java, and is rather variable. Being a very large insect, the figure is necessarily reduced one-half. In some specimens the wings are wholly translucent, as shown in the illustration, and in others they are spotted with brown at the intersections of the nervures. Their whole surface is extremely iridescent.

THE remarkable insect called *Cystosoma Saundersii* is a native of Australia, and is a singular example of imitation, being almost exactly like the Cystocœlia which has been described on page 342.

In this insect the abdomen of the male is extremely large, and quite hollow, the vital portions only occupying a slight streak of thicker substance on the lower surface of the abdomen. The horny cover of the "drum," to which reference has been made, is seen just at the base of the lower wings. The object of this singular structure is uncertain, but some entomologists think that the hollow abdomen may increase the resonance of the sound produced by the drums.

The female has a much smaller abdomen, but it is solid and opaque, whereas that of the male is quite translucent. The

PLATE XVIII.

general colour is green. The upper wings are pale green, with the nervures of the lower surface traced in a brighter green, and

FIG. 473.—Cystosoma Saundersii.
(Pale green.)

the lower wings are translucent and iridescent. Three species of this genus are known, all Australian.

THE accompanying illustration represents one of the most extraordinary of the insect race, the celebrated Lantern Fly, respecting whose luminosity a fierce controversy has long raged. When Madame Merian first described this insect, she mentioned very graphically its wonderfully luminous properties. Succeeding observers, however, flatly denied the luminosity, and attributed it to mere invention on the part of Madame Merian.

The conflicting accounts, however, can be easily reconciled. In all luminous insects the luminosity is capricious, and only endures for a certain time, so that many persons might observe the Lantern Fly carefully and never see its luminosity. There is, however, no doubt that the creature is luminous, as is shown by the fact that a description of the insect has been written by its own light. There are four luminous spots, two on the upper surface of the abdomen, just below the thorax, and two on the under surface. The former give a purple and the latter a green light. Mr. F. Smith has pointed out that the body of the insect is covered in parts with a white efflorescence, like that of our glowworm.

The wings are brown, with a large eye-like spot on each of the lower pair, and the enormous head is as hollow as the

FIG. 474.– Fulgora laternaria.
(Wings brown and chestnut; head crimson, yellow, and blue.)

abdomen of the Cystosoma, and coloured with the most brilliant crimson, yellow, and blue. In Honduras, this insect is popularly called "La Belle."

WE now come to some of those odd-looking insects which are popularly called Chinese Lantern Flies, and are found in every collection of insects brought from China. It is very difficult to judge of the real colours of these insects, as the hues fade almost immediately after death. The form, however, is of more importance than the colour. Like the Lantern Fly, the head of the accompanying insect, which is a native of Java, is largely developed and hollow. Its chief peculiarity is the manner in which it is covered with multitudinous spikes, short, sharp, and sturdy, the use of which it is difficult even to conjecture. The colour of the wings is brownish green, spotted with black.

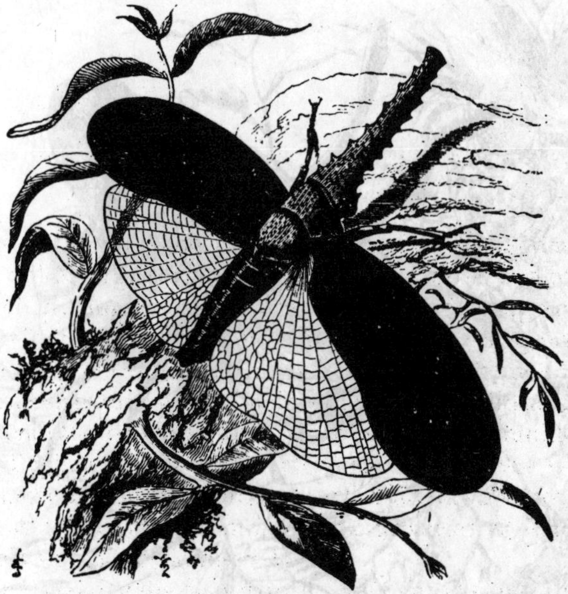

FIG. 475.—Pyrops nobilis.
(Brown, green, and black.)

There are many species of this genus found in Africa, India, and Ceylon, and they vary much in dimensions, some being no larger than the common house-fly.

ANOTHER of these creatures is *Hotinus subocellatus*, a native of various parts of China.

The general colour of the upper wings is pale ruddy brown, with a number of indistinct dark red spots, surrounded with yellow, upon them. Towards the tips they become greenish. There is a reddish patch upon the lower wings, and a somewhat vague pattern in brown.

It is one of the luminous insects. A general officer who was in Hong Kong saw a number of boys throwing stones at an object on the wall, which, according to his account, shone like a star. He hooked the object down with his cane, brought it into the house, and found that it was the species which has been figured.

FIG. 476.—Hotinus subocellatus.
(Brown-green, indistinctly spotted.)

ON Plate XVIII. Fig. 2 is shown another species of this remarkable genus. It is a native of Ceylon.

The upper wings are blackish grey, profusely spotted and mottled with white. The lower wings are grey, changing to black towards the lower edges.

THE pretty insect which is next shown is a native of Venezuela, and is coloured in rather a complicated fashion.

The thorax is green, with a yellow collar. The upper wings are greenish, spotted with white towards the base. Then comes a broad, waving band of cream-white, and the two patches at the tip of the wing are green. The lower wings are orange at the base, and tend to a pale yellow towards the tips.

FIG. 477.—Poicocera combusta. (Golden, white, and orange.)

AMONG the Homoptera, variety of form seems to run riot, and we have in the present instance one of the most singular forms that could be imagined. Anyone

FIG. 478.—Phenax auricoma. (Green, with yellow head-tuft and white processes.)

unacquainted with entomology could hardly believe that it really was an insect and not the creation of some fantastic manufacturer of sham insects. It is a native of Mexico.

The general colour of the insect is pale green, but it has upon its head a crest of long soft, silken, gold-coloured hair. The whole under surface of its body is covered with a white downy secretion, which looks as if the insect had been hastily made from cotton-wool. The long fibres that trail behind the insect are of similar material, and look very much as if they had been made of cotton-wool loosely twisted between the hands. There are many other insects which secrete a similar substance, but we have not sufficient space even to mention them.

We shall now come to several insects of most extraordinary, not to say grotesque, forms, the first of which is called *Hemiptycha punctata.* It is a native of Brazil, and in order to show its peculiar form the figure is slightly enlarged.

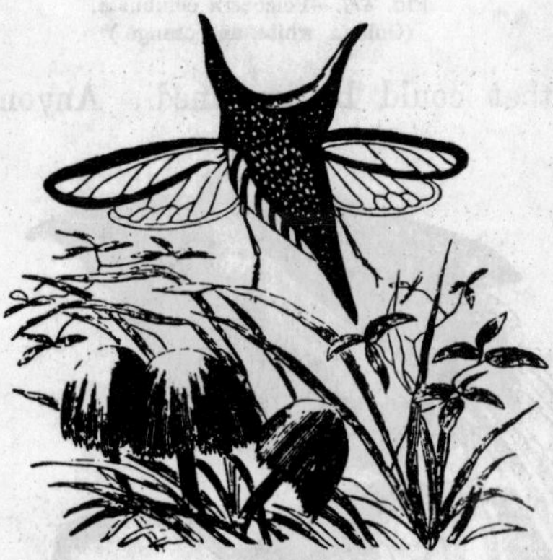

Fig. 479.— Hemiptycha punctata. (Black and yellow.)

The enormous thorax covers the whole upper surface of the insect, widening and stretching out its two horns at the upper end, and projecting in a point at the other end, until it overpasses the abdomen. The colour of the thorax is yellow, mottled with black, and it is thickly and deeply punctured. Along its centre runs a narrow line of shining black, and another line of a similar character runs from the tip of one horn to that of the other.

The upper wings are yellowish in the centre and brown round the edges, and the lower pair are simply pale brown. It is a large genus, and most of the species are Brazilian.

On Plate XVIII. Fig. 3 is shown an insect called *Flata* [or *Pœciloptera*] *circulata.*

It is a native of Java, and is a very pretty insect, the colours of the upper wings being brown and white, and those of the lower pair pure white. Some species of this genus, as, for example, *Flata marginella* of Northern India, have the females flocculent like those of the Phenax, while the males have broad expansive wings, and no flocculence. There are many species of Flata, spread over the warmest parts of Asia, New Guinea, South Africa, and other countries.

HERE is another of the eccentric formations so often seen in the Homoptera. The figure is enlarged to rather more than twice the size of the real insect, so as to show the singular structure. Its body is studded with long and curved spikes, and in this respect it very much resembles the strange little beetle (*Amphisternus Satanas*) which has been described on page 273. Putting the spikes aside, the outline of the insect when seen in profile has a curious resemblance to that of a large ant. This species inhabits the lower Amazons.

FIG. 480.—Heteronotus aronatus. (Pale red.)

The general colour of the insect is pale yellow, with some black streaks on the front of the thorax; and the spikes, together with the two projections in the middle of the body, shining black. In consequence of these long spikes, it has received its specific name. There are many species, of which this is by far the largest, and some are quite tiny.

ANY classical reader will remember the hero Œdipus, and the origin of his name, which signifies "swollen foot." The insects of the genus Œda have received their name from the singular structure of their body. We have seen one or two examples of insects in which the abdomen is swollen and empty, but in these the whole body is little but a skin as empty as a blown bladder the vital and muscular parts being scarcely perceptible.

In these insects the whole body is composed of a material very much resembling the wing of a dragon fly, except that the nervures form two kinds of meshes, the one large and square, and the others small and hexagonal, which fill up the space between the large meshes. In this species the colour is reddish yellow, but in another, *Œda informis*, the creature looks exactly as if it were nothing but the cast skin of some insect, so colourless and translucent is the whole of its structure. Both species are Brazilian. The figure is about twice the size of the real insect.

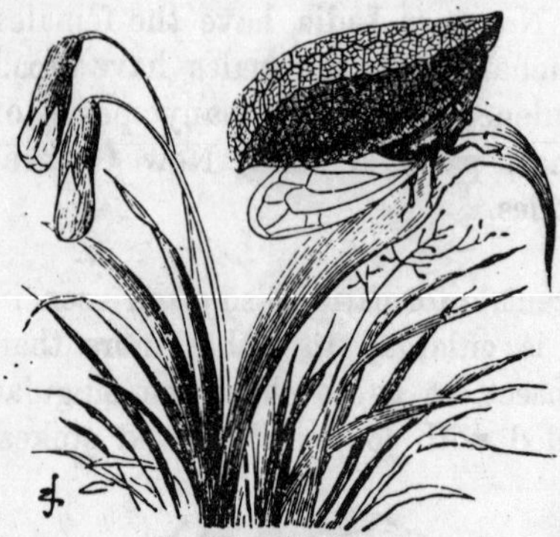

FIG. 481.—Œda inermis.
(Reddish and transculent.)

As will be seen in the two following insects, the thorax is the part in which eccentricity of form seems to have reached its utmost limits.

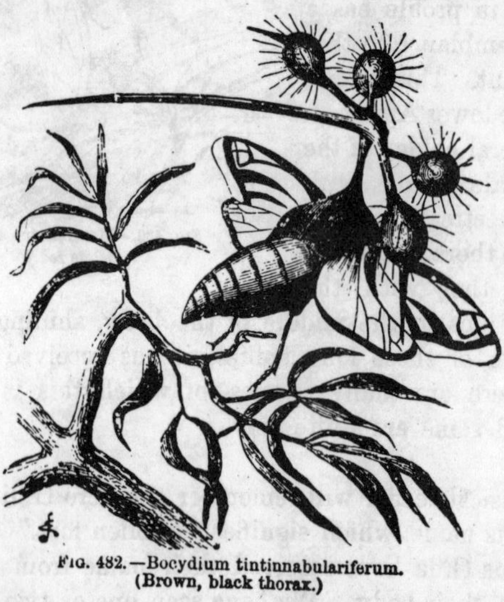

FIG. 482.—Bocydium tintinnabulariferum.
(Brown, black thorax.)

The first of them is *Bocydium tintinnabulariferum*, a native of Brazil. Although the largest of the extensive group to which it belongs, it is but a little creature, being about as long as a common house-fly, but not so stoutly made. The colour of the body is pale brown, while that of the thorax, with its extending appendages, is black. The form of these appendages can be better seen by reference to the illustration than by description. The four round knobs look very much like hawk-bells, and have given rise to the long specific name, which signifies "bell-bearer." They are covered with long black hairs.

THE generic name *Hypsauchenia* signifies "high-necked," and, as may be seen by reference to the illustration, is very appropriate. The figure is much enlarged, the insect being about as

FIG. 483.—Hypsauchenia Westwoodii.
(Brown; black thorax.)

large as the preceding species. It is one of an extensive group all of which are remarkable for the singular development of the thorax, and its division into a fork-like extremity. It is rather variable in point of hue, but the average colour of the body is pale brown, and that of the thorax blackish brown. It is a native of the Philippines. One species, *Hypsauchenia Hardwickii*, has the extremity of the thorax just like a pair of sugar-tongs, the ends of the fork being flattened into a spoon-like shape.

THE genus Cercopis is familiar to English entomologists by means of the pretty Scarlet Hopper (*Cercopis sanguinolenta*), whose scarlet and black wings look so beautiful upon the fern-leaves on which the creature loves to rest.

The present species, which inhabits the Philippines, is a very large and fine one, though it does not possess the brilliant hues of its English relative. The thorax is yellowish brown, thickly and finely punctated and wrinkled. The scutellum is black,

FIG. 484.—Cercopis Theora.
(Blue, black, and yellow.)

and the abdomen yellow. The upper wings are blue-black, with deep yellow marks, and the lower wings are brown, changing to yellow on the upper edge.

CLOSELY allied to the preceding insect is the handsome species which is shown in the illustration. Not long ago it was considered as belonging to the genus Cercopis, but has lately been removed to its present position. It inhabits Brazil, and is one of many species, most of which are natives of the same country.

It is really a beautiful insect. The ground colour of the upper wings is warm chestnut at the base, changing gradually to red at the tip, The bold markings are black, glossed with blue, and the shape of the mark at the base has gained for the insect its specific name, which signifies "forked." The lower wings are

FIG. 485.—Tomaspis furcata.
(Black, scarlet, and violet.

dark brown, edged with very pale brown, and the abdomen is shining metallic violet.

PERHAPS many of my readers may remember the pretty little Tettigonias, that look so much like beetles, and whose brilliant colours are so lovely as the insects march about the white flowers which they love. The insect which now comes before us belongs to this group, and, although not possessing the vivid colouring of its lesser British relatives, is yet a pretty creature, its markings being bold in form and rich in colour.

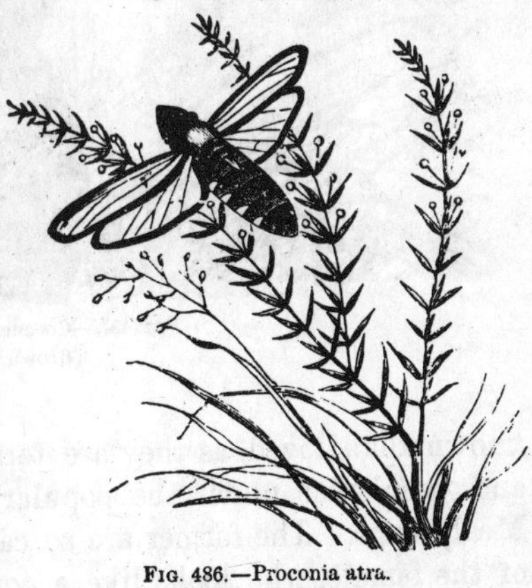

FIG. 486.—Proconia atra.
(Brown and yellow.)

The ground hue of the upper wings is yellow, and upon it are sundry streaks of dark brown, arranged as seen in the illustration. The lower wings are pale brown, without any distinctive markings. The colour of the body is dull blackish brown, very much like that of our glowworm, and along each edge is a row of bright yellow spots. It is a native of the West Indies.

THE group of Homopterous insects known by the name of Coccidæ is a very well-known one. To gardeners it is better

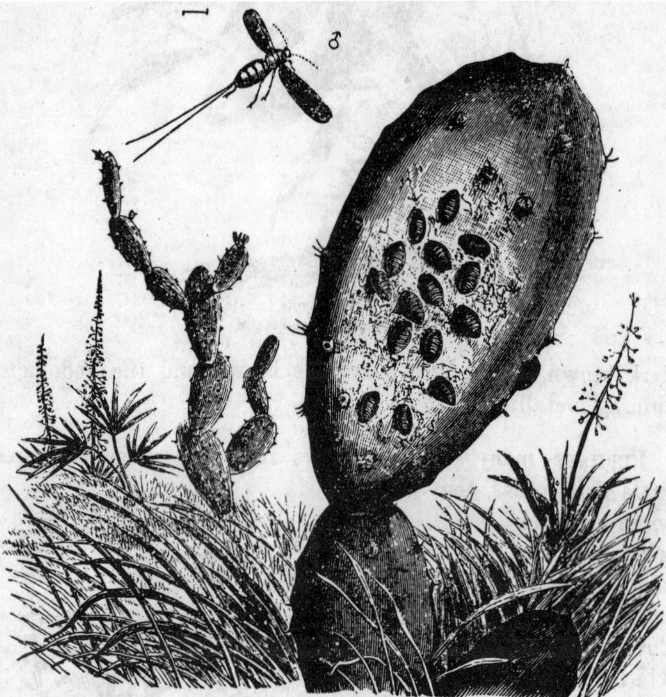

FIG. 487.—Coccus Sinensis.
(Brown.)

known than loved, as they are terrible enemies in the orchard and greenhouse under the popular names of Scale Insects and Mealy-bugs. The former are so called on account of the shape of the female, who looks like a convex scale stuck to the leaf; and the latter derive their name from the flour-like secretion which is copiously emitted from the body.

In trade, the Coccidæ are familiar as being the producers of a sort of wax (which is more used in China than in England), of the useful substance called "lac," and, above all, of the invaluable "cochineal" dye. The first of these species is shown in the illustration. The male is very small, winged, and flies freely in search of a mate, whereas the female is fixed to one spot, dies there, and her withered body becomes the shelter of her young.

From the body of the female is exuded a wonderful amount of a white secretion, which, when collected, melted down, and strained, has many of the properties of wax, and is generally called by that name. In the British Museum there are many specimens of the insect, together with a lump of the wax, which looks almost exactly like spermaceti. There are also specimens of other wax-making Coccidæ, mostly belonging to the genus Ceroplastes, of the Lac Insects, and the Cochineal.

THE last of the Homoptera which can be described in this

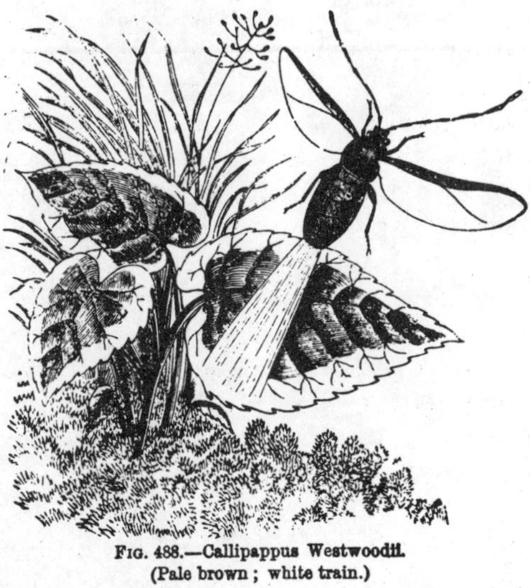

FIG. 488.—Callipappus Westwoodii.
(Pale brown ; white train.)

work is an example of the singular genus Callipappus, a male of which is here shown.

As to the female, she is simply hideous. She is a big, black, plump, flat, grub-like creature almost an inch and a half in length, and looking as if she would burst if touched.

The male, on the contrary, is a beautiful, though not brightly coloured insect. The body and wings are pale brown, but from the tail proceeds a train of soft glistening white threads, looking exactly like the tails of the spun-glass birds which are so popular at bazaars. This species is a native of Australia.

DIPTERA.

DIPTERA.

As their name implies, the DIPTERA possess only two wings. These, again, cannot be folded, and the place of the lower pair is taken by two little winglets or balancers. The mouth is formed for suction. Without going further into technical detail, we will proceed to a short description of the insects which have been selected as examples.

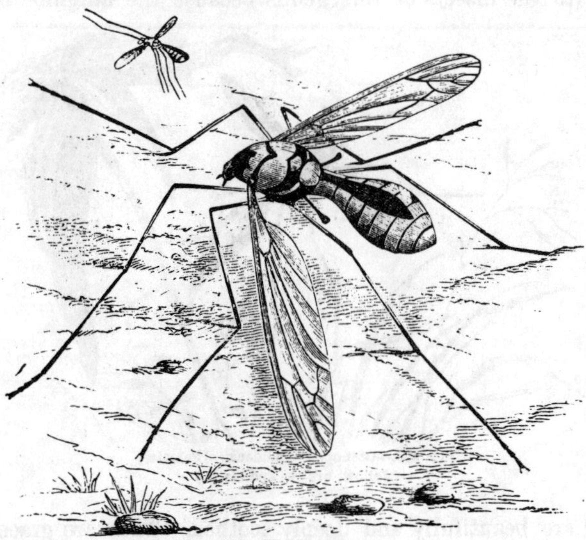

FIG. 489.—Tipula imperator.
(Yellow and black.)

EVERYONE is familiar with the group of flies called Tipulidæ, the various insects known by the popular title of "Daddy Long-legs." These creatures strike unutterable terror into many minds, the generality of people thinking that they possess venomous stings, while others are almost equally terrified by the legs, which to them are inexpressibly revolting. Why anyone should object to an insect's legs is rather unaccountable. That they should fear the sting or the jaws is intelligible enough, but that they should fear the legs more than the wings is not so easily understood.

The present species may perhaps lay claim to being the largest and the handsomest of them all. Its colours are black and yellow, which even extend to the enormously long legs. The mode of flight employed by the insect is very remarkable. Instead of allowing all its legs to dangle beneath it, the creature stretches its two fore-legs in front of it, on the same principle employed by the heron when it stretches out its long neck in flight. This species inhabits Australia.

THE Greek word *Ctenophora* signifies "comb-bearer," and is given to the insects of this genus because the antennæ of the

FIG. 490.—Ctenophora gaudens. [Female.]
(Yellow, brown, and black.)

males are beautifully and deeply toothed. They are gracefully curved, the teeth being inside the curve, so that they look like two delicate plumes. Several species of this genus inhabit England, such, for example, as *Ctenophora pectinicornis* and *Ctenophora bimaculata.*

The figure which is here given represents a female, the male being much smaller. The whole of the thorax and body is yellow, except the end of the abdomen, which is black. The wings are brown, with the exception of a patch of yellow towards the tip. The insect inhabits the Celebes.

THERE is a large group of Diptera, scientifically termed Tabanidæ, and popularly known as Breeze Flies, Gad Flies, or Clegs. Their mouths are developed into a piercing apparatus, which is so powerful that it can be driven through the tough skin of cattle. These insects attack man as well as beast. They made my life a burden to me in the New Forest, until I repelled them with paraffin, even driving their beaks through thick woollen clothing.

FIG. 491.—Pangonia fulvithorax. (Black, with yellow down.)

Our species are bad enough in the way of annoyance, but some of the foreign species are very much larger than ours, and have proportionately powerful means of offence. One of the most important genera of these flies is Pangonia, several examples of which will be given. The first is *Pangonia fulvithorax*, a native of Brazil.

The ground colour of this insect is shining black-brown, but the thorax is covered with a dense coating of golden yellow down, having a silken gloss, and looking something like yellow velvet. The abdomen is without the down except at the end and on the sides, where the yellow hairs are rather sparingly planted. The wings are shining brown.

ON Plate XX. Fig. 1 is shown *Pangonia longirostris*, a native of India.

Its colour is brown, like that of our common Drone Fly, barred with yellow. Its specific name signifies "long-beaked," and, indeed, the proboscis is so long in proportion to the body, that the insect is said to be incapable of attacking cattle except on the wing. In common, however, with many of the Tabanidæ, it draws much of its nutriment from flowers. The proportionate dimensions of the proboscis may be gathered from the fact that whereas an ordinary specimen measures ten-twelfths of an inch in length, the proboscis is two inches and a half long.

ANOTHER of these long-beaked insects is here given, which, as its name implies, is a native of Amboyna. It is a pretty insect,

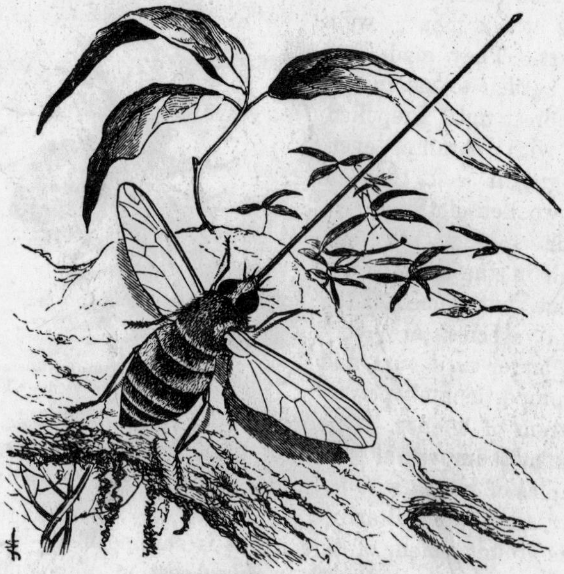

FIG. 492.—Pangonia Amboinensis.
(Brown, black, and yellow.)

with a bee-like aspect about it. The colour is very dark brown, with a coating of yellow down on the thorax, and a black band across the base of the abdomen.

WE now take an example of the typical genus, *Tabanus hilaris*, an East Indian insect.

The general colour is reddish brown. The head is white, the thorax is traversed by two grey streaks, and the abdomen by three similar stripes. The large compound eyes are divided into

PLATE XX.

two distinct regions. The upper region is composed of very large facets, while the remainder is composed of very small facets. This remarkable arrangement of the facets is found in several other insects.

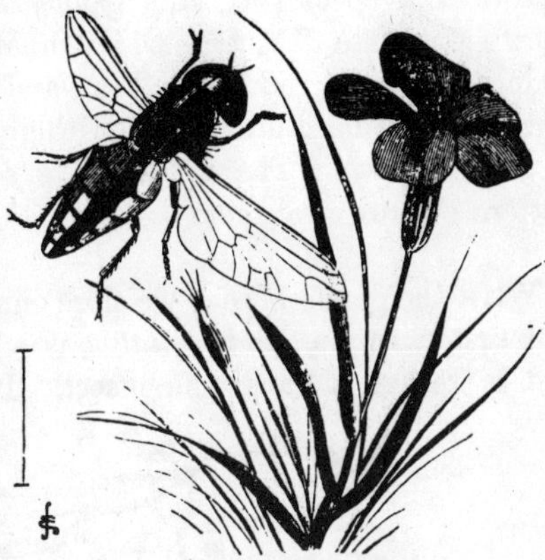

FIG. 493.—Tabanus hilaris. Reddish brown.)

THERE is a genus of Tabanidæ called *Acanthomera,* or "thorn-legged," because a sharp spike projects from the end of the thigh. They are very large insects, and much resemble the grey flies popularly known as Millers, except that they are much larger.

The species which is here given is Brazilian. The abdomen is dark brown, and so is the thorax. The latter, however, is

FIG. 494.—Acanthomera Heydenii. (Brown and silver-grey.)

covered with a coating of silken down, arranged in stripes of silver-grey, black, brown, and white. The eyes are so large that the multitudinous facets of which they are composed are visible even without the aid of a lens, and even in death they retain something of the sheen which makes them so beautiful in life. The pattern on the centre of the wing is yellow and brown.

ANOTHER species of this genus, *Acanthomera magnifica*, is shown on Plate XX. Fig. 2. It inhabits South America. The abdomen is rich ruddy chestnut, and the thorax is silver-grey, striped with dark brown. The thighs are yellow, and the rest of the leg brown. The wings are very pale yellow, with a slight pattern of brown on them.

WITH the genus Mydas we close our account of the Tabanidæ. Our first example, *Mydas filatus*, is a native of North America, and is rather a handsome insect. Its general colour is dark

FIG. 495.—Mydas filatus.
(Brown and yellow.)

brown, relieved by a broad yellow band at the base of the abdomen. The wings are brown and iridescent. One of the most beautiful of the genus is *Mydas dives* of Brazil, in which the body is shining metallic blue.

The largest of these insects is *Mydas giganteus*, also a native of Brazil, which is shown on Plate XX. Fig. 3. It appears at first sight to be black, but in a good light is seen to be of a very deep blue, this colour being imperceptible except with a strong light directed upon the insect from the side. The wings are rather dark brown at the base, and become lighter towards the tips.

Of the family Acroceridæ we shall take two examples, the first of which is *Tricopthalma vetelinea*, a native of Australia.

Fig. 496.—Tricopthalma vetelinea. (Brown, white, and yellow.

This pretty insect is covered with a thick dark brown down, which has a velvety look about it. On the sides of the thorax is long grey down, and the longitudinal stripes upon it are white. The abdomen is also brown, but the edge of each segment is marked out with a narrow ring of short bright golden hairs. There are many species of this genus, most of which are Australasian, though some are found in Southern Africa, and others in Europe.

The rather odd-looking insect which goes by the name of *Exetasis tumens* is a native of Brazil. In order to show its structure the better, the figure has been enlarged about one-third.

Fig. 497.—Exetasis tumens. (Brown and black.)

The ground colour of the insect is shining black, but the whole of the thorax and a great part of the abdomen are covered with thick tawny down, looking very much like the fur of a mole. The edges of the segments of the abdomen, however, are without the downy coating, so that they are shining jetty black, and the same colour extends upwards in a triangular form, as seen in the illustration. The wings are ashen grey. The specific name, *tumens*, signifies "swollen," and is one of the characteristics of the family, which are sometimes called Vesiculosæ, *i.e.* Bladder Flies.

We now come to the Asilidæ, some of the finest of the insect tribes. They prey upon other insects, as can be seen by watching the proceedings of our English species. A Continental

FIG. 498.—Dasypogon spectrum.
(Yellow and black.)

species, *Asilus diadema*, has been seen even to capture and kill the hive bee, in spite of its sting. Some of the larger species are said to attack cattle, like the Breeze Flies. We shall examine several species of this group, one of them a yet undescribed insect.

The first species is a native of China, and is a formidable looking insect. It is entirely yellow and black, the latter being the ground colour, and the former due to a thick coat of bright yellow down distributed in bands across the body. The wings are pale yellow.

There are many species of this genus, some of them exceedingly large insects. One of the prettiest is *Dasypogon Vica* oi Northern India, in which the abdomen is shining black, and the wings are beautifully iridescent, with shifting tints of blue, purple, and green.

THE genus Laphria being a very large and important one, we shall take several species, the first of which is *Laphria alternans*

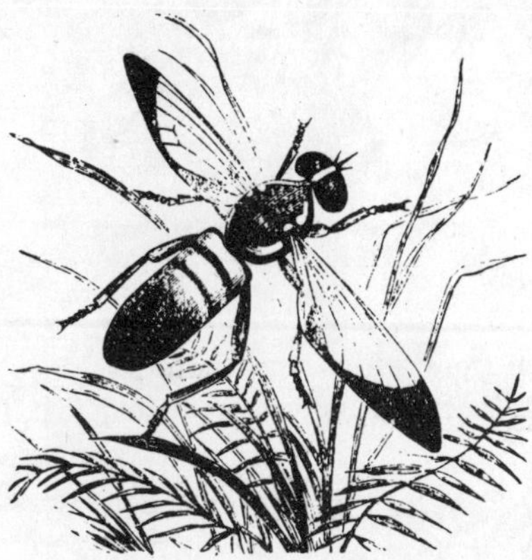

FIG. 499.—Laphria alternans.
(Brown barred with gold.)

of Java, its specific name being due to the alternating hues of its body.

The colour is brown-black, mottled with black, and the abdomen is barred with golden yellow. The wings are rather curiously coloured, being white at the base and changing gradually to pale yellow. The dark marks upon them are brown. In order to show the markings better, the figure has been enlarged to twice the size of the insect.

SEVERAL curious examples of imitation occur in this genus, one of which is called *Laphria xylocopiformis*, from the extraordinary resemblance which it bears, both in shape and colour, to the great wood-boring bees belonging to the genus Xylocopa.

Figures of some of these bees may be seen on page 520 and on Plate X.

FIG. 500.—Laphria xylocopiformis (Blue-black.)

The specimen from which the figure was drawn was taken at Madras. Its colour is wholly blue-black, just like the female of the species described on page 520, or *Xyclopa morio,* which is given on Plate X. The resemblance in form will be seen at a glance by comparing the two figures.

FIG. 501.—Laphria consimilis. New Species. (Black and grey.)

THE insect which now comes before us is an undescribed species, which I call *Laphria consimilis,* on account of its remarkable resemblance to one of the wood-cutter bees of Southern Africa. Indeed, so close is the resemblance, that if a specimen of these flies were placed among a number of the bees, it would probably pass muster except to a very practised eye. It is a native of Natal.

The colour of the thorax is black, and so is that of the abdomen. The latter, however, has a fringe of long grey down. There is a tuft of yellow down on the top of the head, and a patch of the same colour on the tibia of the fore-legs. Those of the hind legs have a fringe of long grey hair running along the inner edge. The rest of the limb is black. The wings are deep blackish brown, and with a strong side light a deep gloss of blue is seen upon them.

OUR last example of this genus is *Laphria horrida* of Sumatra. It is represented in the act of pouncing on a luckless insect, which it will speedily drain of its juices. In these insects the grasping power of the fore-legs is wonderful, and the tenacity with which they stick to their prey scarcely less so. On a windy day, our English hornet-flies may be seen drifting along in the breeze as if without any purpose. No sooner, however, do they come near another insect than they pounce on it, clasp it tightly with their fore-legs, and drive the beak into its body. It often happens that the remaining legs are not sufficiently strong to enable the insect to hol its own against the wind, and so it may be seen rolling over and over, clutching at the grass with the second and third pairs of legs, but never for a moment relaxing its hold of its prey.

FIG. 502.—Laphria horrida. (Black, with yellow wings.)

The present species is almost entirely black. There is a tuft of yellow hairs on its head, and its legs are yellow, but these latter are nearly concealed by the long black hairs with which they are covered. A ridge of yellow hair runs along both edges of the thorax. The wings are shining yellow.

On Plate XX. Fig 4 is seen an insect called *Phellus glaucus*, an inhabitant of Western Australia. The specimen from which the figure was drawn is in Mr. Saunders' collection.

The colour of the thorax is black, fringed with pale yellow hairs. The ground colour of the abdomen is bright deep blue, clothed with short black hairs. The first two segments are also covered with long, thick, yellow down. The legs are black and covered with short black hairs, changing to tawny at the ends of the tarsi. The wings are blackish brown at the base, and the rest is grey, traversed with black veins.

I presume that the accompanying insect derives its specific name from the colours which it wears, which are those of the traditional stage demons. It is a native of Brazil.

Fig. 508.—Asilus infernalis. (Black and yellow.)

Nearly the whole of the insect is black, and it is entirely covered with thick down. At the junction of the abdomen with the thorax there is a semicircular patch of long orange hairs, an there is a broad band of the same hue across the middle of the abdomen. The thighs of the hind legs are fringed with very long black hairs above, and covered with white down below. The wings are smooth, shining brown in colour, and iridescent with various tints of blue and purple.

Our last example of the family is *Asilus coriarius*, a native of New Holland, which is represented as in the act of chasing prey. The specific name *coriarius* is formed from a Latin word signifying "the bark of a tree," and is given to the insect on account of its resemblance in colour to the rough brown bark of the oak or similar tree.

The colour of the abdomen is warm brown, with a black bar at its base, and a series of tufts of jet black hair along the sides.

The thorax is brown, edged with white down, and a large quantity of similar down grows on its under surface. A patch of

FIG. 504.—Asilus coriarius.
(Brown, black, and white.)

grey-white hair occupies the front of the head. The wings are pale brown.

FIG. 505.—Anthrax seniculus.
(Chocolate and yellow.)

OF the family Leptidæ two examples will suffice. These are also predacious insects, and in one species, *Leptis vermileo*, the larva behaves very much like that of the Ant Lion, digging conical holes in the loose sand, remaining at the bottom of them, and then pouncing on the insects that fall into them. Yet, voracious as the creature is, it has been known to survive a total fast of six months.

The species which is given in the illustration is chocolate-brown on the thorax, and blackish brown on the abdomen. There is a very narrow collar of yellow between the head and the thorax. The wings are singularly handsome, being the richest brown by way of ground colour, and having several large translucent spots of yellow. It is a native of Southern Africa.

This is a very large genus, spread about over the whole world, and extending even to England, where we have several species.

The form of *Bombylius analis* must be familiar to every English entomologist, on account of the Humble-bee Flies, as they are popularly called, which are so well known in this country. These insects are spread all over the world, wherever flowers can grow, and they feed, like many of the Hawk Moths, by poising themselves on the wing before a flower, and extracting its juices with the long and straight proboscis.

Fig. 506.—Bombylius analis. (Black and yellow or white.)

The present species is a native of Southern Africa. The thorax and abdomen are covered with long black hair, with the exception of a large patch at the end of the abdomen, which is white in some specimens and golden yellow in others. The wings are nearly translucent, but they are dark brown at the base, and a wavy patch of very pale brown runs parallel with the upper edge.

In the family of the Conopsidæ, the larvæ are parasitic upon other insects, mostly belonging to the bee tribe. One species, *Conops russipes*, was found by Latreille to undergo its transformations within the abdomen of the living humble-bee, and the insect has been seen patiently flying in chase of the bee. The word *Conops* is Greek, and was used to signify a large kind of gnat. The proboscis is incapable of being withdrawn, is powerful, and bent under the head in a sort of elbow-shape.

The insects are nearly all prettily coloured, and the present species, which is a native of Brazil, forms no exception to the rule. At a first glance it appears to be only blackish brown, but a closer inspection shows that the abdomen is clothed with silvery down, while there are gleams as of patches of burnished gold on the legs and forehead. From this latter mark the species receives the name of *aurifrons*, or "golden fronted." The wings are glossy green, with a gold gloss, and darker towards the upper edge.

FIG. 507.—Conops aurifrons.
(Brown, silver-white, and gold.)

THE fine insect which is given in the accompanying illustra-

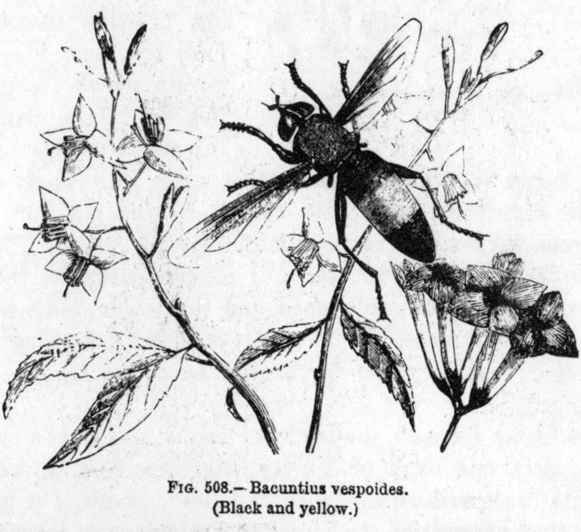

FIG. 508.—Bacuntius vespoides.
(Black and yellow.)

tion belongs to the same family as the preceding insect. It is a native of Singapore.

From the black and yellow which form its chief tints, and which give it no small resemblance to a wasp, it has received the specific name of *vespoides*, or "wasp-like." The thorax is quite black, and the abdomen is nearly so. Across the middle of the abdomen runs a very broad band of deep yellow, just like the colour of the common wasp. The wings are dark brown, with a shining surface. When the insect is alive, the eyes must present a very beautiful appearance, for even when the creature has been dead and dry for years, these organs shine with a coppery lustre that tells of long-vanished beauties.

WE now come to the enormous family of the Muscidæ, in which is included such vast masses of interesting insects, that it is no easy task to make a selection from them. In fact, the whole work might be devoted to this one family alone, and then not nearly exhaust it.

FIG. 509.—Glossina morsitans. (Brown.)

Our first example is the terrible Tsetse Fly (*Glossina morsitans*). No one on looking at this insect could form the least idea of the terrors which its presence inspires. Like many other insects, it attacks man and beast; but it has this peculiarity, that while man is only affected by the slight and brief pain caused by the puncture of the proboscis, horses and cattle almost invariably die. The effect of the Tsetse poison on them is most remarkable, the blood being blackened and thickened, and the whole frame rendered one mass of disease, the strongest muscles becoming so disintegrated that they can be broken to pieces by the thumb and finger.

The Tsetse lives on the banks of rivers, and it is a curiously local insect, one bank of a river being free from it, while the opposite bank will swarm with the flies. There is a long and interesting account of the insect in Livingstone's travels. The colour of the Tsetse is pale brown. It is about the size of the common house-fly, the figure having been enlarged in order to show its structure the better.

THE generic term *Tachina* is formed from a Greek word signifying "rapidity," and is given to the insects in consequence of their swiftness. There are very great numbers of species belonging to this genus, and there is scarcely a part of the world in which they are not represented. None of them are brilliant in point of colour, brown, black, grey, and yellow being the invariable hues.

FIG. 510.—Tachina grandis.
(Brown and yellow, variable.)

The present species is a native of Mexico. Its general colour is black, and even the long hairs which thickly clothe the body are of the same colour. The thorax is black, but is relieved by some lines of silver-grey, with a very slight tinge of blue in them. This is the usual colouring, but the insect is exceedingly variable, both in size and colouring. Some specimens are barely half as large as others, while in some the colour is entirely yellow, in others half yellow and half black, and in others again the colour is entirely black, with the exception of a yellow tip to the tail.

THE genus to which belong the next two insects is rather a large one, and contains some of the most splendidly coloured of the Diptera. The first species, *Dexia effulgens*, is a native of New Guinea. The ground colour of the insect is soft velvety black. Upon the abdomen the black is relieved by a number of interrupted bands, which glow with tints so varying that it is almost impossible to decide which is the real colour. One bar, for example, will seem to be glittering emerald-green, another gold, and another azure; but on shifting the position of the insect it will be found that the same colours pass in turn over each bar, the hue depending wholly on the direction of the light. The wings are dark brown at the base, and the remainder is pale yellowish brown.

The second species is a native of New Holland.

The colour of this insect is wholly green, glossed with gold, very much the hue of our common Rose Beetle, but with much more gold about it. There is a tuft of long black hair at the end of the abdomen. The wings are translucent, with a round patch of dark brown at the base.

Among the notable examples of this genus may be mentioned *Dexia regalis,* also a native of New Holland. This is a much

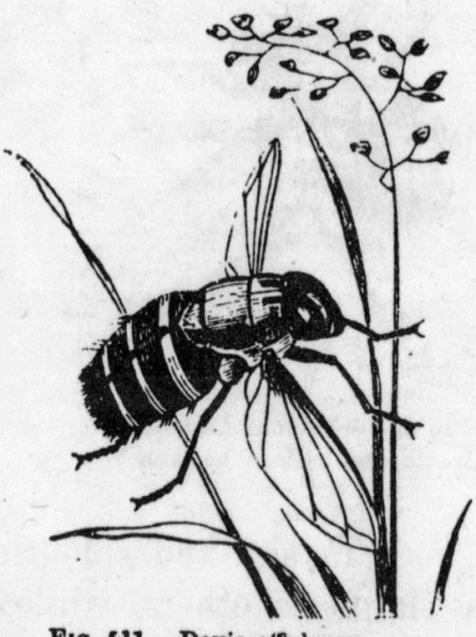

Fig. 511.—Dexia effulgens.
(Black, barred with blue, green, and gold.)

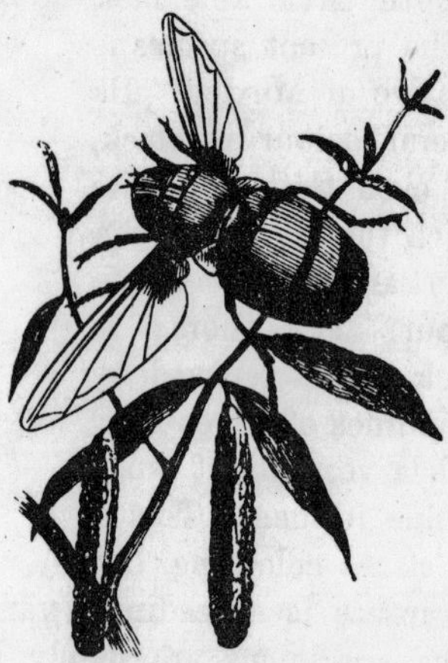

Fig. 512.—Dexia formosa.
(Green, glossed with gold.)

smaller insect than the last species, but is strikingly beautiful, its rich and delicate colouring causing it to stand out boldly from among its brilliant kinsfolk. The gold and the blue are as vivid as in *Dexia effulgens,* but instead of the green, pink is substituted, and, indeed, may be considered as the ground colour.

Another of the rare insects in Mr. Saunders' collection is here given.

The colour of the thorax is chestnut-brown, relieved by four white stripes. The head is darker, and has a coating of grey down in front. The base of the abdomen is reddish brown, and the rest black. In the legs, the thighs are very strong and thick, thus giving rise to the generic name *Rhopalomera*, or "club-thighed." They are covered with hair, and are black, except the knees, which are yellow. The wings are grey clouded with brown. The insect is a native of Brazil.

FIG. 513.—Rhopalomera tibialis. (Chestnut and black.)

No one who was unacquainted with the subject would think that the two insects which are next represented are but the male and female of the same species. Yet this is the case, the insect being one of a small group in which the males are distinguished by some extraordinary appendages to the head, while the females have nothing remarkable about them.

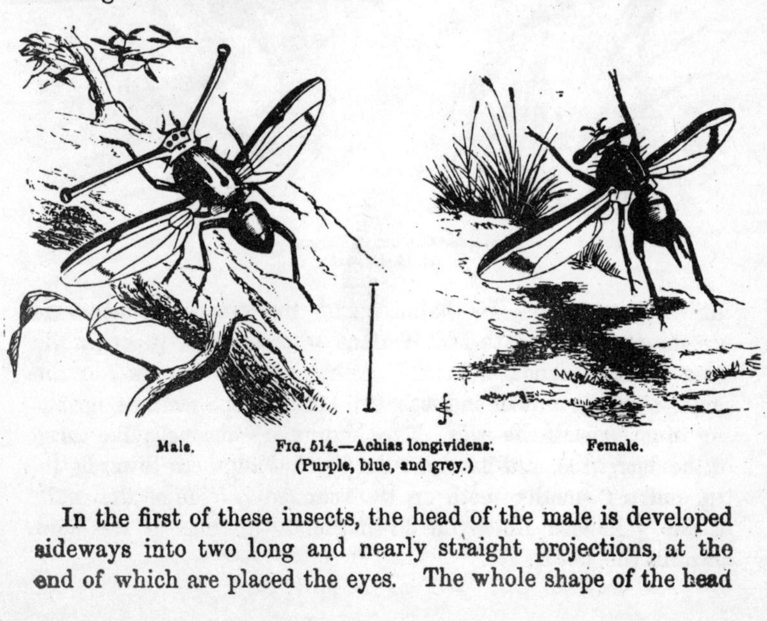

Male. FIG. 514.—Achias longividens. Female.
(Purple, blue, and grey.)

In the first of these insects, the head of the male is developed sideways into two long and nearly straight projections, at the end of which are placed the eyes. The whole shape of the head is almost exactly that of the Sentinel Crab (*Podopthalmus vigil*), in which the footstalks of the eyes are enormously lengthened. This species is a native of Ava. The figure is slightly enlarged.

The head, with its projections, is dark brown; the thorax is very dark purple, variegated with streaks of silver-grey. The ground colour of the abdomen is shining blue, changing to purple in certain lights, and covered sparingly with soft brown hair, so that it is handsome in colour as well as remarkable in form. The wings are translucent, with a slight brown pattern on them. There are several species of this genus, but this is the largest and most conspicuous.

BOTH names of the following species refer to the singular conformation of the head of the male. The Greek word *Elaphomyia* literally signifies "Stag Fly," and the Latin word *alcicornis* sig-

Male. FIG. 515.—Elaphomyia alcicornis. (Reddish brown.) Female.

nifies "Elk-horn." For the insects of this remarkable genus we are mostly indebted to Mr. Wallace, who collected them in the East Indian islands. In the present species the head of the male is ruddy brown, and has two horn-like projections springing from beneath the eyes. These horns are curiously like those of the deer tribe, and have one long projecting tooth towards the tip, and six smaller teeth on the rounded portion of the stalk. A few yellowish lines run down the broad front of the horn towards the teeth.

The thorax is rusty brown, with four long black lines, two parallel with the vertical line of the insect, and two slanting diagonally towards the abdomen. The long legs are reddish brown, and in the middle of the thighs of the fore-legs is a patch of black bristles pointing forwards. The female is coloured much like the male, except that the head and thorax are yellowish brown, and that she wants the patch of bristles on the fore-legs. The illustration is magnified in order to show the shape of the insect, the length of which is about half an inch.

ANOTHER of the insects captured by Mr. Wallace is *Elaphomyia cervicornis*, which inhabits the island of Dorey.

The head is blackish brown above and ruddy brown below. The oddly-shaped horns take their origin just below the eyes, and are black tipped with white. The thorax is yellowish olive above and whitish beneath. The abdomen is modified into a sort of footstalk, which is yellow brown, and the remainder is dusky brown, becoming darker at the tip. The legs are long, and yellowish brown. The female has no horns, her head being simply rounded.

FIG. 516.—Elaphomyia cervicornis. (Yellowish brown.)

This is rather a larger insect than the last, the average length of the male being about six-tenths of an inch.

OUR last example of the Stag-horned Flies is also a native of Dorey.

The head of the male is blackish brown, streaked with yellow in front. The eyes are very protruding, and just below them is a short, rounded, and rather flattened projection which takes the place of the horn. The colour is brownish black, but across the footstalk of the abdomen passes a bar of yellow. The reader will doubtless observe the remarkable shape of the wings. Instead of having the upper edge nearly straight, as is the usual custom with insects, it is much thickened in the middle, and formed into an angular projection. The length of the insect is rather less than half an inch.

FIG. 517.—Elaphomyia brevicornis. (Brown.)

THE remarkable fly which is given in the accompanying illustration inhabits the United States.

It is called *Militaris*, because in its larval state it is parasitic on the "Army Worm," *i.e.* the caterpillar of *Leucaria unipunctata*, which traverses the country in vast hosts, completely devastating whole fields of the grain and grass crops. Nothing stops them but a deep ditch with perpendicular sides, and when such a ditch is cut across their line of progress, it is often found filled to a considerable depth with a seething, moving mass of larvæ.

FIG. 518.—Exorista militaris. (Dark silver-grey.)

Many stupid people, on seeing the Exorista emerge from the Army Worm, took it into their heads that it was the parent of the caterpillar, and so destroyed every fly they could catch, instead of protecting the insect as their best friend.

It is also parasitic on the larva of *Attacus Cecropia*, which feeds on the apple, cherry, plum, and other fruit trees. A peculiarity of this insect is, that instead of causing the larva which it infests to decrease in size, it has just the opposite effect.

For example, a larva of Attacus which was attacked by the Exorista, measured more than four inches in length, was a full inch in diameter, and weighed two ounces. Its body was entirely covered with the empty egg-shells of the fly, the larvæ having burrowed into its body. It died, rotted, and in about twelve days there appeared a vast number of maggots very much like those of the blue-fly. They went into the earth at once, and remained in the larval state all the winter. At the beginning of April they changed to pupæ, and at the end of May emerged in the perfect state. For the Cecropia Moth see p. 670.

THE curious family of the Hippoboscidæ, or Horse Flies, is here represented by an African species which infests the camel. We are all familiar with the English Horse Flies, which cling so tightly to the animal with their powerful legs, and run so actively in any direction if disturbed. These insects are remarkable for their manner of reproduction. They do not lay eggs after the fashion of most insects, nor deposit living larvæ as do several flies. But the female deposits the pupa ready formed, and enclosed within a soft, white, oval case. Exposure to the air soon hardens this case and turns it brown, and the fly, when developed, makes its escape by pushing off one end of the case.

FIG. 519.—Hippobosca camelina. (Brown.)

THE true position of the APHANIPTERA, or Fleas, is still a problem. Systematic entomologists of the present day seem to think that they are least out of place at the end of the Diptera.

From these I have selected the best-known foreign Flea, the Chigoe (*Pulex penetrans*). This insect burrows into the feet of human beings, and, if left undisturbed, forms a globular hollow in which the young are reproduced. Many accounts of this insect have been published, but I give a short and graphic description by one of my brothers.

"You ask me whether I am practically acquainted with the Chigoe. Rather so; just a little; in fact, I may say that we have been on terms of most intimate acquaintance for some years.

"As far as I have read upon the subject, a great deal of rubbish has been written about the Chigoe. It is true that our friend is a great nuisance in his way, but in six years I have never known, or ever heard, of anyone being much the worse for the Chigoe, though I have seen some people too lazy to extract them until their feet were full of their nests. As far as my experience goes, I can only state that for six or eight days after they have made their entrance, there is no trouble beyond a slight itching, and then if they are extracted with any reasonable amount of care, the nest of eggs comes away all correct. If it should be broken, which will happen sometimes, a pinch of snuff is put into the hole, and there is an end of the matter.

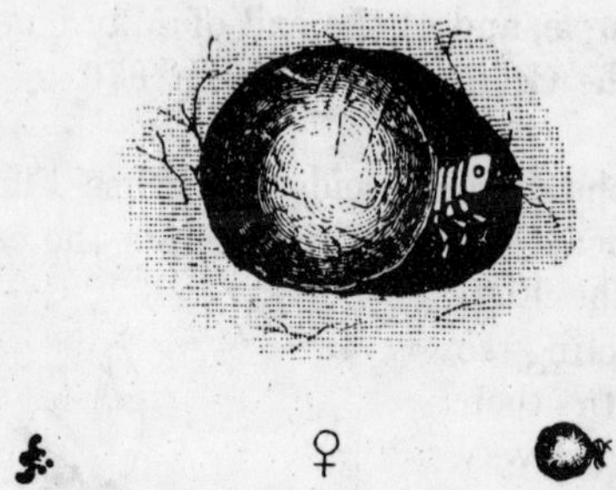

FIG. 520.—Pulex penetrans. (Red-brown.)

"I may be more thick-skinned than other people, and not suffer the same amount of inconvenience, but such is my experience. Since February last, when I came to this house, which is an old Brazilian Fazenda, I have had literally hundreds taken out of my toes. During the past month there would be half a dozen at a time boring away and removed two or three times a day. Some would escape observation for a few days; then out they come on the point of a pin, are put in the candle, and go 'Pop.' Now, after four months' continual washing and scraping of floors, they are so much diminished that I sometimes pass a couple of days without one. Mr. B. has just sent me a fine one for you. I don't know whether it will be of any use to you, but I enclose it. If you want any more, only say so."

INDEX.

ALPHABETICAL INDEX.

ABISPA SPLENDIDA, 487
Abraxas tigrata, 704
Acanthomera Heydenii, 763
— magnifica, 754
Achæa chameleon, 647
Acheta monstrosa, 313
Achias longividens, 767
Acrididæ, 331
Acridoxena Hawaiiana, 325
Acripeza reticulata, 324
Acrocinus longimanus, 243
Aculeata, 417
Adesmia variolaris, 175
Adolias Anosia, 611
— Durga, 611
— Epiona, 612
— Kesava, 609
— Plemius, 611
— Ramada, 611
— Sahadeva, 611
Æsalides, 106
Agarista contorta, 650
Ageronia Alicia, 605
Algaë cœrulea, 518
Agra Megæra, 38
— Moritii, 39
Agrias Phalcidon, 617
— Sardanapalus, 616
Alaus lymphatus, 157
— mœrens, 157
— oculatus, 157
Alurnus marginatus, 265
— thoracicus, 266
Alypia octomaculata, 651
Amarygmidæ, 182
Amblypoda quercetorum, 629
Ambulatoria, 300
Amissus Atlas, 716
— nitidus, 716
Amphisternus hamatus, 274
— Satanas, 273
— tuberculatus, 274
Ammophila melanaria, 460
— opulenta, 461
Ampulex compressa, 467
— hospes, 468
Anaxita decorata, 666
— Sannionis, 665
Andrena holomelana, 598
Anisosis caudatus, 175
Anisonyx ursus, 123
Anomalides, 126
Anomalipus lineata, 191
Antherea Pernyi, 674
Anthia guttata, 47
— sex-guttata, 46
— thoracica, 48
Anthidium Fiorentinum, 515
— manicatum, 514
Anthrax seniculus, 761
Anthribidæ, 195
Antliarhinus Dregei, 206
— Zamiæ, 205
Ant-Lions, 365
Ants, 427
Apate terebrans, 171
Apatura Agathina, 615
— Cherubina, 615
— Iris, 613
— Laura, 614
— Lavinia, 613
Aphaniptera, 771
Aphenogaster barbata, 445
Aplosonyx basalis, 260
— purpurascens, 260
Apocrypta paradoxa, 530
Appias placidia, 575
— Zarinda, 574
Arctia hyperborea, 664
— Isabella, 663
Arrhenodes coronatus, 201
Ascalaphus filipennis, 373
— imperatrix, 371
— Kolyranesis, 372
Asilus coriarius, 760
— diadema, 756
— infernalis, 760
Aspidomorpha mutata, 265
— Novæ-guineensis, 265
— Sanctæ Crucis, 264
Asthenia machaonaria, 667
Ateuchus sacer, 110
Athalia centifoliæ, 386
Atta cephalotes, 441
Attacus Jorulla, 669
— Luna, 673
Attelabus curculionoides, 199
— sumptuosus, 200

BACILLUS NATALIS, 309
Bacteria cornutum, 309
Bacuntius vespoides, 763
Batocera Celebiana, 239
— læna, 240
— lineolata, 240
— Thomsonii, 240
Batonota bidens, 264
Bees, 506
Belonogaster Indicus, 488
— junceus, 488
Belostoma grandis, 727
Bembex rostrata, 471
Bembidiides, 60
Bizarda clarissima, 655
— optima, 655
Blaps mucronata, 178
— polychrestos, 178
Blattidæ, 285
Bocydium tintinnabuliferum, 740
Bolbocerus Reichei, 121
Bombus cajanensis, 523
— eximius, 523
Bombylius analis, 762
Bombyx processionea, 668
Bostrichidæ, 171
Brachelytra, 76
Brachinidæ, 45
Brachinus crepitans, 35
— Sinensis, 37
Brachycerus Algerus, 211
— barbarus, 211
— imperialis, 209
— obesus, 211
— ocellatus, 211
— undatus, 211
Brachygnathus oxygonus, 55

BRA

Brachygnathus pyropterus, 55
Brachypeplus auritus, 90
Brachystethus rubromaculatus, 714
Bracon aureomaculatum, 404
Brahmæa certhia, 676
Brana calopasa, 690
Brenthidæ, 201
Bruchus rufimanus, 195
Buprestidæ, 148
Buprestis feldspathica, 151
— splendens, 149
Burying Ants, 430
— Beetles, 82

CALANDRA sacchari, 225
Callichromides, 241
Callidryas Thalestris, 575
Callimenes dasypus, 323
— oniscus, 322
Callirhipis Childrenii, 169
— Dejeanii, 169
Calliodes orbigera, 695
Callipappus Westwoodii, 745
Callitæra Aurora, 590
Calochroa princeps, 20
Calosoma Indicum, 31
— Mc Leayii, 31
— sycophanta, 31
Camel Cricket, 292
Carabidæ, 28
Carabus Adonis, 30
Cardamyla carinentalis, 699
Cardinal Beetle, 173
Carebara dux, 448
Carpella districta, 653
Carpophagus Banksii, 195
Cassidiidæ, 261
Castnia Diva, 648
— Zerinthia, 649
Catacanthus incarnatus, 713
Catadromus tenebrioides, 59
Catagramma Astarte, 604
— excelsior, 603
— mionina, 605
Catoxantha gigantea, 151
Cellar Beetles, 173
Centris denudans, 519
— dimidiata, 519
— flavopicta, 519
Ceratocampa regalis, 681
Cerberodon viridis, 321
Cercopis sanguinolenta, 742
— Theora, 742
Ceruchus striatus, 106
Cetoniides, 141
Chafers, 124
Chalcophoridæ, 151
Chalicodoma muraria, 512
Chalybs Actæon, 629
— coronata, 628
— Pholcus, 629
Chameleon Moth, 697
Chariesterus mæstus, 724
Charaxes Eudamippus, 618

CHA

Charaxes Fabius, 619
— Jasius, 618
— Kadenii, 618
— Nilebis, 618
Chiasognathidæ, 93
Chiasognathus Grantii, 96
Chigoe, 771
Chinch-bug, 727
Chlæniides, 56
Chlorion lobatum, 466
Chœrocampa Nerei, 638
Cholidæ, 217
Choragus Sheppardii, 195
Chromacris colorata, 340
Chrysantheda frontalis, 518
Chrysis oculata, 416
Chrysochroa Buquetii, 153
— limbata, 153
— vittata, 153
Chrysomelides, 257
Chrysophora chrysochlora, 127
Churchyard Beetles, 173
Cicada adusta, 732
— septemdecem, 731
Cicindela aurofasciata, 15
— octonotata, 19
— Sinensis, 16
Cicindelidæ, 6
Cillenium laterale, 61
Cimbex triangulum, 387
— variabilis, 387
Cimex Banksii, 711
Cladognathus cinnamonea, 99
— giraffa, 97
— inquinatus, 99
— occipitalis, 99
— vittatus, 99
Cleridæ, 169
Clerus formicarius, 170
Clisiocampa castrensis, 679
— sylvatica, 680
Clythridæ, 255
Clytus arietis, 246
Coccinellidæ, 271
Cockroaches, 286
Coccus Sinensis, 744
Cocytia Durvillii, 647
Cœlioxys ducalis, 517
Cœquosa Australasiæ, 644
Collyris acrolia, 23
Componotus compressus, 429
— gigas, 428
— sericeiventris, 430
Conops aurifrons, 763
— russipes, 762
Coprides, 118
Copris Hamadryas, 119
— Laius, 119
— lunaris, 118
Corydalis armata, 374
Cosmisoma ochraceum, 248
— scopipes, 248
Crabro subterraneus, 476
Cratosomus Roddami, 220
— varicosus, 221
Crioceris asparagi, 251

DOR

Cryptocephalidæ, 256
Cryptorhynchidæ, 219
Ctenocerus ramosus, 454
Ctenophora bimaculata, 750
— gaudens, 750
— pectinicornis, 750
Cucujo, 160
Cursoria, 286
Cychrides, 32
Cychrus vidua, 35
Cyclommatus tarandus, 102
Cyclosia sanguifera, 662
— subcyaneus, 662
Cylindrodes Campbellii, 319
Cynips confluens, 406
Cyphocrania Enceladus, 307
— gigas, 307
Cypholoba Ranzonii, 49
Cyphus azurea, 217
— Germari, 217
— gloriandus, 216
— modestus, 217
Cystocœlia immaculata, 342
— Saundersii, 343
Cystosoma Saundersii, 733

DALADER ACUTICOSTA, 717
Damaster blaptoides, 33
Danais insolata, 586
Dasypoda hirtipes, 509
— plumipes, 509
Dasypogon spectrum, 756
— Vica, 757
Deltochilidæ, 117
Deltochilum Icarus, 118
— McLeayii, 117
Deilephila Daucus, 636
Derecyrta pictipennis, 389
Dermaptera, 277
Deroplatys desiccata, 297
Dexia effulgens, 765
— formosa, 766
— regalis, 766
Diadema Bolina, 607
Diactor bilineatus, 724
Dichthadia glaberrima, 421
Dicranocephalus Bowringii, 139
Dictyopterus Aurora, 167
Dinoderus ocellaris, 171
Dinoponera grandis, 437
Dioctes Lehmanii, 57
Dipelicus Cantori, 132
Diptera, 749
Disaulax hirsuticornis, 248
Dismorphia orise, 573
— spio, 573
Diurus furcillatus, 202
Dorcides, 103
Dorcus Antæus, 105
— De Haanii, 105
Dorylus longicornis, 421
Doryphora æneoguttata, 258
— duodecemguttata, 258

Doryphora imperialis, 258
— princeps, 258
— pura, 258
— tesselata, 257
— testudo, 258
Drusilla bioculata, 592
— mylæcha, 591
— Phorcas, 592
Dynastes Hercules, 130
Dynastidæ, 129
Dyticus latissimus, 67
— marginalis, 66

EARWIGS, 277
Eciton hamata, 438
– legionis, 441
— prædator, 439
Ecstatosoma tiriatum, 312
Edessa cornuta, 714
Egybolia Vaillantina, 666
Elaphomyia alcicornis, 768
— brevicornis, 770
— cervicornis, 769
Elephant Beetle, 135
Elephant Hawk-Moths, 637
Elphos hymenaria, 702
Empusa gongyloides, 299
Encaustes verticalis, 267
Enceladus gigas, 42
Endomychides, 271
Entimus imperialis, 207
— splendidus, 206
Entomophaga, 393
Epomis Crœsus, 56
Erasmia pulchella, 661
Erateina Julia, 705
— leptocircata, 705
— lineata, 706
— regina, 707
Erebidæ, 689
Eremiaphila rotundipennis, 293
Erineus monstrosus, 81
Erotylus Guerenii, 269
— histrio, 268
— peregrinus, 269
— Surinamensis, 270
Erycina Atahualpa, 624
— Calphurnia, 624
— ocollo, 623
Eubagis Ines, 602
— Mæon, 602
— Sara, 602
Eucheirus Dupontianus, 126
— McLeayii, 125
Eucyane glauca, 656
— melaxantha, 656
Eudema eximius, 56
— tomentosus, 55
Eudryas grata, 685
Euglossa dimidiata, 521
— Romandi, 521
Euglyphia hieroglyphica, 684
Eumenes armata, 482
— coarctata, 479
Eumenes esuriens, 481
— petiolata, 480
— xanthurus, 480
Eumolpus fulgidus, 259
— vitis, 259
Eumorphus bipunctatus, 273
— dilatatus, 273
— marginalis, 272
Eunomia hæmorrhoidalis, 651
Eupezus nigerrimus, 183
Euphæa refulgens, 361
— splendens, 360
— tricolor, 361
Euplexoptera, 277
Euplæa Diocletia, 588
– hamata, 588
— imitata, 587
— Lorenzo, 588
— Palla, 588
Eupyra principalis, 652
Eurycantha Australis, 305
— olivacea, 305
— Tyrrhæa, 304
Eurytrachelus Titan, 104
Euschema Bellona, 659
— flavata, 658
Evanioceridæ, 185
Exeirus lateritus, 474
Exetasis tumens, 755
Exorista militaris, 770

FATUA WEIDMANNII, 271
Fiddler, 39
Fireflies, 159
Flata circulata, 738
— marginella, 739
Fleas, 771
Forficesila Americana, 281
— gigantea, 279
— longissima, 280
Forficula Petropolis, 279
Formicidæ, 427
Fulgora laternaria, 734

GAGATOPHORUS BOIS-DUVALLI, 214
— Schönherri, 213
Gall-flies, 404
Genussa celenaria, 653
Geodephaga, 6
Geotrupidæ, 121
Glossina morsitans, 764
Goliathus Druryi, 137
Golofa hastatus, 131
Gonatoceri, 213
Gonatopus Celebicus, 411
Graphipterus cordigera, 45
— elegans, 44
— exclamationis, 45
— melanocephalus, 44
— Senegalensis, 45
— variegatus, 43
— Westwoodii, 45
Ground Beetles, 28
Gru-gru, 225
Gryllacris signifera, 330
— spurcata, 330
Gyrinidæ, 69
Gymnetes hieroglyphica, 143
— holosericea, 143
Gynanisa Isis, 676
Gyriosema Leuzotii, 184

HALICTUS QUADRISTRIGATUS, 507
Harlequin Beetle, 243
Hebomoia Glaucippe, 579
— leucogynia, 578
Helæus echidna, 188
— perforatus, 187
Heliconisa impar, 678
Heliconius Hecalesia, 597
— Hermathena, 596
Heliothys armigera, 687
Hemiptera, 711
Hemiptycha punctata, 738
Hesthesis cingulatus, 239
— ferrugineus, 238
Hestia Idæa, 585
— Jasonia, 585
Heteromera, 173
Heteronotus armatus, 739
Heteroptera, 711
Hippobosca camelina, 771
Hispidæ, 265
Hister gigas, 89
Histeridæ, 88
Homalosoma Vigorsii, 60
Homoptera, 731
Homopterus Braziliensis, 73
Hoplia cœrulea, 123
— philanthus, 122
— squamosa, 124
Hoplidæ, 122
Hoploscelis grossipes, 122
Hotinus subocellatus, 735
Humble Bees, 522
Hydaticus festivus, 68
Hydradephaga, 65
Hymenoptera, 385
Hypercampa imperialis, 664
Hyperchirea lineosa, 678
— rubrescens, 677
Hyperion Schroeterii, 51
Hypsa orbicularis, 663
Hypsauchenia Hardwickii, 741
— Westwoodii, 741

ICARIA FERRUGINEA, 489
— variegata, 491
Ichneumon arrogator, 397
Ichthyosoma mirabilis, 251
Idolothrips spectrum, 348
Inea lineola, 145
– Sommerii, 144
Ixias Mariamna, 576.

JULODIDES, 148
Junonia crebrene, 698
— Orithyia, 599

KALLIMA INACHIS, 599
— Paralekta, 600
Kangaroo Beetle, 128

LACON MURARIUS, 157
Lagria basalis, 185
— hirta, 184
Lamellicornes, 109
Lamprima aurata, 95
Languriidæ, 270
Lantern Fly, 733
Laphria alternans, 757
— consimilis, 758
— horrida, 759
— xylocopiformis, 757
Larrada ducalis, 468
— hæmorrhoidalis, 469
Leaf Insect, 314
Lebiadæ, 38
Lenyra Ashtaroth, 633
Lepidoptera, 535
Leptis vermileo, 761
Leptoderus sericeus, 84
Lesina lutescens, 323
Leucopholis bimaculata, 125
Leucospis Aruera, 408
Libellula Carolina, 359
— pulchella, 358
— variegata, 357
Locust Carpenter, 682
Locustidæ, 320
Longicornes, 229
Lophonocerus barbicornis, 247
Loxura Atymnus, 631
— Surya, 630
Lucanidæ, 96
Lucanus cervus, 91
Lycænidæ, 627
Lycidæ, 166
Lycisca Romandi, 410
Lycoperdina bovista, 272
Lycus Bremii, 167
— præmorsus, 167
— scutellaris, 165
Lynx crinitus, 123
— Peritrichia, 123

MACROCHERAIA GRANDIS, 725
Macroglossa triopus, 634
Macrosila cruentus, 641
Magpie Moths, 704
Malacodermi, 166
Mantichora mygaloides, 7
Mantis religiosa, 291
— tinctipennis, 292
Mantispa grandis, 375
Marcius generosus, 725
Meal Beetles, 173
Mecistogaster ornatus, 363
Megacephala Senegalensis, 9
— sepulchralis, 9
Megacerus chorinæus, 134
Megachile centuncularis, 513
— disjuncta, 513
— fasciculata, 513
— lanata, 513
— monstrosa, 513
Megalodon ensifer, 327
Megaloprepus brevistigma, 361
Megalops cephalotes, 79
Megalosoma cephalotes, 79
Megalosoma Actæon, 136
— elephas, 135
Megalyra fasciata, 395
— Shuckardii, 394
Melasoma, 178
Melipona fasciculata, 524
Melitta Eurytion, 633
— pulchipes, 633
Melolonthides, 124
Mesomphalia discoides, 263
— dissecta, 263
— festiva, 263
— illustris, 262
— latevittata, 263
Metacycla Sallei, 260
— turgida, 260
Metalleutica splendida, 294
Metapodius latipes, 721
Methoca ichneumonoides, 423
Micronia astheniata, 703
— justasia, 703
Micropus leucopterus, 727
Mictis curvipes, 718
— symbolica, 718
Mischocyttarus labiatus, 488
Molchina compressicornis, 720
Molobrus purpuratus, 53
— rotundiplanis, 53
Moluris allifrons, 181
— Perretii, 181
— Rouletii, 181
— Rowleyana, 180
Monedula heros, 472
— magnifica, 473
Monobia quadridens, 48[illegible]
Morionidæ, 50
Mormolyce phyllodes, 3[illegible]
Morphinæ, 591
Morpho Cypris, 593
— Peleides, 594
Moths, 632
Mouhotia glorissa, 52
Mutilla armata, 420
— capitata, 420
— cephalotes, 419
— cerbera, 418
— Klugii, 419
— occidentalis, 419
Mydas dives, 754
— filatus, 754
— giganteus, 754
Mygnimia Aspasia, 456
— avicula, 455
Mygnimia ducalis 455
Myrina Phocides, 631
Myrmecocystus Mexicanus, 436
Myrmeleonidæ, 365
Myrmica barbata, 449

NECRODES GIGANTEUS, 86
— osculans, 87
— Necrophaga, 81
Necrophorus grandis, 85
Necroscia annulipes, 311
— roseipennis, 311
— Zeuxis, 310
Necyra Manco, 622
Nelcynda rectificata, 708
Neleus interruptus, 106
Neuroptera, 353
Nitidulidæ, 89
Nomada sex-fasciata, 516
Nyctalea superciliosa, 686
Nyctelidæ, 184
Nyctipao albicincta, 693
Nymphalinæ, 592
Nyssonidæ, 473

ODONTOCHEILA DEGANDII, 21
Odontolabris Cuvera, 101
— dux, 101
Œda inermis, 740
— informis, 740
Oil Beetles, 173
Oncomeris flavicornis, 716
Opatrum sabulosum, 191
Ophideres apta, 691
— dividens, 692
— Salminia, 692
— smaragdipicta, 693
Ophiusa fulvotænia, 698
Ornithoptera Cassandra, 538
Orobites cyaneus, 220
Osmia bicolor, 510
— parietana, 511
Orthoptera, 285
Oryctes nasicornis, 129
Oryctides, 133
Ospryncholus objurgator, 403
Owl Butterfly, 595
Oxynopterus Cumingii, 158
Oxytelidæ, 79

PACHYLIS ACUTANGULUS, 723
— gigas, 722
Pachyrhynchus gemmatus, 212
— reticulatus, 212
Pachytylus migratorius, 331
Palpares Caffer, 370
— immensus, 370
— tigroides, 371

Panacanthus varius, 327
Panagæinæ, 54
Panagra tricolor, 704
Pangonia Amboinensis, 752
— fulvithorax, 751
— longirostris, 751
Paphia Glauce, 620
— Nessus, 620
Papilio Aconophos, 548
— Æneas, 551
— Alebion, 571
— Anticrates, 569
— Antiphus, 563
— Brookeanus, 543
— Caudius, 546
— Cloanthus, 569
— Coön, 565
— Diomedes, 542
— Doubledayii, 563
— Emathion, 543
— Ergeteles, 550
— Erythalion, 552
— Euchenor, 558
— Hierocles, 551
— Joësa, 558
— Jophon, 560
— Krishna, 553
— Laodocus, 541
— Leonidas, 567
— Memnon, 561
— Mencius, 559
— Mezentius, 549
— Œbalus, 555
— Palinurus, 555
— Panthous, 544
— Parmatus, 571
— Patros, 545
— Philippus, 558
— Polycaon, 541
— Polyphontes, 563
— Poseidon, 545
— Pronomus, 540
— Sarpedon, 568
— Theseus, 563
— Victorinus, 566
— Ulysses, 542
Papilionidæ, 536
Parapison rufipes, 470
Paratropes decipiens, 289
— elegans, 289
— melanaria, 289
— orientalis, 289
— pica, 289
Parnassius Charltonius, 581
— Hardwickii, 583
— Stubbendorfii, 583
Paussidæ, 72
Paussus sphærocerus, 73
Pectinicornis, 91
Pelecinus polyturator, 396
Pelidnotidæ, 127
Pelopæus chalybeus, 462
— lætus, 462
Pepsis elevata, 457
— heros, 458
— nigrescens, 459
Pericopis angulosa, 654
Petalocera, 109
Petascelis remipes, 719
Phœnicocerus Dejeanii, 236
Phæophilacris funesta, 322
Phæoxantha Klugii, 15
— laminata, 15
Phanæus lancifer, 120
— melon, 121
— nigroviolaceus, 121
— sulcatus, 121
Phasganophora signator
Phasmidæ, 300
Phellus glaucus, 760
Phenax auricoma, 737
Pherhopalus aplustrifer, 75
— denticornis, 74
Phibalosoma pythonius, 301
Philanthus coronatus, 478
— triangulum, 478
Phlæa corticata, 712
Phrissoma horridum, 245
Phyllium scythe, 314
Phyllocnema mirifica, 243
— phyllopus, 241
Phyllodes consobrina, 693
Phyllonemia paradoxa, 298
Phyllopertha horticola, 127
Phytophaga, 253
Pictus labyrinthicus, 681
Pimelia bipunctata, 189
Pimelopidæ, 132
Pimpla intricatoria, 399
Platycrania edulis, 313
— phelaus, 313
Poiocera combusta, 737
Polistes aterrima, 493
— biguttatus, 494
— Hebræus, 494
— Tasmaniensis, 492
Polybia sericea, 504
Polyergus rufescens, 433
Polyphaga Ægyptiaca, 287
Polyrachis bihamata, 435
— textor, 435
Polyzosteria cuprea, 288
Pompilus atrox, 451
— Gravesii, 452
— nobilis, 453
Ponera contracta, 438
Popilia dorsigera, 126
Poropleura bacca, 257
— chimæra, 257
— cuprea, 257
— monstrosa, 256
Porrorhynchus marginatus, 69
Potamophora Manlia, 694
Præsos Mariana, 659
Praxis corvus, 688
Prepona demodice, 615
Prionidæ, 231
Prionocalus Buckleyi, 233
Prionotheca coronata, 190
Prionus coriarius, 232
— cervicornis, 231
— giganteus, 234
Procerus taurus, 29
Processionary Moth, 668
Proconia atra, 743
Proctotrupidæ, 411
Protocerus colossus, 223
Psalidognathus Friendii, 233
Pselaphanax setosus, 60
Pseudotrimera, 267
Pterinoxylus difformipes, 306
Pterochroza ocellata, 327
Pterosophus complanatus, 37
Pterostichi, 58
Pterygophorus cyaneus, 388
— interruptus, 388
Pulex penetrans, 771
Pygoplatys lancifer, 715
Pyrodes columbinus, 236
— marginatus, 236
— pictus, 235
— pulcherrimus, 236
— Smithianus, 236
Pyrophorus noctilucus, 159
Pyrops nobilis, 735

RANATRA ASIATICA, 726
Raptoria, 290
Rhamphorhina Petersiana, 139
Rhigus Schuppellii, 208
Rhina barbicornis, 221
— palmarum, 224
Rhinastus pertusus, 218
Rhipidocera mystacina, 168
Rhipipteryx marginatus, 319
— nigro-æneus, 320
Rhomalea centurio, 338
Rhomborhina Ruckerii, 142
Rhopalomera tibialis, 767
Rhopelophorides, 248
Rhynchium brunneum, 486
— carnaticum, 485
— nitidulum, 483
Rhynchophora, 293
Rhynchophoridæ, 221
Rhyssa lunator, 401
— nobilitator, 401
Rove Beetles, 76
Rupilia ruficollis, 260
Rypophaga, 72

SAGRA BOUQUETII, 254
— chrysochlora, 254
— empyrea, 254
— nigrita, 254
Saltatoria, 317
Samia Calleta, 671
— Cecropia, 670
Sanaa imperialis, 326
Sand-runners, 9
Satyrinæ, 590
Saüba Ant, 441
Saw-flies, 385
Scaritarchus, 52
Scaritidæ, 52

SCL

Sclerodermà cylindrica, 07
— dux, 406
Scolia bicincta, 425
— flavifrons, 424
— procera, 425
Scolobates, 398
Scutellaria nobilis, 712
Scydmænidæ, 81
Sephina formosa, 717
Serecinus Montela, 583
— Telamon, 572, 583
Shaving-brush Butterfly, 617
Siagonides, 42
Sialidæ, 373
Siderone Archidona, 620
— Isidora, 620
— Thebais, 620
Silpha Americana, 89
— cœlestina, 88
Silphidæ, 82
Sinodendron cylindricum, 105
Sisyphus muricatus, 115
Skipjack Beetles, 146
Smerinthus Dumolinii, 643
Soldiers and Sailors, 166
Sphex argentata, 463
Sphingomorpha fulgurifera, 696
Sphinx quinquemaculata, 639
— satellita, 640
Staphylinus cæsareus, 79
— versicolor, 78
— villosus, 79
Sterculia fulgens, 77
Sterculides, 77
Sternacanthides, 246
Sternotomides, 244
Sternotomus bifasciata, 250
— Bohemanna, 250
— mirabilis, 250
— regalis, 250
Sternocera sternicornis, 148
Sternoxi, 146
Steropus, 58
Stethorectus ingens, 465
Stigmodera variabilis, 154
Stilbum splendidum, 415
Stizus grandis, 474
— speciosus, 473
Storniza pallicornis, 327
Sugar Weevil, 225
Synagris analis, 484
— cornuta, 483
— mirabilis, 484
Synœca cærulea, 503
cyanea, 504

SYN

Synonycha duodecim-punctata, 271
— grandis, 271
— spilota, 271

TABANUS HILARIS, 753
Tachina grandis, 765
Tachytes pompiliformis, 470
— Sinensis, 469
Tanœcia calliphorus, 612
— Pulasara, 612
— Vikrama, 612
Tarsolepis remicauda, 697
Tefflus Megarlei, 54
Telea Polyphemus, 672
Teramocerus barbicornis, 204
Termes dirus, 376
Tenebrio molitor, 174
Tenthredo coccinocerus, 388
Teracolas Hewitsonii, 581
— Ione, 580
— Phlegyas, 581
Teratodes monticollis, 339
Tesseratoma Javanica, 715
— nocturna, 13
— pallipes, 13
Tetracha punctata, 11
Themesia aurisapilla, 255
Therates labiata, 21
Thespis Bœtica, 295
— ingens, 295
— purpurascens, 295
— Xiphias, 296
Thripidæ, 348
Thynnus Australis, 422
Thyreodon cyaneus, 402
Thyreus Abbati, 635
— Nessus, 635
Thyridia Æderia, 590
— Psidii, 589
Thysanoptera, 347
Thysanira Agrippina, 689
Tiger-Beetles, 6
Timarcha tenebricosa, 257
Timetes Corinna, 607
— Crethon, 607
— Egina, 606
Tipula imperator, 749
Tmesisternides, 251
Tomaspis furcata, 743
Tophoderes frenatus, 196
Torneutes pallidicornis, 237
Torneutides, 236
Tortoise-beetles, 261
Tragelophorus contractus, 200

ZYG

Tragelophorus giraffa, 199
Tragocephalus gemmaria, 251
— nobilis, 251
— phosphorus, 251
— pulchella, 251
— variegatus, 250
Tremex Columba, 392
Trichodes crabroniformis, 170
Tricondyla aptera, 23
Tricopthalma vetelinea, 755
Trigona ruficrus, 527
Trigonalys compressus, 497
Trigonodera angulata, 186
Trigonodes maxima, 699
Tropæa Leto, 676
— Mænas, 676
Trypoxylon alternatum, 477
— intrudens, 477
— rejector, 477
Tryxalis unguiculata, 334
Tsetse, 764
Tumble-bug, 113

UMBRELLA ANT, 441
Urania Orientalis, 645
— Sloanus, 626
Uroceridæ, 389

VATES LATIFOLIUM, 323
Vespa cincta, 500
— mandarinia, 498
— Orientalis, 501
Vesiculosa, 756

WASPS, 487
Water Beetles, 67
Weevils, 193
Whirligigs, 69
White Ant, 376

XENOCERUS LINEATUS, 197
Xyleutes Robinea, 682
Xylocopa caffra, 521
— morio, 521
— nigrita, 520
— trepida, 521
Xylotrupes dichotomus, 135

ZEONIA BATESII, 626
— Faunus, 626
Zographus oculator, 249
Zopherus Bremii, 176
Zygænidæ, 651